When Brute Force Fails

When Brute Force Fails

HOW TO HAVE LESS CRIME
AND LESS PUNISHMENT

Mark A. R. Kleiman

PRINCETON UNIVERSITY PRESS

PRINCETON & OXFORD

Published by Princeton University Press, 41 William Street, Princeton,
    New Jersey 08540

In the United Kingdom: Princeton University Press, 6 Oxford Street,
    Woodstock, Oxfordshire OX20 1TW

press.princeton.edu

Fourth printing, and first paperback printing, 2010
Paperback ISBN: 978-0-691-14864-9

THE LIBRARY OF CONGRESS HAS CATALOGED THE CLOTH EDITION OF THIS BOOK
    AS FOLLOWS
Kleiman, Mark.
When brute force fails : how to have less crime and less punishment /
Mark A.R. Kleiman.
    p. cm.
Includes bibliographical references and index.
ISBN 978-0-691-14208-1 (hbk. : alk. paper)
1. Crime—United States. 2. Crime prevention—United States. 3. Punishment—
United States. 4. Criminal justice, Administration of—United States. I. Title.
HV6789.K53 2009
364.40973—dc22   2009019862

British Library Cataloging-in-Publication Data is available

This book has been composed in MT Van Dijck

Printed on acid-free paper. ∞

Work leading to this book was supported by grants from the National Institute of
    Justice and the Smith Richardson Foundation, and by sabbatical support pro-
    vided by the UCLA Department of Public Policy and by the Thomas C. Schelling
    Visiting Professorship at the University of Maryland School of Public Affairs.
    None of the sponsors bears any responsibility for the content.

Printed in the United States of America

10 9 8 7 6 5 4

To Steve Hitchner and Phil Heymann,

who got me pointed at the problem,

and to Tom Schelling, who provided the tools.

Brute force succeeds when it is used.

Effective deterrent threats are never carried out.

—Thomas C. Schelling, *Arms and Influence*

CONTENTS

ACKNOWLEDGMENTS

It is just as well that intellectual debts need only be acknowledged, rather than paid; else we would all die bankrupt. Looking back, I realize that I have been preparing to write this book for most of a lifetime, and my list of creditors is correspondingly long. For the most part, I have attempted to economize by naming each person only once. Within categories, names are listed in no particular order. No doubt some have been omitted by mere inadvertence; I sincerely beg their pardon for the oversight. Some are no longer with us, and I treasure their memory.

☒

Studies of criminal careers all agree: When a young man gets involved with drugs and crime, it is usually because he has fallen in with the wrong crowd. The risk is especially grave if those he admires, and whose good opinion he craves, are themselves caught in the drugs-and-crime net. So it was in my case.

Thirty years ago, I was innocently engaged in running a small policy shop in the Boston mayor's office when Philip B. Heymann was appointed assistant attorney general in charge of the Criminal Division of the U.S. Department of Justice. Phil had taught me—or tried to teach me—politics and public management at the Kennedy School of Government at Harvard. He was, and is, both an inspired and inspiring teacher and a great manager. One of his innovations in the Criminal Division was to create the Office of Policy and Management Analysis (OPMA), and to head it he hired Steven B. Hitchner, Jr. Steve had been a couple of years ahead of me in the Kennedy School master of public policy program and was already marked for greatness; only his tragic early death kept him from reaching the highest level of appointive office. The nation is the poorer for it, and Steve's many friends continue to regret his untimely passing.

When Steve invited me to work with him and try to figure out how to prosecute public-corruption cases, I had no particular interest in the topic. I did, however, have in mind the advice every college freshman hears, "Don't take courses; take professors." The chance to work with and for Steve and Phil was too good to pass up. So I joined OPMA, and my career in crime was launched. I have never reformed.

The Criminal Division was a high-morale, high-performance, high-integrity organization. In addition to treasured colleagues in OPMA, including Bud Frank, Bill Fisher, Irvinia Waters, and Julie Samuels, I learned from a dazzling array of fine lawyers and dedicated public servants across the division: Mark Richard, Irv Nathan, David Margolis, Mike DeFeo, Alec Williams, Bill Corcoran, Eric Holder, Kate Pressman, Ruth Wedgwood, and most of all the legendary Jack Keeney. Peter Bensinger and his colleagues in the Drug Enforcement Administration, including John Coleman, taught me the drug business and were remarkably tolerant of my fumbling attempts to make sense of how drug law enforcement could make a difference.

When Phil left at the end of the Carter administration, he was replaced first by Lowell Jensen and then by Steve Trott, who continued my education and earned my deep admiration. I began to collaborate with Peter Reuter at RAND and Susan Ginsburg at the State Department; those two partnerships remain among my most prized resources.

॰

I came to the Justice Department pig-ignorant about its work, but well prepared to learn, thanks to many teachers, starting with my parents, who raised me to prize understanding and to believe in public service. My formal education took place at Elementary School #64, at Pimlico Junior High, at Baltimore City College (actually a high school), and Northwestern High School.

Rhoda Bennett, my first and second grade teacher, taught me that learning could be a source of joy; a child who learns that will eventually learn whatever else he needs to know.

Several people taught me how to write and (the essential prerequisite) to care about writing and to tell good writing from bad; if there is a more demanding art form than English expository prose, I can't imagine what it might be. Mrs. Hergenroeder (I don't think it occurred to me that she might have a first name) who taught seventh grade American history,

assigned—and corrected—an essay every night for an entire year, starting with a sentence and working up to 250 words. Her corrections were
as much about writing as they were about history, and by the end of the
year I could write three consecutive paragraphs without gross errors of
grammar or style. Berniece Baer in eighth grade English diagrammed sentences, although the official curriculum no longer allowed it. Stephanie
Miller, whose subject was chemistry but who also served as adviser to the
school newspaper, initiated me into the mystery of journalistic prose and
into the attitude that all writing, including my own, is mere "copy," capable of being improved, and needing to be improved, by editing. It was
not until later that I heard the Golden Rule of prose—"There is no such
thing as good writing, only good re-writing"—but it was as the copyeditor of the *Pimlico Pacesetter* that I learned the attitude it expresses. The
book you hold is, on average, about a fifth draft.

It was about then that I began to encounter the masters of expository
and argumentative writing, whose skill I have been trying to emulate
ever since: Bertrand Russell, John Kenneth Galbraith, George Orwell,
C. S. Lewis, Michael Walzer, Thomas C. Schelling, and Abraham Lincoln.

Angelo Fortunato, in a single class on the economic origins of the Ref-
ormation, gave me a taste for both historical analysis and political economy. Eileen Henze, in the course of teaching Shakespeare, started me on
my lifelong love affair with English history. Herbert Bernhardt opened
my eyes to the beauty of mathematical reasoning. I recall with affection
schoolmates including Arthur Cohen, Steve Krafchik, Ellen Rothman,
Stuart Levine, Jeff Liss, Susan Michaelson, and Judy Shub.

All of this took place in a big-city public school system, which makes
me impatient both with those who argue that public education must necessarily be deficient and with those who insist that its current state is
satisfactory, or even acceptable.

At Haverford College I had a dazzling array of brilliant and dedicated
teachers. In chronological order, I encountered Sara Shumer, Holland and
Helen Hunter, Ashok Gangadean, Frank Connolly, Bob Gavin, Paul and
Rosemary Desjardins, Sid Waldman, Tad Krauze, Wyatt MacGaffey, Ar-
iel Kosman, Louis Green, Richard Bernstein, and Roger Lane, as well as a
brilliant philosophy of science teacher who was only there for a year and
whose name I have forgotten, without ever forgetting what he taught me.
I learned as much from my classmates, including Tom Gowen, Susan Bell,

Jon Delano, Peter Goldberger, and Eric Sterling, and most of all my room-mates: Gary Emmett, Dave Hsia, Steve Harvester, and Marc McClaren (from whom I first heard the ironic maxim "When brute force fails, you're not using enough").

At the Kennedy School, I studied analytic methods with Edith Stokey, Dick Zeckhauser, Howard Raiffa, and Mike Spence; economics with Tom Schelling and Francis Bator; statistics with Will Fairley and Fred Mo-steller; and politics and public management with Richard Neustadt, Phil Heymann, and Mark Moore. Kip Viscusi, Don Shepard, and Steve Hitch-ner were especially inspired teaching assistants. With such teachers, it would have been difficult not to learn.

Every one of my 24 classmates in the MPP program, and many of my near-classmates, taught me something important; I think especially of Ken Miller, Chris Edley, Kitty Bernick, Michael Eliastam, and Mark Iwry. I learned just as much from housemates Dick Friedman, Jeremy Paretsky, and, most of all, Joel Schwartz.

Harvard also allowed me to take breathtaking courses in political theory with Judith Shklar, Louis Hartz, Harvey Mansfield, and Michael Walzer. Walzer, despite his profound disapproval of my decision to study policy analysis rather than becoming a theorist, gave me my first oppor-tunity to teach, as a section leader for his introductory lecture course on modern political thought. The experience gave me a taste for teaching that has never left me; Walzer's lectures, and Mansfield's, set a standard I have never been able to match.

After finishing the master's degree, I continued my postgraduate edu-cation in three positions before landing at the Justice Department. Les Aspin of Wisconsin hired me as a legislative assistant on Capitol Hill; I learned much about both policy and politics from him and from my daz-zling colleagues there, including Bill Broydrick, Gretchen Koitz, and Ed Miller. That was not my first Capitol Hill experience; Parren Mitchell of Maryland had introduced me to congressional life one summer during college. That experience followed an exciting shoestring election cam-paign in which I wound up as the press secretary, and in the process met Tom Edsall, who taught me a great deal both about politics and about the practical business of reporting and who has been a good friend ever since. I doubt I earned my keep that summer, but I learned much, with George Minor and Elinor Bacon trying their best to keep me out of trouble and Sandy Rosenberg helping me make trouble.

My next job after Aspin's office was at Polaroid Corporation, where I was special assistant to Edwin Land, with Carl Kaysen—acting on Francis Bator's recommendation—as my sponsor and mentor. Working for Land was a liberal education in itself; Kaysen helped me interpret what I was experiencing, which was not at all the profit-maximizing firm of the economics textbooks. Bill McCune, Mac Booth, and Shelly Buckler all expanded my mind in various ways.

From Polaroid I went to the Boston job mentioned earlier, running the policy and management shop in the Mayor's Office of Management and Budget. I worked for Jerry Mechling, and with Zack Tumin, Ronnie Levin, Jack Lew, Jim Young, and Bo Holland. That was my first experience of management, and my colleagues did their level best to make up for my many limitations. Joe Jordan, then Boston's police commissioner, taught me the rudiments of police management and introduced me both to his two star lieutenants, Al Sweeney and Bill Bratton, and to his civilian adviser, Bob Wasserman, who were helping to give birth to what was later called "community policing."

After four years at the Justice Department, I returned to Harvard to complete my long-deferred dissertation. Mark Moore was my thesis chair, and Tom Schelling, Phil Heymann, John Kaplan, and Peter Schuck also served on the committee. Phil also gave me an office at the Harvard Law School Center for Criminal Justice, where I encountered Donald Black, whose *Behavior of Law* profoundly shaped my thinking. Lesley Friedman, then an undergraduate, provided invaluable help—bordering on collaboration—in the painful process of writing down my thoughts in thesis form and then turning that thesis into a book.

About then I had the idea of starting a firm to sell policy analysis as a consulting service. BOTEC Analysis Corporation was a professional, though not a commercial, success, and I remain grateful to my long-suffering colleagues in that enterprise, including Jenny Rudolph, David Cavanagh, David Boyum, Richard Mockler, Andrew Chalsma, Ann-Marie Rocheleau, Kerry Smith, Sarah Chayes, Doug Wilson, and the unforgettable Fred Hayes. Kevin Burke, then district attorney of Essex County in Massachusetts, gave us our first assignment, an evaluation of the Lynn Drug Task Force, which started me thinking about the dynamics of enforcement crackdowns. Subsequent clients included the Office of National Drug Control Policy, where John Carnevale and Ross Deck gave us great scope to do sometimes unconventional thinking, and the National

Institute of Justice, where Bud Gropper, Ed Zedlewski, Thom Feucht, Lois Mock, and Jeremy Travis provided intellectual as well as financial support.

My first teaching job after graduate school was a one-year fill-in assignment at the public policy program of the University of Rochester. The program was housed in Rochester's political science department, then the epicenter of the rational choice earthquake that shook American political science to its foundations. Bruce Bueno de Mesquita was our chair, and I learned much from my colleagues, including William Riker, Richard Fenno, David Weimer, Bruce Jacobs, and Chuck Phelps. (Alas, part of what I think I learned was that, except in the hands of a genius such as Riker, "rat-choice" was mostly a dead end.)

From Rochester I returned to the Kennedy School, where the efforts of Tom Schelling and Mark Moore secured me a teaching post and a research affiliation with the program in criminal justice policy and management. There I met, collaborated with, and learned from Frank Hartmann, George Kelling, Bill Spelman, Anthony Braga, Susan Michaelson, and David Kennedy. Among my teaching colleagues, I benefited especially from Glenn Loury, Steve Kelman, Ron Ferguson, Arthur Applbaum, Anne Piehl, Fred Schauer, Al Carnesale, Joe Kalt, Dennis Thompson, and Mike O'Hare. The participants in the executive sessions on community policing and on prosecution, including Ben Ward, Steve Goldsmith, John O'Hair, Dennis Nowicki, Ed Flynn, and Norm Maleng, were generous in sharing their knowledge of the nuts and bolts of the criminal-justice system. While at Harvard, I had the pleasure of serving on the MIT thesis committee of Jonathan Caulkins and of starting Rick Doblin on his way toward a doctorate, and was assisted by a succession of dazzling undergraduates, especially Aaron Saiger and Rebecca Young.

The interdisciplinary project on drugs and drug policy of the university-wide program on Mind, Brain, and Behavior, brought me into contact with such luminaries as Steve Hyman, Gene Heyman, and George Vaillant, and with younger research workers, including Will Brownsberger and Deborah Harlow. Jim Harpel was not only a generous donor but a participant in our deliberations.

My next—and current—teaching assignment took me to the then-new public policy department in the equally new UCLA School of Public Affairs, where I have experienced the pleasure of helping to build an academic enterprise and of working with people genuinely interested in sharing ideas and happy to see me succeed. Archie Kleingartner, our founding dean, and his successors Barbara Nelson and Frank Gilliam, as well as academic dean Fernando Torres-Gil, have been generous in supporting our department and my work in particular, as have chancellors Chuck Young, Al Carnesale, and Gene Block. On the administrative side, VC Powe, Minne Ho, Mari Hatta, Karen Kovacs North, Vincent Riggs, Jim Tranquada, and Bill Parent have gone above and beyond the call of duty to advance my work. Tom Plate was more responsible than anyone else for persuading me to make the move to UCLA, and he has been a firm friend ever since.

Karen Friedman has been trying valiantly for more than a decade now to keep all of my balls in the air, and has done so with astounding competence, cheerfulness, and patience.

I am inordinately proud of my current and former colleagues in the public policy department: Dan Mitchell, Arleen Leibowitz, Mark Peterson, Michael Stoll, Sandy Jacoby, Eric Monkkonen, Allen Scott, Meredith Phillips, J. R. DeShazo, Andy Sabl, Amy Zegart, Eric Patashnik, Tom Kane, Sarah Reber, Matt Kahn, Aaron Panofsky, Joel Aberbach, Michael Dukakis, Joel Handler, Sandy Jacoby, Lynne Zucker, and Rob Jensen. And the departmental staff, including Ken Roehrs, Maciek Kolodziejczak, Kyna Williams, and Ronke Epps, has done more with less than seemed humanly possible. Among colleagues from the social welfare and urban planning departments I would be remiss not to mention Rob Schilling, Jorja Leap, Stuart Kirk, Don Shoup, Ted Benjamin, Paul Ong, Joe Nunn, and Zeke Hasenfeld.

UCLA students, including Phil Carter, Myles Collins, Thomas Tran, Amy Hu, Terri Patchen, Paul Fishbein, Alex Sange, Hasmik Badalian, Celeste Drake, and Jack Clift, have assisted and inspired me in various ways.

In the spring of 2000, I was diagnosed with advanced-stage Hodgkins disease. Without treatment by Christos Emmanouilides and the advice of Gary Emmett and Alan Rabson, I might well not have survived to write this book. Both my chances of recovery and my spirits were boosted by an astounding outpouring of love and support. Although I mention specifically the help of Lowry Heussler, Sally Satel, Leonard Pickard, Roy McKinney, Mitch Marcus, Barb Maynard, Tracey Trautman, and Al

Carnesale, that is not to slight the help of many, many others. My department and my school made every possible accommodation when I was too sick to teach.

The great and pleasant surprise of being at UCLA has been the extent to which collaboration across departmental lines is a way of life. Due in large part to following the lead of Jack Hirshleifer, who seemed to be connected to most of the centers of intellectual vitality at UCLA, I have found stimulation in a wide variety of settings:

- the seminar on political economy, including Harold Demsetz, Lynn Stout, and Al Harberger;
- the program on awe-inspiring experiences, funded by the Metanexus Institute, and including Susanne Lohmann and Bob Jesse;
- the behavior, evolution, and culture group, including Dwight Read, Dan Fessler, Rob Boyd, Clark Barrett, Jeff Brantingham, Alan Fiske, Martie Haselton, Joan Silk, and Francis Steen;
- the project on complex human systems, of which John Bragin has been the entrepreneur;
- the Marschak colloquium, under the direction of Mike Intriligator, through which I met, and learned from, such giants as Colin Camerer and George Loewenstein;
- the Integrated Substance Abuse Programs, including Doug Anglin, Rick Rawson, Walter Ling, Yih-ing Hser, Tom Ungerleiter, and Doug Longshore;
- the faculty Tanakh study group (now named in Jack Hirshleifer's memory), a model of truly interdisciplinary activity, starring Chaim Seidler-Feller, Steve Yeazell, Joe Ostroy, Carole Goldberg, Arthur Cohen, Arthur Rosett, Deborah Kennel, Gershon Hepner, César Ayala, Max Novak, Marvin Smotrich, Harry Jerison, Shelley Salamensky, David Rapoport, and Monica Osborne; and
- the seminar series of the philosophy department, where Seana Shiffrin, Barbara Herman, David Kaplan, Joseph Almog, and Calvin Normore have made me welcome and where speakers including Jerry Cohen and Tim Scanlon have delighted me.

In addition to the visible institutions that have housed me, I have been a member of three "invisible colleges," the informal networks that carry on the enterprise of building knowledge through journals, conferences, and exchanges of unpublished work. My three "colleges" are the groups that work on drugs and drug policy, crime and crime policy, and public policy and management generally. Unlike the invisible colleges in purely scientific endeavors, these groups include practitioners and journalists as well as scholars.

Among those engaged in research and practice around the drug issue, I have learned from Jerry Jaffe, Bob DuPont, Norman Zinberg, Bob Schuster, David Courtwright, David Musto, Harriet de Wit, Eric Wish, Rob MacCoun, Alison Ritter, Robin Room, John Strang, Marsha Rosenbaum, Michael Farrell, Harold Pollack, Kathleen Kennedy Townsend, Beau Kilmer, Steve Alm, Ann Shulgin, Sasha Shulgin, Maia Szalavitz, Roland Griffiths, Bill Richards, Rick Doblin, Keith Humphreys, Rob Bonner, Herb Kleber, Amanda Fielding, Alexandra Hill, Ana Maria Salazar, Francisco Thoumi, Rosalie Pacula, Adele Harrell, Karyn Model, Mike Isikoff, Peter Kerr, Aric Press, Mark Schoofs, Michael Massing, Steve Morral, Andrew Golub, Karst Bestemann, John Walsh, Chris-Ellyn Johanson, Bob Millman, Herb Okun, John Pinney, Martha Gagne, Mitch Rosenthal, Lew Seiden, and Alan Trachtenberg. The International Society for the Study of Drug Policy represents one visible face of this community of knowledge-seekers.

Among those who study crime and practice crime control, I am indebted to Frank Zimring, Jerry Skolnick, Phil Cook, Jay Carver, John DiIulio, Jan Chaiken, Marcia Chaiken, Joan Petersilia, Laurie Robinson, Adam Gelb, Samuel del Vilar, George Tita, Jake Horowitz, Charles Ogletree, Eric Lotke, Charlie Beck, Fox Butterfield, Grace Mastalli, Jose Cerda, and Amy Solomon. Jim Wilson has been especially generous in the face of our sometimes profound disagreements.

In the broader world of public policy and management, I have benefited from association with Steve Teles, Tom Garwin, Gene Bardach, Steve Fetter, Doug Besharov, Mort Halperin, Jeremy Stone, Suzi Levi-Sanchez, Hilary Bok, Amitai Etzioni, and Gene Smolensky.

Ever since Eugene Volokh suggested that I try my hand at a new literary form called "blogging," I have been a devotee. James Wimberley, Jonathan Zasloff, Jonathan Kulick, Robert Frank, as well as some others mentioned above, have contributed to *The Reality-Based Community*; Eugene, Andrew Sullivan, Kevin Drum, Ezra Klein, John Amato, Megan

McArdle, Matt Ygelsias, John Cole, Brad DeLong, and Arianna Huffington have been generous in helping to draw attention to my thoughts.

Some of my heaviest obligations do not fit into any of the categories above: to Newell Mack, Siena Kirwin, Ram Dass, Clare Frank, Mary Ellen Lawrence, Jordan Peterson, Cecily Rayburn, François Lalonde, Alex Desjardins, Margaret Desjardins, David Nielsen, Hope Nielsen, Jim Fadiman, Missy Craig, Alice Schelling, Inna Naletova, Mary Edsall, Robin Krauze, Ruth Albert, David Albert, Beth Albert, Dana Albert, Hilary Albert, Jane and Brett Summers, and last, but never least, my sister Kelly.

I have run up additional debts in the process of writing this book. Financial support came from the National Institute of Justice, under grants OJP-2000-173M and 2001-IJ-CX-0033; Thom Feucht, Christine Crossman, and Marlene Beckman served as admirably nondirective project officers. Of course that sponsorship does not constitute endorsement of the ideas expressed here. UCLA provided additional support in the form of sabbatical leave, and the Urban Institute made me welcome as a visiting scholar for a year. The School of Public Policy at the University of Maryland honored me with the first Thomas C. Schelling visiting professorship.

Kevin Barry, Karen Parker, Patricija Petrac, Elizabeth Dodd, Kelsey Yu, Eric Gorin-Regan, and Sam Boyd provided able research assistance; Steve Davenport did most of the heavy lifting in calculating incarceration-to-offense figures. Kris Kastinova of UCLA's Young Research Library worked miracles of information-finding in response to the merest hints about what was being sought.

Angela Hawken read an entire early draft and provided both much-needed encouragement and several important corrections. David Hsia, Andrew Holmer, Katherine Moore, Nisha Mehling, Kenny Casebere, Greg Midgette, and Julie Quinn also read and commented on the manuscript in whole or part; Rob MacCoun, Rick Tuttle, Kevin Barry, Keith Humphrey, and a person currently behind bars whose cellmate might not approve provided especially thorough and helpful comments. At the invitation of Glenn Loury and with financial support from the Criminal Justice Policy Foundation, an all-star team consisting of Glenn himself, Phil Heymann, Jonathan Caulkins, Will Brownsberger, Phil Cook, David Boyum, and Corey Brettschneider assembled at Brown University for two days of unrestrained criticism. That process led me to reorganize the volume, rewrite substantial parts of it, and add the chapter on what might go wrong.

At Princeton University Press, Chuck Myers as the acquiring editor and Terri O'Prey as the production editor have been wonderfully supportive and tolerant; Jennifer Malloy performed admirably as the copyeditor; and Richard Comfort prepared an exemplary index.

I hope that this volume will show those mentioned above, and those not mentioned due to my faulty memory, that I have not entirely wasted their gifts.

▨

Note to the paperback edition: The discussion of nurse home visitation on page 127 was written before the publication of a study showing no decrease in crime among the boys in the Elmira study by their twentieth birthdays. In light of that finding, the optimism expressed about nurse home visitation as a crime-control measure needs to be reined in; since males commit the vast bulk of crime, a program that does not reduce crime among males has sharply limited value in crime control, whatever its other benefits. See John Eckenrode, Mary Campa, Dennis W. Luckey, Charles R. Henderson, Jr., Robert Cole, Harriet Kitzman, Elizabeth Anson, Kimberly Sidora-Arcoleo, Jane Powers, and David Olds, Long-term Effects of Prenatal and Infancy Nurse Home Visitation on the Life Course of Youths: 19-Year Follow-up of a Randomized Trial, *Arch Pediatr Adolesc Med*. 2010;164(1):9–15.

When Brute Force Fails

How to Have Less Crime
and Less Punishment

Engineers have a sardonic saying: "When brute force fails, you're not using enough." For three decades, in the face of the great crime wave that
started in the early 1960s, we have been trying to solve our crime problem
with brute force: building more and more prisons and jails. Recently, the
crime problem has diminished—though the downtrend stopped around
2004—but we still have a huge crime problem, to which we have now
added a huge incarceration problem: there are now 2.3 million people behind bars at any one time, and that number continues to grow.[*]

Is there an alternative to brute force? There is reason to think so, and
pieces of that alternative approach can be seen working in scattered places
throughout the world of crime control. But the first step in getting away
from brute force is to want to get away from brute force: to care more
about reducing crime than about punishing criminals, and to be willing to
choose safety over vengeance when the two are in tension.

Developing a consequence-focused approach to crime control would
require that we blunt the emotional edge that debates about crime often
have and ask the simple question: what are the stakes in crime control? If
for a moment we thought about "crime" as something bad that happens
to people, like auto accidents or air pollution or disease, rather than as
something horrible that people do to each other—if we thought about
it, that is, as an ordinary domestic-policy problem—then we could start
to ask how to limit the damage crime does at as little cost as possible in
money spent and suffering inflicted.

---

[*]Except as noted, all statistics about crime rates, incarceration rates, numbers of arrests, probationers, parolees, and criminal-justice budgets are drawn either from the annual
Bureau of Justice Statistics *Sourcebook of Criminal Justice Statistics* or the annual FBI Uniform
Crime Reports (published as *Crime in the United States*). Detailed page and table references and
extensive methodological notes are available. See http://press.princeton.edu/titles/9018
.html.

The answer to that question will not be the only factor that influences, or should influence, crime-control policy. Justice both requires and limits punishment. Laws, customs, and institutional arrangements—including the Constitution and ideas such as "innocent until proven guilty"—limit, and ought to limit, the range of options. Still, thinking about the advantages and disadvantages—what economists quaintly call "benefits" and "costs"—of different approaches to crime control is one place to start the inquiry.

Crime causes damage: directly to victims, and indirectly as people incur costs, and impose costs on others, to avoid victimization. The value of the total damage is hard to reckon, but serious estimates (even excluding "white collar" crime) run as high as $1.4 trillion per year: more than 10 percent of GDP.[1] Furthermore, this damage falls most heavily on the poor and socially marginal people least able to bear it; crime not only concentrates around social disadvantage but also sustains it, increasing costs for consumers and employers alike and thereby driving away resources and opportunities.

One possible way to reduce the amount of crime is to detect, apprehend, convict, and punish criminals. All of those actions cost money— currently about $200 billion per year nationwide—and do other kinds of harm, imposing suffering not only on those punished, but also on their families and friends. That the United States, with about 1 percent of its adults behind bars, now has the highest level of incarceration per capita in the world is not something to be proud of.

Nor are the conditions of incarceration. Some of the defenders of torture at Abu Ghraib, Bagram, and Guantánamo, and in the secret CIA prisons, argued that what was being done to detainees abroad was no worse than what goes on all the time in domestic prisons. That was false. But it was closer to true than it ought to have been. Twenty-five thousand prisoners in the United States live in long-term solitary confinement in "super-max" prisons, and tens of thousands more in "administrative segregation," sometimes for years on end. Prolonged isolation is one of the nastier ways of driving someone mad.[2]

Those harms, too, fall disproportionately to the lot of those already disadvantaged by poverty, social exclusion, and, not least, crime itself. "Criminals" and "victims" are not two distinct populations. Many victims commit no crimes, but few criminals avoid victimization, and most were victims before becoming perpetrators. Victimization is criminogenic.

One way to frame the general problem of crime-control policy is, "What set of actions would result in the least total harm and cost, from crime and crime-control efforts combined?" Neither across-the-board lenity nor maximum severity offers the right answer to that question.

The right answer, as far as the operations of the criminal-justice system are concerned, will use the minimum amount of punishment necessary to achieve any given level of crime control. That in turn requires that most punishments be swift and certain, rather than severe. Theory and evidence agree: swift and certain punishment, even if not severe, will control the vast bulk of offending behavior. One problem with the brute-force, high-severity approach is that severity is incompatible with swiftness and certainty. Severity means using a large share of punishment resources on a (relatively) few offenders, and (as the American experience with capital punishment since its reintroduction illustrates) the more severe a sentence is the more reluctantly it will be imposed and the more "due process"— and therefore the more time—it will require.[3]

The resources of the current criminal-justice system, matched against the volume of crime, simply do not allow it to punish, even modestly, all offenses or all offenders. Trying to control everything and everyone—the tough-sounding "zero tolerance" approach—leads to sporadic and delayed punishments as the system overloads. The result is great quantities of punishment, much of it severe, and effective control of nothing and no one except those actually behind bars: a bad bargain.

That implies two additional design principles for enforcement regimes to add to the use of swiftness and certainty in place of severity: concentration of resources, and the direct communication of deterrent threats to likely offenders.

Concentration exploits a central, but poorly understood, phenomenon: positive feedback in rates of offending.[4] (See chapter 4.) In a group of generally well-behaved individuals, enforcement can concentrate on a small number of miscreants, delivering swift and certain sanctions, and the resulting high probability that any offense will lead to punishment will make misbehavior an unattractive option.

The same amount of enforcement attention applied to a badly behaved population will lead to only delayed and sporadic punishment, because the level of offending will "swamp" the enforcement response.[5] As individuals learn that the most likely result of offending is getting away with it, offense rates will tend to rise, aggravating the inadequacy of the enforcement response. Both high and low levels of offending will be self-sustaining, and increases and decreases in offending levels will tend to be self-reinforcing. Positive feedback (the technical term for self-reinforcement) generates both vicious circles—bad situations getting worse—and the opposite: what might be called "virtuous circles." Sometimes both extremes are stable, but no place in the middle is stable: a "tipping" situation.[6]

Then the problem, once caught in a vicious circle, is how to move from the bad, high-violation equilibrium to the good, low-violation equilibrium. One way to do that is to add enforcement capacity so that it is possible to convincingly threaten even a large number of offenders. Since a low violation rate, once achieved, tends to be self-sustaining, it will not be necessary to maintain that additional capacity forever; a level of enforcement activity inadequate to suppress a riot is ample once the riot is under control. The challenge is to find, even temporarily, enough additional capacity to do the job.

One approach to finding those resources might be called "dynamic concentration." Start somewhere: with a geographic region, a set of offenses, or a set of offenders. Borrow existing capacity from other areas, offenses, or offenders to concentrate on the chosen target. Once offenders have gotten the message that, in the words of the old music-hall song, "You can't do that there here," and reduced their level of activity accordingly—once that original target has been "tipped" from high offending to low offending—the temporary increase in enforcement directed at that sector can be relaxed without letting the target "tip" back. That frees up those extra resources for a new target, which tips in turn. Continue until the cost of the enforcement activity required to maintain good behavior where it has been achieved exhausts the available resources. Only at that point will it be true that achieving more compliance will require inflicting more punishment.

Right now the U.S. criminal-justice system is a long way from that point: we could have much less crime, and many fewer people behind bars, than we now do, simply by applying dynamic concentration. ("Simply," of course, in concept only; actually doing it is hard.)

The cost of "tipping" a high-violation situation to the alternative low-violation equilibrium depends on how quickly offenders respond to the new level of deterrence. That transition cost can be reduced—to the benefit of law enforcement and offenders alike—by warning offenders in advance. Actual crime control, unlike the playground game of "cops and robbers," is not a zero-sum game where any gain to one side must reflect a loss on the other side. Since punishment—as opposed to the crime reduction punishment intends to bring about—is a cost, not a benefit, to the public, officials who design and carry out crime-control efforts share a common interest with the people whose behavior they are trying to control: both sides would gain by reducing the level of punishment. (See chapter 4.)

That makes it in the interest of real cops, as opposed to playground cops, to warn potential lawbreakers of the consequences of lawbreaking. In some situations, the warnings alone can do most of the work, but they need to be backed up with the capacity to deliver on the threat when necessary. As any parent knows, a warning that turns out to be a bluff devalues future warnings.[7]

The same principles that apply to controlling the behavior of actual and potential offenders in general apply, but with even greater force, to controlling the behavior of offenders under "community supervision": parolees (under supervision after incarceration), probationers (under supervision instead of incarceration), and those released on bail or their own recognizance while awaiting trial (a special case, given that they are still presumed innocent).

As things stand, the community-corrections system reproduces the flaws of the larger criminal-justice system, having more rules than it can reliably enforce and imposing sporadic but sometimes severe sanctions; a parent who acted the way the probation system acts—letting most misconduct go unpunished, but occasionally lashing out with ferocious punishments—would be called both neglectful and abusive. A small set of rules—each clearly linked to the goal of reducing re-offending—adequate capacity to monitor whether those rules are being observed, and a system of swift, reliable, and proportionate sanctions to back up those rules would perform much better. If we can make community corrections a genuine alternative to incarceration—in other words, if we can learn how to punish people and control their behavior when not paying for their room and board—we can have less crime and less incarceration, to the benefit of victims and offenders alike.

The good news is that programs embodying these principles are beginning to spring up around the country and in all parts of the criminal-justice enterprise. H.O.P.E., CeaseFire, and High Point aren't yet "celebrity" ideas, but they deserve to be.

Of course, crime levels respond to factors other than punishment: both social services and social reforms can reduce crime. (See chapter 7.) But not every social program or reform, not even every worthwhile one, is crime-reducing. Since a relatively small number of people account for a very large proportion of all crime, broadly distributed social services have low "target efficiency" as crime-control measures.

For example, since high-school dropouts have higher crime rates, on average, than people from similar social backgrounds who manage to graduate, it makes sense that improving educational outcomes, especially for students from high-crime neighborhoods, would tend to reduce crime.[8] But there is no convincing evidence that increasing spending on public education by 10 percent would actually improve educational outcomes enough to measurably reduce crime, while 10 percent of the public education budget is more than a quarter of the *total* criminal-justice budget. So while there are many good reasons to want to improve K-12 education, it is unlikely to be a cost-effective means of crime control.

There are things that non-crime-control agencies can do to reduce crime, many of them with much more effect per dollar spent than routine criminal-justice activities. Some of them do not even cost money. If high-school classes started at 10 a.m. rather than 8 a.m. and ended at 5 p.m. instead of 3 p.m., after-school crime would be greatly reduced, and there is no reason to think that pre-school crime would rise correspondingly. But since no one thinks to blame the school superintendent for after-school burglaries, school systems face no pressure to make the change. Similarly, teaching first-grade teachers techniques of classroom order maintenance demonstrably improves not only learning, but also pupils' behavior outside the classroom well into adolescence, if not beyond.[9]

Only social programs that are either very cheap or very effective are likely to be worth doing universally for their crime-control benefits alone. But it is not very hard to spot people, even fairly young children, whose behavior and social circumstances mark them out as high-risk for criminal activity. The ranks of serious and persistent adult offenders are drawn largely from juveniles with records of misconduct in school and a succession of increasingly serious juvenile arrests.[10] Most of those active juvenile offenders will not develop into high-crime-rate adults, but enough of them will do so to warrant targeting them in crime-prevention efforts. Services that would not be cost-effective as crime control if scattered may look much more attractive if focused on those most likely to become serious criminals when they grow up.*

On the other hand, because crime is so very expensive, any modest-sized social program with measurable crime-control benefits is likely to pay for itself many times over. Positive feedbacks in the system create synergies between social programs and enforcement programs; reductions in crime due to social programs increase the efficacy of the law-enforcement system by reducing the number of crimes competing for enforcement attention.

Nurse home visits for expectant mothers, high-quality preschool programs (and perhaps even Head Start[11]), and reducing children's exposure to lead have all demonstrated that they can reduce crime, some of them quite spectacularly compared to their costs.[12] (See chapter 7.) Yet social-service programs get very little attention in the discussion of how to control crime, and crime-control benefits tend to be peripheral to the way such programs are designed and evaluated.

The bad news is that current policies leave us with unnecessarily—unforgivably—high levels of both crime and incarceration. The good news is that the knowledge of how to do better grows from year to year. This book is intended to push that learning process one step forward, and to help create public pressure for public agencies to do what is needed to shrink both the crime problem and the population behind bars.

---

*This is the other side of the Schuck and Zeckhauser (2006) "bad apples and bad bets" analysis. Donohue (2007, p. 390) argues that targeting by race and poverty would be fairly efficient, but notes the difficulty of openly doing so.

The Trap

How did we get where we are? If we look back half a century, the United States had much less crime and much less punishment than it has today. What went wrong? What has gone right since 1994? And where do we go from here?

Starting about 1963, crime began to rise quickly after a long plateau at historically low levels.[1] Demography explains part of that change: in 1963, the first wave of the post-war Baby Boom generation reached the age of seventeen, which meant that the oldest Boomers were entering their prime crime-committing years. Even had age-specific crime rates stayed stable, having larger cohorts in their high-crime years would have pushed up crime rates. But in fact age-specific crime rates soared, perhaps because the sheer size of the Boomer generation made it less responsive to its elders.[2] ("With the birth of the third child," it has been said, "parents have to move from man-to-man coverage to zone defense." The same principle seems to apply at the macro level.) Rising crime rates, like the unholy trinity of sex, drugs, and rock 'n' roll, partly reflected the greater rebelliousness enabled by the Boomers' greater numbers.

While the drugs most associated with the cultural upheaval known as "the Sixties"—cannabis and the hallucinogens (such as LSD)—had little if any connection with predatory crime, the mid-1960s also saw the sudden rise of heroin addiction in poor, and especially racial-minority, urban areas, further exacerbated in the later 1960s by the return of soldiers who had acquired the heroin habit in Vietnam to those areas. Heroin use was widespread among American troops while in the theater of war , but those who returned to neighborhoods where heroin was not easily available or widely used mostly gave it up once they got home.[3] (The heroin wave of the 1960s, which had its effect on crime largely through inducing income-producing crime among heroin addicts, was only a warm-up to the crack epidemic of the late 1980s, which generated not only economic crime by users but massive violence among dealers.[4])

The wave of urban riots that started in Watts in 1965 and climaxed in the summer of 1968 following the King assassination left behind it higher rates of day-to-day crime, worsened legitimate economic opportunities, and police departments concerned—especially after the Kerner Commission report[5]—that aggressive tactics against routine street crime might spark more riots.

Thus demography, sociology, and history combined to set the stage for an explosion in crime rates.

At the same time, a combination of ideological and historical factors acted together to reduce the country's prison capacity. By then, penologists had figured out that the "Big Houses"—the mega-prisons built after World War I, holding thousands of prisoners each—were too big, and that smaller prisons were easier to control. So when those mega-prisons hit the forty-year mark that was understood to be the end of their designed useful life, the impulse was to shut them down rather than renovating them. Back then, not many communities wanted prisons as neighbors, so siting new prisons was difficult, especially in high-population-density states.

Prison administrators, who were losing both self-confidence and support within the political system, had little desire and even less capacity to insist on matching increases in crime with increases in prison capacity. They had built up the idea that prisons were centers for rehabilitation: "penitentiaries" in the original sense of that term. But a growing body of research suggested that sending someone to prison did not, on average, reduce his subsequent criminal behavior, other than by keeping him off the streets for a while.[6] That was interpreted—not very accurately—as meaning that rehabilitative efforts within prison were wasted effort. An equally plausible but less popular interpretation of the same results was that some aspects of the prison experience were likely to be criminogenic, while others tended to be rehabilitative, yielding a net effect near zero but allowing for the possibility that more or better rehabilitation could reduce recidivism. But the conventional wisdom among decision-makers treated the claim that "Nothing works" as an established fact of penology.[7]

If the goal of prison was rehabilitation, and if prisons did not rehabilitate, then there seemed to be no good reason to keep building them, or even to replace the ones that had passed their "use-by" date. So the 1960s and early 1970s saw the nation's total prison capacity shrink by 10 percent even as crime soared. If we set the 1962 ratio of the incarceration

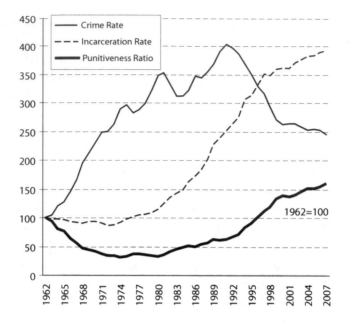

Figure 1. Crime and punishment, 1962–2007

rate to the crime rate—what might be called the "punitiveness index"—equal to 100, by 1980 it had fallen to 32, and did not return to its 1962 level until 1996. (See figure 1.)

At the same time, judicial decisions and the civil rights revolution made it less and less possible for police to inflict illegal summary punishment, known among beat cops as "street justice."* To add to the mix, the wave of "de-institutionalization" of patients in state mental hospitals, combined with the failure to build the community mental-health system that was supposed to replace them, released to the streets a group of people who, though relatively few of them committed serious crimes, generated enough low-level public-order offenses to increase the strain on police and jails.

---

*This does not imply that extra-legal punishments were justifiable; it is possible to abhor lawlessness by law enforcers while acknowledging that cracking down on it had, at least temporarily, perverse effects on the underlying crime problem. Even from a strictly "practical" viewpoint "street justice" had high costs in the form of creating hostility to the police in high-crime neighborhoods.

At that historical moment, conservatives both in the academy and the political system started to challenge what they saw as the liberal orthodoxy about crime: that the key to fixing crime was to change the conditions of social deprivation that were its "root causes"; that controlling lawless behavior by the police was as important as, or even more important than, controlling street crime; that punishment should be designed primarily to rehabilitate rather than to incapacitate or to deter; and that the public's fear of crime was exaggerated and reflected racial fears stirred up by demagogues.

A key voice on the academic side was that of James Q. Wilson, then in the government (political science) department at Harvard University. Wilson's *Thinking about Crime*[8] proposed to replace what its author saw as liberal muddle-headedness with what seemed to Wilson, and to many who did not share his other political opinions, like plain common sense.

Crime, in Wilson's view, had both characterological and social roots, but was fundamentally the product of individual choice rather than irresistible socioeconomic forces or psychological compulsions. Individuals' inadequate capacity to defer gratification, their preference for idleness over work and self-indulgence over responsibility, and a climate of opinion that supported the expression of those character traits as "liberating" rather than deploring them as depraved all played a role. The country was experiencing an increase in crime, according to Wilson, largely for two interrelated reasons: because we had gotten into the habit of "understanding" crime and thereby explaining away the moral onus on criminals, and because we were failing to vindicate the maxim "Crime doesn't pay." Due to the laxity of the criminal-justice system, said Wilson, crime *did* pay, and young men who noticed that, and who lacked the social or characterological resources to resist temptation, became criminals.

The prescription of *Thinking about Crime* was straightforward: convincingly reassert the middle-class virtues as against the "do-your own-thing" spirit of the Sixties, and ramp up the capacity of the criminal-justice system to deliver punishment in order to make crime no longer pay. Then we would see crime recede, even without delivering on the Great Society promise of redress of long-standing social, and especially racial, grievances.

Though Wilson's tone and analytic apparatus were different, the themes of his work were consistent with the "economic theory of crime" being developed contemporaneously by Gary Becker of the University of Chicago economics department.[9] To Becker, criminal activity, like all human activity, reflected the responses of selfishly rational actors to the incentives created by their desires and opportunities. People would offend, according to Becker, if and only if the rewards of offending, net of the risks of being punished, exceeded the rewards of not offending.

The arithmetic seemed to support the Wilson/Becker view.[10] The punishment for any given crime is largely random, and likely to be zero: that is, most offenses never even lead to an arrest. Still, it is possible to compute the average punishment per crime by dividing the total amount of punishment for any given crime (measured in person-days of incarceration) by various measures of the frequency of that crime. Assuming as an approximation that the number of prisoners is constant across any given year, the year-end count of the number of persons behind bars for any given offense, multiplied by 365, yields the aggregate number of person-days of incarceration being served for that offense. Divide that number by the total number of offenses of that type committed that year (eliding the fact that not all of the prison time served in any year results from offenses committed that year and, conversely, that most of the punishment for offenses that year will take place in future years) and the answer is the average number of days incarcerated per offense committed for that crime type. That number is what statisticians call an "expected value": that is, a probability-weighted average.

The answers were astonishing. In 1974, at the low point for punishment-to-offense ratios, there were about 6 million burglaries.* At the end of 1974, American prisons and jails housed just under 60,000 burglary arrestees and convicts. On average, then, each burglary resulted in about 1 *percent* of a year—about four days—behind bars.† (See chapter 5.) In light of these rather trivial punishment levels, high and rising crime rates did not seem very surprising.

Obviously, there was and is no such thing as a four-day sentence for a burglary, any more than there is a family with 2.7 children living at home

---

* About half of all burglaries are reported to the police; this calculation uses the higher survey-derived estimate.

† This calculation is complicated by the fact that about half of all burglaries were committed by juveniles; the risk facing an adult burglar would have been about eight days.

or an at-bat that results in .280 of a hit. Most burglaries never lead to an
arrest, so the punishment suffered by those burglars is zero. Of those that
lead to an arrest, some cases are never filed, some are dismissed, some are
"pled out" to lesser charges, and some (a tiny fraction) lead to acquittals.
Of burglars who plead guilty or are convicted, some get probation, some
get jail time (i.e., less than a year), and some get prison time. In addition,
many burglary arrestees spend time in jail awaiting trial.

The four-day figure represents the average of all those results for burglaries in 1974: most burglars not punished at all, a few getting multiyear
prison terms.

That result seemed to vindicate the Wilson viewpoint: the (average)
punishment was grossly inadequate to the crime. Punishments for the
other Part I offenses were equally unimpressive: 8 days per aggravated
assault, 28 days per robbery.

The combination of rising crime rates and shrinking prison capacity
over the decade 1964–74 meant that the "price" of a crime—in the form
of punishment—had been falling in the teeth of a crime wave. Clearly,
the falling punishment-per-crime ratio was partly the result of that crime
wave, since for any fixed amount of prison capacity more crimes meant
fewer cells available per crime. But the converse might be the case as
well; falling punishment-to-crime ratios might make crime even more attractive to potential criminals by reducing the risks they faced, thereby
accentuating the uptrend. That is the vicious circle of "enforcement
swamping," in which rising levels of crime so overtax the capacity to
punish as to make the uptrend self-reinforcing.[11]

While critics faulted the U.S. criminal-justice system as overly punitive because of its high ratio of prisoners to population, the picture looked
very different if the focus was on the ratio of punishments to crimes.
Western European countries indeed had much smaller prison populations
than did the United States compared to their total populations, but the
U.S. led in crime by a margin even greater than its lead in punishment.

As a result, the punishment per crime was actually higher in most
countries in Western Europe than it was here, just as the ratio in the
United States itself was higher in the low-incarceration (but low-crime)
1950s than it is today.

In that context, there seemed to be a reasonable case for building more
prisons in order to restore deterrence levels while also preventing crime

through the purely mechanical "incapacitation" effect: putting offenders behind bars separates them, albeit temporarily, from potential victims. Indeed, in the intervening three decades we have built prisons, and built prisons, and then built still more prisons, until some of us who supported expanding prison capacity from its low 1970s levels have started to feel like the Sorcerer's Apprentice, vainly looking for the "off" switch on a mechanism gone completely out of control.

After half a century in which U.S. incarceration per capita hovered around 150 per 100,000 population—higher than the rest of the developed world, but not grossly so—the past thirty years have seen that number grow to an astonishing—not to say appalling—700 per 100,000, the highest rate in the world. We now have 2.3 million people—just about 1 percent of the entire adult population—behind bars at any one time.[12] That increase accounts for part of the rather spectacular crime decrease the country has experienced since about 1994: how much is a matter of heated dispute.[13]

The combination of higher incarceration and lower crime has greatly multiplied incarceration-to-offense ratios, as shown in figure 1. The punitiveness index, which fell by 68 percent from 1962 to 1974, quintupled from 1974 to 2007. The punishment-price of a burglary, which fell from fourteen days in 1963 to four days in 1974, reached sixteen days in 2007.

But the political, ideological, legal, and administrative impetus behind the prison-building boom, which developed when crime was frighteningly high and rising, has not noticeably dissipated now that crime has decreased. On the contrary, the growth in the number of people whose livelihood comes from incarceration—building prisons, staffing prisons, serving communities for which a prison is an economic lifeline—and the rise of the prison guards' unions and the private prison industry as political forces supporting the policy of high incarceration have given the prison boom great momentum; it is only now being slowed by fiscal crises in state governments.

The devastation wrought by incarceration itself—on the prisoners most of all, but also on their families and the neighborhoods where their absence is an important demographic fact—is now too great to ignore. The prisons have not gotten better at reforming their inmates as they have grown larger; rather the reverse, as tight budgets and growing populations lead to more crowding and less rehabilitative programming.

Gang activity and violent ethnic conflict spill over from the institutions to the streets, and there is reasonable fear—though not, yet, much hard evidence—that the prisons may be a source of a problem Europe has to deal with but the United States has, until now, been spared: home-grown Islamic terrorists.

Incarceration rates in some population subgroups are now so high that having been in prison has lost much of its local stigma.[14] Not only is prison experience regarded as more or less normal in some neighborhoods (though it remains a great barrier to finding legitimate employment); it even confers a sort of prestige. The flood of prison returnees—600,000 per year, two-thirds of whom will be back "inside" within three years—now constitutes a major social problem in its own right.[15]

Arguably, if the choice were between high incarceration and the high crime that results from too little deterrence and too many criminals running around loose, the country would be better off accepting high incarceration. But at some point, surely, the cure is more painful than the disease. With the crime rate 15 percent lower today than it was in 1974 and the incarceration rate four times as high, the average prisoner today must be far less criminally active than his counterpart thirty years ago, suggesting that further expansion will hit the law of diminishing returns.[16] Beyond some level—and we may well have passed that level[17]—the scale of imprisonment can generate so many perverse effects that additional incarceration becomes, on balance, a contributor to the problem rather than the solution. (For a discussion of the problem of "mass incarceration," see chapter 6.)

Yet crime remains a central social problem, especially in poor, black high-crime neighborhoods. The burden of crime, and the burden of crime control, are alike hard to bear. Is there a way out of the trap?

Thinking about Crime Control

To think clearly about crime-control policy, we need to weigh the gains from reducing crime, and the threat of crime, against the costs—in money, in liberty, and in suffering—of crime-control efforts. That weighing requires us to consider how much damage crime now does.

By contrast with illicit drug abuse—where three decades of study have convinced me that, aside from the link with crime, there is much less to the problem than popularly supposed*—crime has been a badly underestimated problem (more so among scholarly experts than among ordinary citizens or elected officials), especially in terms of the damage it does to otherwise disadvantaged groups.

Since it is hard to imagine a world entirely without crime, it is hard to give a meaningful answer to the question, "How much total damage does crime do?" The practical question before us is always how to value the change in the level of victimization risk—which is distinct from the crime rate[1]—that would result from some policy intervention.

Since the obvious losers from crime are victims, the most straightforward approach to measuring the social cost of crime is to add up the damage to victims. Crime victims lose property, incur medical expense, miss time from work, and experience pain, suffering, disability, and residual fear, all of which they would pay something to avoid if they could. In principle, we could try to sum up the direct financial costs and the "willingness-to-pay" associated with the non-monetary losses from victimization to determine the total damage. But it does not make much

---

*Addiction can be a horror for both the addicted person and his or her family, friends, coworkers, and neighbors. But only a minority of illicit drug users ever develop substance-abuse disorders, and most of those problems resolve themselves over a period of months or a few years. At least three-quarters of the people in this country who are addicted to an intoxicating drug are addicted primarily to the one legal intoxicant, alcohol, which also accounts for most of the drug-related crime, disease, job loss, accidents, and fetal damage. Aside from its substantial contribution to crime and incarceration, the abuse of illicit drugs is a human tragedy but not a major threat to the social order. (See chapter 9.)

sense to ask someone, "What would you be willing to pay not to be shot?" still less "What would you be willing to pay not to be murdered?"

What does make sense is to ask what someone would be willing to pay to reduce a 1/10th of 1 percent chance of being shot (or robbed, or even killed) sometime this year to a 1/20th of 1 percent chance of the same event. After all, people in effect voluntarily accept small risks of victimization routinely, as they voluntarily accept the risk of a crash every time they get into an automobile.

As we look around, though, the measurable losses from crime do not seem to be especially large compared to the measurable losses from other sources of risk: surely not large enough to account for the level of public concern over crime.

THE COST OF BURGLARY

Residential burglary illustrates the puzzle. Surveys estimate that there are about 2.7 million completed residential burglaries in the United States. About 60 percent of those burglaries are reported to the police: presumably these are disproportionately burglaries involving larger property losses, since reporting a burglary is part of the process of making an insurance claim. The average reported property loss in those burglaries is slightly less than $2000. That puts the total loss to homeowners from burglary at about $5.4 billion per year, spread among 110 million households. Thus the average burglary loss per household is just under $50: about $4 per household per month.

And yet, people asked in a survey[2] how much they would be willing to pay out of their own funds to reduce burglary in their community by 10 percent gave an average answer of $100 per year (in current inflation-adjusted values).* Why in the world would people pay twice the total annual expected burglary loss to reduce burglary risk by only 10 percent? (Put a different way, it looks as if householders in the aggregate would be willing to pay $28,000 per burglary avoided, compared to an expected property loss of $2000.) That suggests either that householders over-value

---

*The survey, conducted in 2001, reported an average valuation of $83; adjusting for inflation, the $83 figure would be $100 in 2009 dollars.

burglary risk by a factor of about 15, or alternatively that they are valuing something other than broken windows and lost television sets.

One possibility is that "contingent valuation" survey methods fail to elicit a true willingness-to-pay estimate. Such surveys are notoriously difficult to interpret when asking about "ideal interests" such as saving whales or preventing distant famine, at least in part because the hypothetical choices the surveys ask people to make are so remote from their day-to-day experience. But the question about reduced burglary risk is perfectly concrete and personal; people hunting for apartments or houses routinely ask about the risks of crime. So there is no particular reason to think that the survey answers fail to capture respondents' actual preferences as expressed in their actual decision-making. The reader may wish at this point to introspect: would you be willing to add 1 percent to your rent check or mortgage payment to reduce your own risk of being burglarized by 10 percent?

A different concern is that respondents failed to distinguish between a 10 percent reduction (for example, reducing the risk from 3 percent per year, roughly the national average, to 2.7 percent per year) and a 10 *percentage point* reduction. Since very few apartments or houses face a risk as high as 10 percent per year to start with, the 10-percentage-point interpretation would not be a reasonable one, but perhaps respondents either had no firm belief about the actual starting risk and took their cues from the questions, or merely accepted the question as a hypothetical and tried their best to answer it as they thought it was being asked. Or perhaps someone asked to imagine an apartment facing a smaller risk of burglary imagines an apartment in a neighborhood more desirable in many ways: not only less burglary, but lower risk of other crimes, better schools, lower noise levels, and so forth. It is also possible that the respondents were valuing the safety of other households as well as their own, though the question specified that every household would have to pay the same amount.

While the measured level of victimization loss is not consistent with the attention paid to burglary in particular and crime in general in local political campaigns, the survey-estimated willingness-to-pay is. If householders actually valued their risk of being burglarized at no more than $50 per year, it is hard to see why burglary should be a major campaign issue, while much larger variations in other household costs—utility bills, for example—are so much less salient politically. A cultural critic might accept both that the survey results reflect actual willingness-to-pay and that they are unreasonably high, and explain the inconsistency in terms of irrational fear of crime, linked in part to discomfort about ethnic heterogeneity, and promoted by crime-obsessed mass media (especially local television news[3]) and politicians.

While any of these factors might account for some of the difference between the measured property-loss figures and the survey-estimated willingness-to-pay to avoid burglary risk, it seems hard to imagine that any of them, or all of them together, could account for such a huge disproportion between observable victimization losses and the reported intensity of individual and political concern.

One difference between victimization losses and other costs is that victimization doesn't just *happen*. Victimization is *done* to someone by someone else. Being singled out—even anonymously—by another person for ill-treatment is a different experience than being the victim of mere happenstance. "Even a dog," said Justice Holmes, "knows the difference between being stumbled over and being kicked."

This is so in part because a deliberate act sets a precedent in a way that an accident does not: having been once a victim naturally raises fears of further victimization, with no assurance that subsequent crimes will not be more serious than the original. Burglary victims often report feeling less safe at home thereafter, and that feeling of insecurity represents a real, and sometimes very substantial, loss even if difficult to measure in dollar terms.

In addition, all victimization includes insult as well as injury, because to victimize someone is to treat that person as one whose rights can be violated and whose interests can be disrespected. There is evidence that being victimized (but not suffering accidental loss) tends to reduce the victim's standing in her own eyes and in the eyes of those around her, and that the effect is worse if no retribution is exacted from the perpetrator.[4]

THE COSTS OF AVOIDING VICTIMIZATION

Using victimization losses as an estimate of the social cost of crime omits the losses crime inflicts on those who are never actually victimized.

Those losses provide a straightforward explanation for what would otherwise seem an unreasonably high willingness-to-pay to avoid what is, in strictly financial terms, the fairly modest risk associated with residential burglary. Some of those losses are intangible, in the form of anxiety. Some are diffuse and hard to measure, such as the damage crime does to interpersonal trust, which is an important contributor to collective social capital* and the contribution of crime to ethnic and social-class tensions. But one class of nonvictim losses is easily observable: the costs of efforts to avoid victimization.

At the very simplest, doors have locks, and people carry keys to open them. The costs of the locks, the keys, the anxiety associated with forgetting or losing one's keys, the inconvenience and expense of occasionally locking oneself out: these are all costs of avoiding crime. At a more elaborate level, there are high-security windows, burglar alarms, and commercial neighborhood security services: the annual expenditure by homeowners (as opposed to landlords) on this class of devices and services exceeds their total property losses from actual burglary.

But the dominant form of crime-avoidance cost comes from shaping one's behavior in order to reduce victimization risk. In the case of residential burglary, that means, primarily, moving to a safer neighborhood, or not moving to a riskier neighborhood despite its other advantages. The economic geography of every metropolitan area provides testimony to the importance of crime as a factor shaping residential (and business) location decisions. How else could one account for the coexistence of housing abandonment and new housing construction only a few miles apart? There are many reasons for moving to the suburbs, but surely crime is high on the list.

Crime-avoidance behavior imposes costs even on those who do not themselves engage in it. It would be unusual, in adding up the social costs of crime, to include the cost of long commutes on crowded highways and the land-use, air-quality, and energy-consumption consequences that flow from those commutes. But it would be a mistake to omit them; average commutes would be shorter if fewer people fled the cities and the inner

*Also called "collective efficacy," collective social capital measures the capacity of a group, such as a neighborhood, to get its members to make contributions for the good of the group. See the discussion of "Broken Windows" in chapter 6.

suburbs to avoid crime, and every commuter adds to the time other commuters spend caught in traffic. The secondary consequences in the form of ethnic and social-class segregation and ethnic tension are even harder to measure and value, but not necessarily less important. Of course race prejudice is one source of the fear of crime, but it is hardly plausible that the fear of crime does not help support race prejudice.

The direct and secondary costs of crime avoidance dwarf the immediate costs of victimization. Even the highway construction costs generated by the sprawl which in turn is generated by the desire to avoid being burglarized doubtless exceed the $5 billion per year in property taken by burglars.

Turning our attention from residential burglary to other crimes, we find similar phenomena: victimization losses that seem too small to justify the level of public and private concern, unless we take moral outrage at injustice, fear, and the cost of precaution into account. About 17,000 Americans each year die from criminal violence; about 46,000 die on the highways, and auto accidents involve a higher ratio of long-term disability to death than do gunshots.[5] Even accidental poisoning accounts for as many deaths each year as homicide,[6] yet no one considers accidental poisoning a major social problem, while even modest movements in the homicide rate make headline news.

PRIVATE BENEFITS AND SOCIAL COSTS IN CRIME AVOIDANCE

It might seem that if avoidance costs exceed victimization losses, the avoidance costs must be irrationally high. Not so. The victimization losses we observe are those that remain after potential victims have taken countermeasures in the forms of locks, burglar alarms, gated communities, and suburban addresses. One reason crime has fallen in the past decade is that potential victims—households and businesses—have moved away from high-crime neighborhoods into low-crime neighborhoods.

Much crime-avoidance behavior is wasteful from a social perspective, but not from an individual perspective. If my putting a burglar-alarm sticker on my front door simply leads a burglar to break into my neighbor's home instead, the victimization loss is shifted rather than avoided, and in effect I incur a real resource cost to make sure that someone else suffered the cost of being burglarized. Socially, the alarm represents a waste of resources. But that fact makes putting up the sticker no less rational for me as an individual. For any given level of actual burglary, in my selfish private calculation I would prefer to have more of the risk fall on you and less on me. In this way, precaution against crime sometimes illustrates Robert Frank's category of "smart for one, dumb for all."[7]

Crime-avoidance behavior can impose costs on others beyond shifting crime risk. Even putting aside the environmental, traffic, and land-use costs of suburban sprawl, residents fleeing high-crime neighborhoods generally make things worse for those who stay behind; abandoned houses make bad neighbors, and on average it is the more successful who are able to escape areas of concentrated poverty, to the detriment of the remaining poor. The effects of business-location decisions driven by crime-avoidance considerations can be equally severe; businesses that move out or restrict their hours deprive neighborhood residents not merely of convenient services but also of job opportunities.

This is a particular problem in low-income urban minority neighborhoods. Whether the "spatial mismatch" between the location of the unemployed and the location of unfilled jobs is an important cause of high minority unemployment remains a contested question,[8] but there can be no doubt that having to commute farther to work is, at best, an inconvenience, especially for teenagers who would be working only part-time in any case and whose attachment to the labor market may be weak. And those disadvantages tend to accumulate, since teenagers with less work experience become less attractive employees as young adults. Worst of all, anything that makes licit employment less attractive will tend to make its illicit alternatives more attractive;[9] and a criminal record can be a very substantial barrier to subsequent employment in the licit economy.

Crime to job loss to poverty to crime is a positive-feedback loop: high-crime neighborhoods tend to be low-opportunity neighborhoods, low-opportunity neighborhoods encourage criminal activity by their residents, and that criminal activity makes the neighborhoods even less attractive places in which to live and do business, and some of the residents less attractive as potential employees. Loss of residents, especially the relatively prosperous residents most likely to be able to afford to move out, makes a neighborhood less attractive to retail businesses, and the loss of retail services in turn makes the neighborhood a less attractive place to live for those who have other options.[10]

THE UNEVEN IMPACTS OF CRIME

That poverty is a cause of crime is a commonplace, though the mechanisms involved are complex and poorly understood. That crime is a sustaining cause of poverty is no less true, though in the past it has been much less remarked on. The poor are victimized directly; the probability of criminal victimization rises steadily with income. They are victimized again as a result of crime-avoidance behavior that limits their opportunities and blights their neighborhoods. Philip J. Cook sums up the new consensus: "Safe streets are a necessary platform for neighborhood growth and prosperity . . . the notion that poverty is the mother of crime has been turned on its head."[11]

The picture is worst for African Americans; even adjusting for overall lower incomes, African Americans suffer much more crime than do members of other ethnic categories.[12] Homicide provides the most dramatic example; representing less than 15 percent of the population, black people suffer more than 50 percent of the murders.[13]

Here again, the problem tends to be self-sustaining. Since enforcement and prosecution resources are much more equally distributed than is crime, an offender who commits a crime where crime is common is less vulnerable to arrest, vigorous prosecution, and a stiff sentence than an offender who commits the same crime in a more law-abiding neighborhood. Given strong patterns of residential segregation by race, the average African American grows up in a higher-crime environment than the average white American at the same income level. The current system fails to fulfill the constitutional mandate of "equal protection of the laws," if "equal protection" means that a crime against a poor or black person will be investigated as diligently, prosecuted as forcefully, and punished as severely as the same crime against a rich or white person.

Assuming that the threat of punishment has some deterrent effect, growing up where that threat is smaller—and licit economic opportunity less available—should be expected, other things equal, to lead to a higher rate of criminal activity. And indeed that is what we find. African Americans are far more heavily victimized than others, but not as a result of cross-ethnic aggression; crime is overwhelmingly intra-racial.

Add to this the observation that witnessing and experiencing victimization is itself criminogenic, and we need not search for any deep cultural—still less biological—explanation for the vast racial gap in rates of crime commission. Even at the lower per-crime punishment risk that results from committing crimes in high-crime locations, the much higher level of criminal activity among African Americans leads to much higher rates of arrest, conviction, and incarceration: black people account for approximately half of all prison inmates, three times their proportion in the overall population.[14]

Paradoxically, then, efforts to reduce the racial disproportion in the prison population are likely to intensify the implicit racial discrimination among victims that results from lower per-crime rates of punishment, leaving African Americans even more exposed to victimization. The critique of the current system in terms of imposing prison terms and the consequent social stigma on a much higher proportion of African Americans than of whites[15] is fully justified by the facts, but the mechanisms involved are far more subtle than conscious, or even systemic, racial discrimination by officials against black perpetrators.

Indeed, racial disproportion in incarceration has grown even as racial prejudice and discrimination have become less marked, in part at least because the criminal-justice system has become more diligent about punishing crimes against black victims. Providing something closer to actual equal protection of the laws[16] would make the problem of disproportion in punishment worse, not better, unless and until higher per-crime punishment risks caused African American crime rates to fall. In some ways it would be better if, as is often asserted, systemic racial bias, in the form of more severe punishment for black offenders, lay at the root of the problem; then eliminating racial bias could eliminate disproportionate incarceration. But if the actual problem is the positive-feedback loop from high criminal activity to low punishment-per-crime back to high criminal activity, no such fix is available. The standard critique portrays a melodrama; the reality is a tragedy.

WHAT CRIME RATES FAIL TO MEASURE

If the bulk of crime-related loss is not victimization loss, then the rate of completed victimization—the crime rate—is not a good proxy for the seriousness of the crime problem. A neighborhood abandoned due in part to crime, or where residents stay inside behind locked doors for fear of muggers, or a park that many people are afraid to enter after dark, may have a lower rate of completed crime than a safer neighborhood or park, simply because so many fewer people are at risk. Even before the spectacular crime decrease of the 1994–2004 period, New York City actually had a relatively low burglary rate compared to other big cities, but the public impression that burglary risk was higher in New York was nonetheless probably correct: as a visitor might easily notice, New Yorkers were habituated to being much more careful about burglary-proofing their homes than was common in cities where burglary was less on residents' minds.

The paradox that more safety can actually lead to more injury by increasing the extent of the underlying activity is well known to safety engineers, who call the phenomenon "risk-compensation."[17] Perhaps its most familiar illustration is the increase in average highway speed, and therefore in the average seriousness of auto accidents, when drivers are persuaded to wear their seat belts. In that case, risk-compensation is undesirable, because those faster-moving drivers are imposing risks on others as well as accepting risks for themselves. But in the absence of such external costs, and assuming workably rational behavior by those subject to the risk, risk-compensation is a feature, not a bug, of safety engineering. If safer ski bindings reduce the risk of broken legs among skiers, leading to so much more skiing that the total number of broken legs goes up, there is no particular reason to think that the skiers are making a mistake. If today's airplanes were as dangerous as the airplanes of 1920, so few people would fly that the number of air-crash fatalities would be lower than it actually is, but that would hardly represent an overall improvement. Formally, risk-compensation is the same phenomenon as increasing total expenditure on some commodity in the face of a price decrease, due to greater sales; we would not in general say that consumers had been made worse off by falling prices for cell phones or personal computers simply because their total spending on those items increased.

The extent of risk-compensation is an empirical question. Sometimes the effect will be small, and the total incurred loss will fall just about proportionally to the decrease in risk. Other times the effect will be greater, and risk-compensation will mean that total incurred loss does not fall very much, or even rises, in the face of decreased risk.

Crime-control policy creates benefits not so much by reducing the number of completed crimes as by reducing the victimization risk in various parts of the social environment, and thus the costs, direct and indirect, of crime-avoidance behavior and fear, especially where crime risk is currently greatest. Unfortunately, victimization risk is much harder to measure than the frequency of completed crime, because avoidance behavior is hard to observe.* Thus practitioners, politicians, and scholars alike tend to think in terms of actual victimization rather than victimization risk. Yet it is the criminal riskiness of the social environment, not the number of completed crimes, that matters most.

Valuing Changes in Criminal Riskiness

How big is the crime problem overall? Or, since no real-world policy could make crime go away altogether, what would it be worth to reduce the size of the problem by some specified percentage?

The survey[18] that asked about how much additional housing expense people would be willing to pay in order to live with a 10 percent smaller risk of burglary asked the same question about four other crimes: homicide, armed robbery, rape and sexual assault, and other serious assault. All the answers fell into the range between $100 per year and $150 per year, yielding a total per-household willingness-to-pay for a 10 percent reduction in the risk of those five crimes alone of $640,† or something greater than $50 per household per month.

If the survey was properly designed and the respondents understood what they were being asked, that ought to reflect the value to them, as they see it, not only of reduced risk of actual property loss or personal injury but also of reduced avoidance cost and reduced residual fear. Whether the respondents took into account the benefit to them of reduced crime-avoidance behavior by other households is not entirely clear, but they were not prompted to do so by the question. Nor were they told to consider the costs crime and crime avoidance impose on businesses.

---

*Conceptually, the level of victimization risk in the social environment is measured by what the level of actual victimization would be, holding crime-avoidance behavior constant. How many hours could a pedestrian walk around this particular neighborhood before her risk of being mugged once reached 10%? How many nights can an automobile with a suitcase on the back seat be parked on this particular street before it had a 50% chance of being broken into once? (See above, "What Crime Rates Fail to Measure.")

†In dollars of 2009 purchasing power.

Minor assault, auto theft, larceny, and the whole range of public-order offenses from drug dealing to public excretion were omitted entirely, as were shoplifting and all "white collar" crimes.

Nonetheless, the sum is impressive: $640 per year times 110 million households comes to just more than $70 billion per year as the value of a 10 percent reduction in the five designated crime categories. If people are willing to pay five times as much for a 50 percent decrease as they are for a 10 percent decrease—a question that remains to be explored—the crime decline from 1994 to 2004 for those five crimes alone added about $350 billion per year (about 3 percent of gross domestic product) to the total well-being of American households, even ignoring external costs and the effects of minor crimes and crimes against businesses.

If anything, that sum should be an underestimate, since the willingness-to-pay survey was done after the bulk of the crime decline was already behind us. Adding back the other crime categories, external costs, and the impact of crimes against businesses on the availability and cost of goods and services and on the well-being of workers could easily bring the total welfare impact of crime on residents of the United States to $1 trillion per year: about $9000 per household per year, or $750 per month.

By contrast, the total expenditure on criminal-justice activities—police, prosecutors, defense counsel for indigents, courts, jails, prisons, probation, and parole—amounts to only $200 billion per year. That is a substantial sum—as the late Senator Everett Dirksen is inaccurately quoted as saying, "A billion here and a billion there, pretty soon you're talking about real money"—but not especially large as a proportion of GDP (about 1.5 percent) or compared to other objects of government spending. Public elementary and secondary education costs $550 billion per year; defense and intelligence spending about the same, even putting aside the costs of the wars in Iraq and Afghanistan. The public contribution to health-care costs is $1 trillion per year, about half the nation's total annual health-care expenditure of something more than $2 trillion. (The public crime-control budget does exceed the budget for public *higher* education, about $150 billion.)

Of the $200 billion per year in criminal-justice spending, about 60 percent is the cost of police services, about a quarter the cost of prisons and jails, and the final 15 percent accounts for everything else: courts, prosecutors and publicly paid defense counsel, and community corrections (probation and parole).

Police services loom large in local government spending. Prisons take a substantial and growing share of state budgets; with much of those budgets already committed by law to K-12 education, Medicaid, transportation, and debt service, rising prison budgets have tended to crowd out higher education, the other big discretionary item in state spending. At the federal level, criminal-justice operations are minor, dwarfed by health, defense, and Social Security.

If crime is a $1-trillion-per-year-problem and if public spending on criminal-justice activity is a $200 billion budget item, then it would seem to follow that a substantial increase in the criminal-justice budget could be cost-justified by a rather modest impact on crime: a 10 percent increase in the budget would only need to produce a 2 percent decrease in crime to have benefits equal to its costs. Of course, such a calculation would neglect the non-monetary costs, to offenders and non-offenders, of investigation, arrest, prosecution, and punishment.

"THREE STRIKES AND YOU'RE OUT" FROM A
BENEFIT-COST PERSPECTIVE

A famous RAND Corporation study of California's draconian "Three Strikes and You're Out"* legislation[19] estimated that the cost of implementing the law—that is, building and staffing the additional prisons required to house the additional prisoner-years generated by the harsher sentences provided for in that law—would come to $6.5 billion per year. The authors of the study clearly regarded that as a frightening figure, a good reason not to pass the law.

And yet that study estimates that full implementation of "Three Strikes" would have reduced crime in California by nearly one-third just by getting criminals off the streets, ignoring any deterrent effect. That

---

* "Three Strikes" is the commonly accepted label for the law, passed by a voter initiative in 1994, which mandates extremely long prison terms for anyone previously convicted of two "serious or violent" felonies (including residential burglary) who is convicted of a third felony, even something as minor as a petty theft (which can be charged as a felony in California if the defendant has a prior misdemeanor conviction). In fact, much of the law's impact on prison populations comes from two other provisions: one doubling the prison sentence for a second "strike" and the other limiting parole release for all violent offenders.

$6.5 billion cost, divided by 11.5 million California households, would have amounted to $565 per household per year, or just under $50 per household per month. But if the burden of crime amounts to $750 per household—that figure might have been higher in 1994, at the very crest of the long crime wave—a reduction by one-third ought to be worth $250 per household per month. If so, the crime-reduction benefits of "Three Strikes" as estimated by the RAND team would have been five times as high as the cost to taxpayers.

Now, that does not prove that "Three Strikes" was a good idea; it almost certainly was not, because there were alternatives—sketched in the RAND report—that would have prevented more crime at less cost in money and suffering. But if indeed "Three Strikes" was a bad idea, that was because we could have done better, not because it was "too expensive" from the taxpayer perspective.

If we imagine the overall size of the California state budget as fixed by other factors and not likely to grow or shrink as a result of passing or not passing the Three Strikes law, perhaps "Three Strikes" was too expensive in the sense that the benefits of the programs it crowded out of the state budget—chiefly higher education—would have been greater than the benefits of the crime reduction due to "Three Strikes."[*] Since "Three Strikes" seems to be about the dumbest possible implementation of the selective incapacitation idea (see chapter 6), and we could have had the same crime reduction with fewer additional prisoners by allocating those extra prison spaces to create more incapacitation and deterrence, then certainly "Three Strikes" was inefficient. If, as is also probably true, spending the same money on strengthening community corrections would have produced much greater crime-control results, that too is a reasonable critique of the law. The same might be true of adding more police, but even a large percentage cut in prison spending would finance only a modest increase in policing, simply because the policing budget is more than twice as large as the corrections budget.

---

[*]This assumes that the overall size of the state budget is shaped by other factors and did not go up as a result of the costs of "Three Strikes" law, so additional prison spending came out of other spending rather than increased taxation. That assumption is probably a good approximation.

But the RAND study strongly suggests that the money taxpayers spent on those extra prison cells did the taxpayers more good than they could have done for themselves had the cells not been built and taxes cut (or not increased) as a result. If "Three Strikes," for all its flaws—it is often cited, not unfairly, as the prototypical excess of the "lock 'em up" school of crime-control thinking—nonetheless produced enough crime-control benefit to justify its financial cost, there is a strong reason to think that the current overall criminal-justice budget is too small. Given how much damage crime does, and how relatively little of our total resources we spend on criminal-justice operations, budget cost will not, generally, be a good argument against some proposal to expand the criminal-justice system.

NONMONETARY COSTS

Money, however, is not the only thing to be economized. The imposition of suffering is also to be avoided. Having fewer prisoners is desirable not, primarily, because prisons cost money, but because prisons are horrible places. They impose misery on, and probably do long-term damage to, not only those confined in them but also the people who care about those prisoners: their families, their friends, and their neighbors. The notion that deserved suffering somehow "doesn't count" is a piece of mere hand-waving with no rational basis in terms of benefit-cost analysis; desert may be, morally, a reason to punish, or a limit on punishment, but it cannot be a reason to ignore the fact that punishment hurts. And in the usual case the suffering of the families, friends, and neighbors of prisoners is entirely undeserved.

The monetary equivalent of the suffering inflicted on the typical prisoner and those who care about him by having him confined may well exceed the $100 per day or so it costs to lock him up; as far as I know, the appropriate survey has never been done.*

---

*Technically, this is a "willingness-to-accept" rather than a "willingness-to-pay." A family that could not actually pay $35,000 to keep one of its members out of prison for a year might not willingly accept that amount as compensation for his incarceration. The problem is complicated by the fact that prisoners and their families tend to be poor; on the other hand, even poor prisoners often have non-poor relatives and friends.

Policing and community corrections involve a higher ratio of threat to actual punishment than do prisons or jails. That means that non-prison spending should be preferred to prison spending if they achieve the same crime reduction. If an extra million dollars' worth of police protection prevents as much crime as could be prevented by spending the same amount on incarceration, then the total cost per crime prevented—counting the suffering inflicted as a kind of cost—is lower for policing than it is for incarceration. The same is true when comparing incarceration to community corrections.

Expanding even these less punitive parts of the system has a cost in terms of liberty, and that too should be economized. But we should keep in mind that living under the threat of crime is also liberty-reducing; "freedom from fear" applies to more than fear of arrest.

At least as far as juveniles are concerned, there is evidence that the public prefers less punitive to more punitive measures that have the same crime-control efficacy. Whether that preference reflects concern for the individuals punished or worry about the long-term impacts of punishment on future criminal behavior is not clear; nor is it clear how much that preference carries over to the population of adult offenders. But at least to some extent public preferences seem to match the results of benefit-cost analysis: since suffering is bad, we should prefer to impose less of it, even on offenders.

The nonmonetary costs of criminal-justice operations—being surveilled, stopped, questioned, frisked, arrested, booked, held pending arraignment, held pending trial, jailed, imprisoned, and made subject to the rules of probation and parole and the orders of probation and parole officers, bearing the stigma of a criminal record, and having all of those things happen to one's family, friends, and neighbors—are not equally distributed across the population. Like crime, criminal justice hits hardest at those who already have the least: the poor, the homeless, and members of otherwise disadvantaged ethnic groups, above all African Americans.[*]

The very same neighborhoods where crime takes its highest toll also bear the brunt of enforcement and punishment. In the same census tracts in which homicide is a leading cause of death for males 15–35, nearly half of the men who have reached age thirty have at least one felony conviction.

---

[*]The direct burdens of criminal-justice operations also weigh disproportionately on men rather than women, and on young adults rather than juveniles or older adults.

That probably reduces the deterrent effect of criminal-justice operations for the residents of those neighborhoods; as arrest and incarceration become routine rather than extraordinary, they must lose some of their fearsomeness, without, unfortunately, losing their power to damage future licit economic opportunity. And someone who has already been to prison has less to lose by going back than someone who has never been to prison has to lose from his first felony sentence.

If the arguments made up to this point are correct, merely easing up on enforcement and punishment in those areas would do their law-abiding residents no favor. But the moral imperative of finding ways to reduce criminality other than by imposing suffering is especially potent where the criminality and the suffering are currently the greatest, and where all the positive feedbacks are working in the wrong direction.

"ROOT CAUSES"

While crime goes along with bad social conditions—poverty, discrimination, unstable family structure, unstable housing, poor educational outcomes, exposure to toxins such as lead—the claim that "fixing the root causes of crime" can substitute for effective criminal-justice operations as a primary means of crime control, and do the job at an equivalent dollar cost, seems far-fetched. Better educational outcomes for young people otherwise at high risk of criminal activity would, no doubt, reduce the average crime rate among those young people, but there is no evidence that simply increasing the budget of a big-city school system by 20 percent would have any substantial crime-control effect, and a 20 percent increase in public education spending would cost the same amount of money as doubling the police budget.

That said, however, it remains the case that controlling crime by providing services, where it works, is greatly preferable to controlling crime by threatening or inflicting damage. That is so partly, but only partly, because the long-term effects of services are likely to be on balance crime-reducing, while the long-term effects of punishment seem to be at best a wash. The primary argument is moral, not "practical" in the narrow sense. We incarcerate 1 percent of our adult population at any one time, and a much larger percentage than that of social groups that suffer other kinds of disadvantage as well. William Stuntz of Harvard Law School calculates that the incarceration rate among African Americans exceeds the Soviet incarceration rate at the peak of the Gulag.[20] That ought to bother us. And the positive-feedback nature of the crime problem means that services, though they may compete with criminal-justice operations for budget dollars, are synergistic with criminal-justice operations in the field. Whatever shrinks the baseline level of offending increases the pressure on the remaining offender population from any given criminal-justice effort.

The problem is to find actual, feasible, scalable social programs that actually reduce crime, for amounts of money comparable to the cost of reducing crime using force and the threat of force. Given the extent of social gains from reducing crime, any substantial crime reduction we could bring about just by spending practicable amounts of money—without at the same time imposing suffering—will be cheap at the price. An expenditure of $1 billion per year would be justified by a crime reduction of as little as 1/10th of 1 percent: not a very high hurdle to clear, especially considering that non-enforcement programs that reduce crime generally do so by making people better off in other ways.

Hope

Three very different programs point to the practical possibility of having less crime and less punishment, while spending no more money than we now spend on the criminal-justice system and doing only things we already know how to do. All illustrate the simple principle that the more credible a threat is, the less often it has to be carried out.

ENFORCING PROBATION IN HAWAII

Judge Alm had a problem. Probation officers were sending him reports of probationers—on probation for all manner of felonies from burglary to auto theft, from sexual assault to drug dealing—who were continuing to use methamphetamine, Hawaii's number-one problem drug. The files fairly bristled with violations: probationers accumulated multiple missed or positive drug tests, often as many as ten, before a report was made to the court. Those violations reflected very high levels of drug-taking, since tests were given only when probationers came in to meet their probation officers, and those meetings were scheduled weeks in advance: a probationer could avoid being caught simply by not using the drug for the three days before he was due to meet his probation officer. Nevertheless, one-fifth of all tests came back positive, and another one-tenth of the probationers called in for testing on any given day simply failed to show up. (Those numbers were consistent with findings from probation offices in a diverse set of counties in California.[1]) Either those probationers really could not quit, even for a few days, or they simply did not regard violating probation rules as anything to worry about.

Under the Hawaii system, each felony probationer had a long prison term hanging over him: typically five or ten years. Revocation of probation meant sending the probationer back to serve the "open term," which seemed unnecessarily drastic to both probation officers and judges, especially in light of the state's prison-crowding problem.

Alm, newly appointed to the state trial court bench in Honolulu after a career as a prosecutor culminating in a term as the United States Attorney, was frustrated and puzzled. Why, he asked the probation officers, was he only hearing about the continued drug use of these probationers when it had gotten completely out of control? If this is the tenth violation, what happened the first nine times?

The probation officers politely explained the realities of the system. Each of them had a caseload of about 180 felons. Most probationers are at least sporadically noncompliant. The probation officers could not possibly write up a violation report for every missed or positive test, every missed appointment, every failure to appear for drug treatment or anger-management class. Not only would writing those reports use up all of their time—a 30 percent monthly violation rate, out of caseloads of about 180, would have meant a dozen violation reports per probation officer per week—the resulting probation-revocation hearings would use up all of the judge's time. A revocation hearing, at which the probationer potentially faces being sent to prison for the number of years remaining in his sentence, is always strongly contested by the defense attorney, who wants to cross-examine the probation officer, and is therefore a time-consuming process. Moreover, the "open term" was simply not a plausible response to an occasional violation of probation conditions. As the probation officers saw it, probationers will be probationers, and the job of the probation officer is to jawbone those who will listen back into compliance and refer to the court only those who will not listen, after they have accumulated violation records that make a strong case for revocation.

Well, that made a kind of sense. But, Alm thought, it didn't make the right kind of sense. You wouldn't train a puppy that way. You wouldn't bring up a child that way. You'd have clear rules, and clear consequences for breaking them, and those consequences would happen right now, not in the sweet bye-and-bye.

After all, said the judge to the probation officers, probation is supposed to be a deal between an offender and the court: the probationer avoids a prison term in return for a promise to abide by the probation rules. Alm wanted to know every time that deal was broken.

Impossible, they explained. Writing up a violation report takes a couple of hours. There simply are not enough hours in a probation officer's day to write all those reports, or enough hours in a judge's day to hold all the hearings.

Judge Alm did not know it, but he was not the first to try to deal with the problem. The historical record offered examples, both good and (mostly) bad, and scholars had pointed out the elements of a workable system.[2]

For thirty years, Project Sentry had been operating in Lansing, Michigan, using frequent drug tests and immediate sanctions to reduce drug use and recidivism among probationers.[3] And for thirty years, the rest of the country had paid no attention. The District of Columbia Pretrial Service Agency seemed to get good results by drug-testing bail releasees,[4] but that innovation also failed to spread. A randomized controlled trial in Washington, D.C., comparing testing-and-sanctions within a drug court to the routine drug-court process including mandatory treatment, showed better behavior and lower costs in the testing-and-sanctions group.[5] But once the experiment was over the D.C. drug court went back to its old routine.

The Structured Sanctions Program for probationers in Multnomah County (Portland), Oregon, had established a structure so elaborate that the assigned sanction for the first five violations was one or another variety of warning; the result was no change in violation rates.[6]

In Maryland, a similar attempt, under the label Break the Cycle, had achieved mixed results: the testing part of the program had worked properly, and substantially reduced drug use rates among participating probationers, but failure to get the judges "bought in"—itself the result, in part, of a decision to start out the program at full blast with 17,000 probationers, rather than starting small and shaking it down before going to mass scale—had resulted in only sporadic enforcement of the intended sanctions. When a program participant with scores of violations who had never been sanctioned for any of them killed a police officer, Break the Cycle was effectively over, and along with it the political career of its sponsor.

But without knowing any of this, Judge Alm was convinced that the existing system had things backwards. He proposed a compromise to the probation department. He said, in effect, "Let's start with the people you're already writing up. I'm not inclined to send them away, but clearly they need tighter supervision. So let's select a group of scofflaws, and make it the rule that each one of them gets written up every time he violates from now on. I won't revoke probation, but I can modify the terms of probation, imposing a short jail sentence: maybe seven days to start with, escalating if the violations don't stop. Then the guy comes right back to your caseload, and with any luck he'll be in a more compliant mood. And why should it take two hours to write up a violation notice, since we're not thinking about a revocation and don't have to consider the probationer's entire history? Mostly the reports are going to be about missed or positive drug tests. How does today's report differ from yesterday's? Just the name, the date, and the drug. Let's design a short fill-in-the-blanks report form that you can fax to my chambers." That last step solved the probation officers' workload problem by reducing a process that would otherwise take hours to one that takes a few minutes.

Grudgingly, after much pushing, the probation office agreed to give the new system a try. Alm held a contest among the probation officers to find a name for the new program, and the winning entry was "Hawaii's Opportunity Probation with Enforcement": H.O.P.E.

In the meantime, Judge Alm—who has a much better management imagination than the typical judge, or for that matter the typical manager—had been thinking about all the moving parts in the probation-enforcement machine.

First, he needed to get swift reports from the probation officers. That seemed settled, at least tentatively.

Second, he needed to make time in his calendar. If he was going to use relatively mild sanctions, they needed to be immediate to be effective. Fortunately, unlike many probation departments, which send out specimens for drug testing, Honolulu tests them on the spot. That made it technically possible to hold a hearing the day of the dirty test, or at worst the next day. Alm was willing to make the time: even if he was in trial, the hearing could happen before or after the court day, or during a recess. Again, since the facts were simple—Did the test come back positive?—and the consequences not very drastic, the hearings could be fairly quick. So he instructed his staff to schedule probation modification hearings immediately: a probationer testing positive in the morning would come before the judge that afternoon, while the same result in the afternoon would lead to a hearing the next morning, with the probationer in jail overnight.

While Hawaii's probation officers have arrest powers and could in-
struct a probationer not to leave their offices, someone had to physically
take the person into custody. Judge Alm persuaded the sheriff to assign
his deputies to that duty. And, in case a H.O.P.E. probationer failed to
come in voluntarily, he got the U.S. Marshal to agree to use the Fugitive
Task Force to bring him in. Despite the chronic crowding problem in the
Honolulu jail, the judge was also able to convince the manager of the jail
to make space available right away for H.O.P.E. sanctions.[*]

Even a probation-modification hearing requires a prosecutor and a
defense attorney. But big-city criminal lawyers are busy, and holding a
hearing right away means having the lawyers available right away. So
Judge Alm, working on the principle that participation generates "buy-
in," brought in a supervisory deputy prosecutor and the public defender,
along with the probation department, to help craft the program. The
deputy prosecutor designed the short probation modification form. He
and the public defender volunteered to cover the initial hearings. That
soon changed to simply enlisting any assistant district attorney and any
assistant public defender that happened to be handy to act as prosecutor
and defense attorney for a modification hearing. Again, the facts were going to be simple enough, and the stakes low enough, so that no elaborate
preparation would be needed.

The supervising deputy prosecutor was enthusiastic and the public
defender, intrigued with the idea that it might be possible to use the probation system to get some of his office's repeat-business clients back on
the straight and narrow path, was also willing to cooperate. But he asked
what turned out to be the crucial question: "You're going to warn them,
aren't you?" To switch probationers from the easygoing process of routine probation to the unbending H.O.P.E. regime without letting them
know in advance would, he said, be both unfair and unlikely to work well.

That seemed reasonable to the judge, so he invented a new court
proceeding, called a "warning hearing." A probationer selected for the

---

[*] Alm, as a former local prosecutor and U.S. Attorney, had much more clout with the
rest of the criminal-justice system and the rest of the state's political process than the average state trial court judge. And Hawaii has a more collegial public-management culture
than do many other states, as well as better-educated probation officers (most with master's
degrees in social work and training in cognitive-behavioral therapy). That leaves it an open
question how much of this could be exported to the mainland, along with the pineapples and
the thousands of prisoners Hawaii sends to for-profit mainland prisons.

H.O.P.E. program—generally as a result of violating probation terms several times—would be called in for a hearing in open court, with the probation officer, defense counsel, and prosecutor all present.

At the hearing,* the judge would make a speech, which he subsequently reduced to a script that other judges could use. A short version of that speech would be:

"Everyone in this courtroom wants you to succeed on probation. But you're not doing your part. When you went on probation, you made a deal with the court: instead of going to prison, you were going to comply with the terms of your probation. You haven't been doing that. I could send you to prison to serve out your original term. But instead, I'm putting you on the H.O.P.E. program. Every time you miss a meeting with your probation officer, every time you test positive, every time you don't show up for treatment, there's going to be a sanction: you're going to spend some time in jail, right away. You'll be arrested on the spot. If you don't come in, a police officer will come to get you, and the sanction will be tougher. Now maybe you'll decide to smoke some meth on a Thursday when you have a meeting with your probation officer that Friday and your baby's first luau is planned for that Sunday. If that happens, you're going to miss your baby's first luau, because *you decided to miss it* when you decided to break the rules. You are a grown-up, and it's time for you to take responsibility for your own actions. I hope I don't have to see you again. Good luck."

H.O.P.E. started with thirty-five probationers, identified by their probation officers as chronic violators. They were brought in for a group warning hearing. And the system braced itself for a flood of violations. After all, these were worse-than-average probationers in a system where the average probationer either failed to show up for a test or tested positive about three times in ten, even when the tests were scheduled far in advance. If thirty-five people got tested the next week, with a violation rate of 30 percent per test, that would mean about ten hearings that week.

But a very strange thing happened: the dog did not bark in the nighttime. That first week there were three hearings, not ten. In the month after that first warning hearing, exactly eight of the thirty-five H.O.P.E. probationers committed a violation. That meant that the actual new workload

---

* All of the H.O.P.E. procedures are described in detail in a "Bench Book"—a sort of judges' manual—prepared by Alm.

for probation officers, court staff, sheriffs, police, prosecutors, defense counsel, the judge's staff, the judge himself, and the jail was perfectly manageable. The biggest strain was on the probation officers: not because they were writing up violation reports, but because they could no longer count on having slack in their schedule because of no-shows for appointments. In fact, in the year after that hearing, fewer than half of the thirty-five problem probationers had to be called in for a sanctions hearing at all. Even more impressively, of those who were sanctioned a first time, fewer than half earned a second sanction.

After six months Alm tightened up the drug testing regimen. Now all H.O.P.E. clients were all to be tested weekly, on randomly assigned days. Each probationer was given a color, and required to call an automated "hot line" after midnight each day. If his color came up, he had until 2 p.m. to show up for a drug test.

The violation rate among H.O.P.E. probationers continued to fall with every additional month they spent on probation, eventually reaching a level more than 90 percent lower than the level for the three months before they were put on H.O.P.E.[7] By contrast, in a comparison group of probationers who would have been assigned to H.O.P.E. had they been among Judge Alm's cases but chanced to have other judges, the violation rate went up over time, as if they were learning how much they could get away with. H.O.P.E. participants were rearrested for new crimes less than half as often as the comparison group, and on less serious charges, promising not only reductions in crime but also savings in future prison costs. And the revocation rate was so much lower among the H.O.P.E. group than among the comparison group that H.O.P.E. participants wound up spending less total time behind bars than the comparison group.

Probation officers, skeptical at first, became true believers as they discovered the satisfaction of exercising in fact the authority they have on paper. And the probationers themselves, even those who have been sanctioned more than once, regard the system as fair; some of them give it credit for finally prying them away from chronic drug abuse.

In some ways, H.O.P.E. resembled a drug court: it was designed to keep drug-involved offenders out of prison, it involved the active supervision of a judge, it used—as some but not all drug courts do—immediate sanctions for breaking the rules. In other ways, it was utterly unlike a drug court: it was mandatory, where participation in a drug court is usually voluntary; it involved offenders already assigned to probation, not those whose alternative was prison; it was open to all probationers, where most drug courts carefully screen their participants and exclude those with histories of violence; it involved court appearances only to deal with violations, not for routine status updates.

Most of all, drug courts are built around treatment; every client is given a needs assessment and assigned a treatment plan; drug testing, if used at all, is thought of as monitoring treatment compliance. That, and frequent meetings involving the judge, the client, the probation officer, and the treatment provider, make drug courts profligate users of scarce resources: much cheaper than prison, of course, but still expensive, and in some areas absorbing so much of the available treatment capacity as to "crowd out" those voluntarily seeking treatment.

H.O.P.E., by contrast, is built around compliance, and specifically compliance with the rule "Stay away from illicit drugs." Treatment is available, and sometimes mandated for those who have repeatedly failed to comply with the rules, but the goal is not to get probationers to enter and remain in treatment; the goal is to get them to stop using, and to comply with other probation conditions. Since H.O.P.E. is much less expensive and much less time-consuming for the judge and the judge's staff, it can—where drug courts cannot—be expanded to mass scale. By the end of 2008, more than one in eight of all the felony probationers on the island of Oahu were assigned to H.O.P.E.: more than 1,000 people, or about one H.O.P.E. probationer per 800 residents, and still growing. At a national scale, that would be equivalent to about 400,000 participants. By contrast, two decades after the introduction of drug courts, the national drug court client count at any one time is still below 100,000.

Squeegee Men, Turnstile Jumpers, and Drunken Drivers

Among the crime problems that plagued New York City in the early 1990s, squeegeeing did not rank very high. But it was an annoyance, a drain on police resources, and a potent symbol of a city out of control.[8]

The "squeegee men" were, in effect, something between aggressive beggars and low-grade extortionists. They would approach cars stopped at red lights, clean their windshields, and then ask to be paid. Drivers feared, accurately or not, that a refusal would lead to their cars being damaged, and enough of them paid to make the practice worthwhile for those who engaged in it. Perhaps some drivers appreciated the service and did not mind paying for it, but the majority, or at least the ones who made themselves heard, regarded the experience as unpleasant and even frightening. The squeegee operators concentrated on the entry points to Manhattan, especially the exits from the tunnels, giving visitors an unpleasant welcome.

The activity was illegal, but its very triviality made it seemingly impossible to control. The offense was seen as too minor to warrant a full custodial arrest, with the time and expense involved in taking the offender to a lockup, booking him, and holding him for arraignment; instead, police issued Desk Appearance Tickets (DATs): merely orders to show up for a hearing later. The squeegee men frequently ignored the DATs—known to New York police officers as "disappearance tickets" for the high no-show rate of those ticketed—and even a squeegee artist who decided to show up in court was unlikely to face any substantial punishment. In a city averaging between five and six homicides per day, the notion of devoting substantial police resources to curbing what was at worst a nuisance seemed absurd, and Police Commissioner Raymond Kelly became the target of mockery when he announced that he was going to put an end to the squeegee problem.

Kelly announced (and his successor William Bratton continued) a "zero-tolerance" policy for squeegeeing. "Zero tolerance" as a slogan is frequently a thought-substitute; manifestly, given the range of illegal behavior in a big city, no police department could possibly make an arrest every time some law is broken. Even if there were enough police, there are not enough holding cells, prosecutors, courtrooms, or capacity to punish all lawbreakers, whether by collecting fines, keeping them in jail, or supervising them on probation. And since squeegeeing was certainly no more obnoxious than much other behavior that the NYPD perforce tolerated, the justification for singling it out for zero tolerance seemed hard to find.

What "zero tolerance" meant in practice was that officers were instructed to look out for squeegee activity, especially at the entrances to Manhattan where it was concentrated, to arrest every person seen engaged in it, and, most important, to make a full custodial arrest—handcuffs, trip to the lockup, mug shot, fingerprints, and booking—rather than issuing one of the despised DATs. Given the jammed court system, that meant at least a night in jail, and maybe more, before the arrestee was even arraigned.

Instead of merely starting to make the arrests and wait for the squeegee men to notice, Kelly and Bratton made a big public fuss about the program, and the squeals of outrage from editorialists and talk-show hosts who poured scorn on the NYPD for fiddling with squeegeeing while the city burned helped give the program publicity.[9]

Unsurprisingly, this level of enforcement pressure, maintained for a few months, drastically reduced the volume of squeegee activity. The perception that there were hordes of squeegee men—a perception fostered by the fact that no matter how many DATs were issued the squeegee operations never ceased—turned out to be false. Actually, what had seemed an intractable problem consisted of fewer than 100 offenders. And their earnings from the activity were not high enough to keep them active once the costs of squeegeeing came to include even a little bit of jail time. After a few months, the activity had dropped to a tiny fraction of its prior level. The NYPD was then able to maintain the "zero-tolerance" stance at a trivial cost in resources; since there was no longer much squeegee activity, there were not (and are not) many arrests, and the cost of surveillance is no higher than driving past the relevant intersections every once in a while.

Compared to dabbling, concentration actually saved police resources over time; devoting some focused attention to squeegeeing for long enough to accomplish that transition meant that the department could then devote near-zero attention to it from then on.

Broadly speaking, the effort to combat turnstile-jumping in the New York City subways followed a similar pattern: a somewhat resource-intensive burst of enforcement, followed by a rapid decline in the prevalence of the behavior and consequently in the demands that effort put on the transit police workforce. In each case, the result was virtually a "free lunch": a time-limited resource commitment achieved a lasting change in problem behaviors.

By contrast, drunk-driving checkpoints, which constitute a demonstrably effective approach to reducing the incidence of driving under the influence (DUI) and the rate of DUI-related accidents, remain resource-intensive even after they succeed in changing driver behavior. The cost of staffing the checkpoint does not fall with the frequency of driving drunk, and the efficacy of the effort does not extend much past the specific route or routes it targets. As a result, checkpoints are a costly means of dealing with the drunken-driving problem, and while many police departments use them they are always targeted at high-accident routes and high-accident occasions such as New Year's Eve.

Breaking Up Street Drug Markets

The Hard Way: Operation Pressure Point

By 1990, Alphabet City (an area of Manhattan's Lower East Side so far east that the avenues have letters rather than numbers) had been home to a vibrant, open-air drug market for a quarter of a century. Users literally stood in line outdoors to buy heroin and crack.[10] Neighbors complained, the police made arrests, some dealers went to jail or prison, and the market just kept rolling along. If a dealer was jailed, quit, or died—none of them unusual events—he was quickly replaced. The market was self-sustaining, both because the sheer concentration of dealing activity tended to protect buyers and sellers alike from arrest and because, once Alphabet City became known as the place to connect, it became the logical place to go for any dealer looking for customers and for any user looking for drugs.[11]

As it happened, New York City Police Commissioner Ben Ward, a transplant from Atlanta, had to drive through Alphabet City on his way to and from police headquarters. After a few months, seeing that massive open-air drug market twice a day was more than Ward could stand, and he announced a massive crackdown, dubbed "Operation Pressure Point."[12]

The numbers were impressive: 1,000 officers, six months, 17,000 felony arrests (which overwhelmed the capacity of the New York City criminal courts). At first, the dealers thought that Pressure Point was just one more "street sweep" operation, a familiar hazard of the trade. One dealing organization even sent its employees to Puerto Rico for two weeks' vacation, expecting that by the time the street dealers returned the police would be gone. But Ward was determined, and slowly the pressure began to drive dealers and users away from the market.* After six months, the operation ended, and the area went back to more or less normal levels of drug enforcement. But those levels turned out to be sufficient to keep the pressure on the reduced volume of dealing activity, and the market never bounced back. In part because Pressure Point had made Alphabet City safer, the area "gentrified," and the new look of the neighborhood made it even less attractive as a dealing spot.

Naturally, other neighborhoods with big drug-market problems demanded similar programs, but the resource demands—not so much on the police as on the court system—simply could not be sustained, and the lower-intensity Tactical Narcotics Teams that succeeded Pressure Point had much less dramatic results.[13] The take-home lesson seemed to be that a massive crackdown could have lasting benefits—unlike routine street drug law enforcement, which produces many arrests over time but leaves the market in place—but at a cost that the system could not bear very often.

The Smart Way: High Point, N.C.

Five years ago, High Point, N.C., was a small-to-medium-sized city (population 100,000) with big-city drug-market problems: three neighborhoods with concentrated and persistent dealing activity, mostly of crack cocaine.[14] Those markets had not yielded to almost twenty years of diligent routine enforcement; as usual, arresting and imprisoning one dealer simply created a market niche for a replacement.

Police identified the worst of those neighborhoods; careful mapping of nondrug crimes—scarce in the few blocks where the dealing took place, but concentrated in a ring around that area—confirmed the intuition of narcotics-squad officers about where the problems were most severe. The worst zone was in High Point's African American West End; the city overall is about 60 percent white, 40 percent black. A history of tension with the largely white police department had left the residents of the West End intensely suspicious of police activity even as they were also

---

*Some dealing moved geographically; some became more discreet; some of the less sophisticated and less committed out-of-town buyers may never have found another place in New York where they felt it safe or convenient to "score."

outraged by the ongoing blight the crack trade created for their neighborhood. (The suspicion and the outrage joined together in the belief that the police were complicit in the crack trade and willing to tolerate it as long as it was confined to black neighborhoods: a common belief among poor urban African Americans.)

The police department, advised by David Kennedy,* decided to tackle the community-relations problem head-on as a preliminary to launching a crackdown. Over several months of often painful dialogue, opinion in the neighborhood was won over to agreement with three propositions:

- that the drug trade itself was an intolerable burden;
- that it was conceptually separable from all the neighborhood's other grievances and from the wider pattern of racial injustice; and
- that the local young men who made a living dealing crack were doing so much damage to their neighbors that the community as a whole had the right and the duty to tell those young men to stop.

Amazingly enough, that turned out to be the difficult part. Given neighborhood support, actually suppressing the market turned out to be fairly cheap and easy.

The first step was identifying the dealers, which required no more than consulting police officers, their criminal informants, and some of the newly mobilized West End community leadership. As with the squeegee men in New York, the number of crack dealers turned out to be startlingly small; only the fact of constant replacement had made them seem numerous.

Of the twenty men identified as having dealt crack in the West End over the previous year, only sixteen were still active. Three were identified as not merely drug dealers but persistent violent criminals, targets for long prison terms if the police could arrange for them. The others

---

*David M. Kennedy, now a professor at the John Jay College of Criminal Justice and the director of its Center for Crime Prevention and Control (previously a Research Fellow at the Kennedy School's Program in Criminal Justice Policy and Management), has been applying ideas about focused and directly communicated deterrent threats—the strategy he calls "pulling levers"—to some of the most difficult problems in urban policing, with remarkable success (Kennedy 2009).

were simply drug sellers, who might be armed in the course of business but had no habit of violence.

For three months, the police did what they routinely do: they made undercover buys to establish cases against the identified dealers. What they did *not* do was follow up those cases with arrests. Instead, when there was a case ready to prosecute against every identified West End dealer, they did something completely unexpected: they sent out teams consisting of a police officer and a community leader to the homes of the suspects and . . . invited them in for a meeting.

At that meeting, the dealers received three messages from three different sources. Their neighbors told them that the dealing had to stop, but that the neighborhood was ready to support their efforts to go straight. Social-service providers offered a smorgasbord of assistance, from dental work to tattoo removal to job training. Then the police and prosecutors delivered the final message: "As of tomorrow morning, the market is closed." Each dealer was given a three-ring binder with all the material needed to send him away—down to an arrest warrant ready for a judge's signature—while a video screen showed a montage of covertly filmed undercover transactions. "Raise your hand," said the police chief, "when you see yourself committing a felony."

The three identified "bad actors" had already been arrested and faced long prison terms. Three other dealers who did not respond to the invitation were also arrested, as was one dealer who tried to enter the business to take advantage of the sudden dearth of competitors. But the others, facing the certainty of prosecution, simply quit. (Whether the prosecutors could have found the hours and the courtroom capacity to actually prosecute all of those dealers remains an open question; since the threat was credible, not much of it had to be carried out.)

What hundreds of arrests over most of two decades had failed to do, credible, concentrated warnings backed up by only seven arrests did: they broke up the market. While taking out one dealer simply made a job available to another, taking out all the dealers at once created a dealing desert, where buyers no longer came and any remaining sellers stood out, easy targets for enforcement. Five years later, that market is still closed, and the other markets in town fell to similar tactics. Not only are crime and dealing markedly down, allowing law-abiding West Enders to reclaim their streets for normal life, but arrests are down, too.

Not all of the young men who stopped dealing drugs went straight; several have been arrested for nondrug crimes. And the crack buyers did not have to go without their drugs; dealing activity reportedly moved to strip clubs on the edge of town. But dealing in the clubs does not disrupt ordinary life or lead to violence, and none of the lap-dancers has complained. The crackdown did little if anything to reduce drug abuse, but it did take control of the streets away from the dealers and their customers and return it to the other residents of the West End. Thus the High Point low-arrest crackdown generated all the benefits of a Pressure Point–style high-arrest crackdown, at a tiny fraction of the cost.[15]

For those of us interested in making the criminal-justice system deliver better crime control with less punishment, H.O.P.E., the squeegee crackdown, and High Point pose two simple questions: What is the magic ingredient? And can you bottle it?

Tipping, Dynamic Concentration, and the Logic of Deterrence

How could we design a crime-control strategy that reduces crime using as little actual punishment as possible?[*] To illustrate the underlying logic of the problem, imagine an offender who is fully rational in the economic sense of that term: capable of choosing from among alternative courses of action the one that best serves his preferences. Some of the implications of that simple model will be reinforced if we consider the imperfectly rational behavior characteristic of actual human beings; others will need to be qualified. For example, the imaginary rational actor will break a rule if and only if the (perceived) personal benefit of rulebreaking exceeds the cost. Most actual human beings behave differently: they are influenced by conscience, custom, and habit, by thoughts of what is fair, and by impulses that lead them to act in ways that, at some level, they "know" not to be optimal.[†]

The Basic Logic of Deterrence for a Single Rational Actor

Imagine, then, an economically rational, conscience-free actor subject to some rule. If he breaks the rule, he pays a fine F. If he complies, he pays compliance cost C. For instance, a firm subject to an environmental regulation might have to decide between obeying it and incurring higher production costs, or violating it and paying a regulatory penalty. Or the

---

[*] This chapter provides a formal model of the ideas about positive feedback, tipping, and concentration sketched in the introduction and the previous chapter. Readers whose eyes glaze over at such expressions as "$F > C > F / 2$" may wish to skim; the final part of the chapter explores in non-mathematical language some limitations of this approach. An animated version of the simulation model can be viewed at http://whenbruteforcefails.com.

[†] The distinction between "Econs" and "Humans" is discussed in Thaler and Sunstein's *Nudge* (2008).

"cost" of compliance could be a forgone benefit: something the subject wants—someone else's television set, for instance, or a methamphetamine binge—that can only be obtained by rulebreaking.

Holding the cost of compliance constant, what happens as the penalty increases? As long as the fine is below the cost of compliance (F < C), the rational subject will violate the rule, and pay the fine F. So as F grows from 0 to C, the rate of violation stays constant—the subject violates every time—and the total penalty inflicted increases in line with the penalty-per-violation. If the cost of compliance is $10, as the penalty moves from 0 to $9.99 the subject's behavior is unaffected and the amount of penalty actually imposed therefore grows. Within this range, sanction looks entirely futile. (See figure 2.)

But something strange happens when the amount of the fine goes from just under the cost of compliance to just above the cost of compliance: from $9.99 to $10.01.* A perfectly rational subject will never violate if he is certain to be punished and if the fine for breaking the rule is above the savings or gain from doing so. Therefore, as the fine imposed in case of a violation crosses the threshold, the violation rate goes from unity (a violation every time) to zero, and the total amount of fines collected also falls to zero, because the rule is not violated and therefore no fine is actually imposed. This illustrates economist Thomas C. Schelling's principle that the perfect threat never needs to be carried out.[1] Having more punishment available can lead to imposing less actual punishment.

Now, in the real world, few penalties are certain; there is usually a chance, often a good chance, of getting away with some nominally forbidden behavior. What happens if the amount of the fine stays fixed, but the probability varies? Again, if the fine F is less than the cost of compliance C, the rule will be broken every time. So the interesting case is where the penalty for getting caught is greater than the cost of compliance, but the probability of getting caught is less than unity. If, for example, the cost of compliance is $10 and the fine is $20, then the rational decision-maker, if he is also risk-neutral, will calculate the "expected value" of the sanction, given a violation, by multiplying $20 by the probability (call it p) of being punished if he offends. In this case, if the risk of sanction is greater than one-half, he will comply; if it is less than one-half, he will violate.

---

*To be precise, from $10 − ε to $10 + ε.

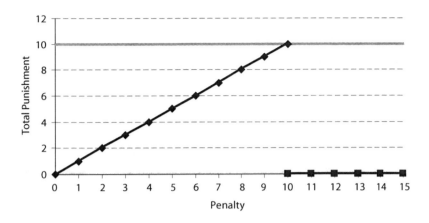

Figure 2. Stiffer penalty, less actual punishment

So as the probability of sanction grows from 0 to $1/2^*$ the subject's behavior does not change, and the expected sanction per turn grows from 0 to the probability multiplied by the fine (p times F). (See figure 3.) But as soon as p is high enough so that the value of the sanction risk is greater than the compliance cost (this is, when p times F, the expected value of the penalty, is greater than C, the cost of compliance)—as soon, that is, as crime does not pay on average—our imagined perfectly rational subject will stop breaking the rule, and the amount of fines collected will fall back to zero. Again, more sanction capacity leads to less actual sanction.

Of course, that assumes that the potential offender is not merely perfectly rational, but perfectly informed. If he cannot observe the risk of sanction directly, but has to infer it from experience, then the penalty may actually have to be imposed a few times before he "gets the message" and starts to comply. Probability theory includes a formula, called Bayes's Rule (sometimes called "Bayes' Theorem"), by which a rational actor, starting with some belief about the probability of some event, adjusts that original idea in the face of experience.[2] Assuming that the potential offender is a Bayesian updater, and also that the cost of compliance or gain from successful violation varies from round to round, softens the implausible "knife-edge" result where the violation rate falls suddenly to zero at

* In general, from 0 to C/F.

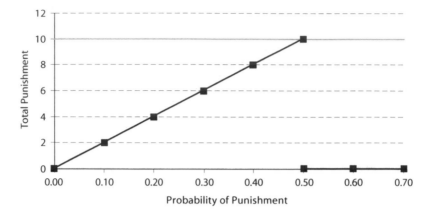

Figure 3. Higher probability of punishment, less actual punishment

some critical value, but the basic pattern remains the same: increasing the capacity to sanction, if it lowers the violation rate, can reduce the amount of sanction actually used.

MULTIPLE RATIONAL ACTORS AND INTERDEPENDENT DECISIONS

The problem grows more complex when more than one actor is subject to the rule, and where the enforcing authority does not have enough capacity to punish all of the subjects if all violate. Then the selfishly rational choices of the subjects may be interdependent.

For example, consider a situation with two subjects but only one available penalty, where the enforcement authority acts on an equal-opportunity basis—which, after all, seems fair—and chooses at random which one to punish if both violate. In that case, the probability of sanction, conditional on violation, is unity—the penalty is certain—if only one subject violates, but if both subjects violate it falls to 1/2. If the fine is greater than the cost of compliance, but less than twice as great*—for example, if the compliance cost is $10 and the fine is $16—then two rational, risk-neutral subjects would each prefer it if both violate (each being

*F > C > F / 2.

	B violates	B complies
A violates	A pays 8 (best)	A pays 16 (worst for A)
	B pays 8 (best)	B pays 10
A complies	A pays 10	A pays 10
	B pays 16 (worst for B)	B pays 10

Figure 4. The compliance game as a "stag hunt"

punished half the time and therefore paying, on average, $8 for each viola-tion) rather than if both comply (paying $10 with certainty).

If the two move simultaneously, the situation is the one game theo-rists call the "Stag Hunt" (first described by Rousseau in the *Discourse on Inequality*).* If both violate, both are better off than if neither violates, but if only one violates he does even worse. So there is no clear answer to the question, "What will rational players do?" The choice of each depends on what he expects the other to do, in an infinite regress, as shown in fig-ure 4. The question is whether the two players trust each other enough to risk violating the rule.

But if the choice is made in sequence, then the actions of the two play-ers are clear, under the conventional game-theory assumption of "com-mon knowledge": that each one knows the rules and is rational, and knows that the other knows the rules and is rational, and so on.

Reason it through from the viewpoint of the player who moves first: Call him Al. He wants to violate if and only if the second mover, Bob, will also violate. So Al has to think through Bob's decision. If Al violates, then Bob can violate knowing that his risk of sanction is only 50/50. Those are acceptable odds to Bob, and Al knows it. So if Al violates, he can be

---

*Suppose three hunters are chasing a stag, and that if all three persist they will take the stag. But suppose also that it is possible that one or more of them may, in the course of the hunt, spot a rabbit he can bring down unassisted. If that hunter were to leave the group in order to chase the rabbit, the remaining two hunters would be unable to bring down the stag, leaving them with nothing. And suppose that a third of the meat of a stag is worth more than a whole rabbit. If you were one of the three and spotted a rabbit, what would you do? It depends on what you think your partners would do if one of them spotted a rabbit, which in turn depends on what they think you might do.

sure that Bob will violate. Therefore Al wants to violate, because then his chances are also 50/50. The result: both violate, and one is punished. In terms of creating compliance, the sanction does no good whatever.

But something surprising happens if the sanction constraint is relaxed: that is, if the enforcement agency has enough capacity to punish both subjects if both violate. In that case, each of them faces the certainty of sanction if he violates, no matter what the other one does. So both comply, and neither is punished. Once again, increasing the capacity to punish reduces the amount of sanction actually inflicted. It sounds paradoxical, but—within the model—it is true nonetheless. That result depends on the fact that violations do not happen automatically or at random, but are choices made by decision-makers capable of imagining and responding to the consequences of their actions: that is, capable of adapting to their environment.

DYNAMIC CONCENTRATION

It turns out, in this artificial system, that a clever enforcement agency can make one penalty do the work of two. The trick is to concentrate on one subject, instead of being "fair" by choosing at random which to punish if both violate. For example, the enforcement authority could announce that if both Al and Bob violate, sanctioning Al has priority over sanctioning Bob. That will make Al comply; whatever Bob does, if Al violates he is sure to be punished, and Al would rather pay the compliance cost C than the fine F.

Now at first blush you might expect that concentrating on Al would allow Bob to run wild. But the opposite turns out to be the case. If Al is the first mover, then Bob, seeing that Al has complied, will himself comply; otherwise Bob knows that he would certainly be punished. So giving priority to Al actually *increases* the pressure on Bob.

And the same result holds if the punishing authority decides to threaten the second mover rather than the first. Imagine that you are Al, and know that Bob has priority for sanction. Your first thought is "Great! Now I can get away with it." But your second thought is different. You know that, whatever you do, Bob will comply, because if he violates he is certain to be punished. But if he complies, and you violate, then *you* are certain to be punished. So the only sensible thing for you to do is comply as well.

The same is true if the two players move simultaneously rather than sequentially. If we give Al priority for sanction, he will certainly comply, if he knows what is good for him. And as long as Bob knows that Al is the target and—more important—*as long as Bob knows that Al knows that Al is the target*, Bob will comply as well.

Bob, knowing that Al is certain to be punished unless Al complies, can predict correctly that Al will comply. But if Al complies, then the one available sanction will be left over to use on Bob if Bob violates. So Bob complies. Result: zero violations and zero sanctions, just as if the enforcement authority had two sanctions available.

What if there are three subjects, Al, Bob, and Charlie? Not a problem, in the frictionless world of game theory. The enforcement authority just has to stick with the alphabetical-order rule. Then Al will certainly comply. Based on the reasoning above, so will Bob; his risk depends only on Al's behavior, not on Charlie's. And Charlie, knowing that Al and Bob are both going to comply, also complies. The result generalizes—again, in the idealized world of game theory—to, literally, as many subjects as you can count.

That is the logic behind the legend about the lone Texas Ranger, with only one bullet left in his gun, facing down an angry mob that wants to storm the jail and lynch the prisoner inside. Even if the mob knows that he is down to his last bullet, he can still prevent the lynching by saying, "Whoever takes the first step forward, *dies*." If everyone in the mob believes him, no one steps forward first. And if no one steps forward first, then no one steps forward at all, and the prisoner is saved.*

---

*Game theorists will notice that the Ranger's strategy is not subgame-perfect; the Ranger, who will be helpless once he fires, will not want to carry out his threat even if someone does step forward. Therefore, if the crowd assumes that he is rational in the economist's sense of the term, his threat is not credible, and the crowd, knowing that, will walk on past him. (Someone might be surprised if the Ranger's pride or anger leads him to fire all the same.) Even without such a sophisticated crowd, the Ranger's strategy is not robust to mistakes. What if someone in the crowd is too dumb, angry, or drunk to draw the appropriate games matrix? Or what if some clever tactician in the second rank of the crowd deliberately pushes the person ahead of him?

BEYOND PERFECT RATIONALITY: SIMULATION RESULTS

Leaving that dream-world for a more realistic world where decision-makers, instead of being omnisciently rational, learn from experience and apply the simple rule of increasing the frequency of successful behaviors and decreasing the frequency of unsuccessful ones, it still turns out that the strategy of concentration outperforms the strategy of equal-opportunity enforcement. Simulation models give us a glimpse into that dynamic world.

Start with Al and Bob again. They move simultaneously, still facing a compliance cost of $10 and a penalty of $16. Each player starts out with some belief about the risk of sanction (technically, a "prior probability"). Each time a player violates, he learns something about the world; if he gets punished, his estimate of the risk of sanction—his "posterior probability"—shifts upward, while if he gets away with the violation, then his estimate of the sanction risk falls.

Under those circumstances, if the sanction constraint is set to one—if either can be punished, but not both—then the outcome is sensitive to the initial conditions, and in particular to the initial beliefs of Al and Bob about their risks of being punished if they offend.

If, for example, each one starts with the belief that the risk of sanction is 1/2, then that belief will be self-fulfilling; each round, both will violate, and one will be punished. Experience will therefore validate their initial beliefs, and they will therefore continue to violate.

On the other hand, if each one starts with the belief that the risk of sanction is any greater than 5/8, which it will be if the other player complies more than a quarter of the time, then neither will violate. That is so because when the risk is 5/8 the expected value of sanction—the probability-weighted average—is exactly $10 (5/8 of $16); at any higher estimate of the sanction risk, on average it will be cheaper to comply than to violate.

Even if we change the model slightly so that Al and Bob each occasionally "experiments" with violating after a period of non-violation, just to test the waters, and does so more often if his subjective probability is near the critical value of 5/8, those experiments will—except in the unlikely event that both players experiment on the same round—lead to the experimenter's being sanctioned, increasing his original subjective probability of sanction. So "both violating constantly" and "neither violating except occasionally" are both stable situations; which one of them becomes the actual equilibrium result depends on initial conditions, and, if the initial condition is near the critical value (also called the "tipping point"), on chance.*

If we start at the "both-violate" equilibrium, we can use simulation to test the effects of changes in sanction capacity and policy. What we find matches the game-theory results:

- Allowing a second sanction each round will drive the situation to the low-violation equilibrium. Each time either player violates, he gets punished, so his subjective probability of being punished always goes up, never down. How long the process takes depends on how low the initial subjective probabilities were and how quickly the players adjust their opinions in the light of experience. In the long run, having a second sanction available will lead to less actual punishment than having only one sanction available. Once the low-violation equilibrium has been established, the second sanction is not needed; a single available sanction will suffice to maintain compliance in the face of occasional experimentation.

- Even with a single sanction, establishing a priority order will drive the system to the low-violation equilibrium. If Al has priority, his expectation of sanction will only go up, never down. Once his subjective probability is above the critical value of 5/8, he will (experimentation aside) stop violating. Then Bob will start to feel the pressure, and his subjective probability will start. Eventually—again, how long it takes to get to "eventually" depends on how low the probabilities start and how quickly the players update—Bob, too, comes into compliance. Note that Bob's feeling the pressure does not result from any change in the sanction-priority rule: Al always gets punished when he violates, even if Bob also violates. So—this is a subtle, but crucial point—it is not the case that Al can go back

---

*This assumes that the players start out with identical beliefs. If one starts more fearful and therefore refrains from violation, the one who started out estimating a lower prior possibility will, at first, violate, and will be punished. That will raise his estimate of the risk of punishment to the point where he too complies.

to violating because the punishing authority has its sights on Bob; the authority seems to have its sights on Bob *precisely because Al is not violating*, and it can switch back instantaneously.

So we find in simulation, as in pure game theory, that more sanction capacity can lead to less actual sanction, and that concentration outperforms equal-opportunity sanctioning. In addition, we see that anything that increases the subjects' fear of being punished or the rate at which they adjust their opinions in the light of new experience—for example, a warning—will reduce the total number of violations committed and the number of sanctions imposed on the way to the low-violation, low-sanction equilibrium.

LARGER POPULATIONS

Now expand the population from two to 100, which would be on the low end of the range of probation-officer caseloads. Let us assume, as a simplification, that the officer has perfect knowledge of who violates and who does not.* For example, drug testing can provide nearly certain knowledge about drug use, and position monitoring using cell-phone or GPS technology can do the same for violations of curfews and restraining orders.

Every week some clients violate the rule. The probation officer must then decide which of those violators to punish, but can not punish more than (to choose a number arbitrarily) eight of them each week because there is not enough time to write up any more than eight reports, or because the judge has a limited tolerance for hearing violation motions. The penalty for a violation is fixed, and does not involve revoking probation; in this simple model, the client population is stable, with no one entering and no one leaving.

Let each probationer start with some initial probability of violating on any given day, varying randomly among probationers. The probability

---

*If monitoring is imperfect, we can consider just those violators who have been detected. The same results emerge, though less sharply. When monitoring costs outstrip enforcement costs, that creates a different situation entirely, calling for a different strategy.

rises every time a probationer gets away with a violation and falls every time the probationer is sanctioned for a violation.

The actual risk each probationer faces of being punished depends on how many others violate, just as it did in the two-player game. The more probationers who comply, the greater the risk to those who violate. If most violate, violation is relatively safe. If most comply, violation is relatively risky. That makes both high and low violation rates self-reinforcing.

We can represent each probationer by one square on a ten-by-ten grid, where the shading of each square represents the probationer's estimate of the risk of sanction: light gray represents high subjective risk (and therefore low probability of violating), while dark gray represents the opposite.

Each round, each probationer either violates or complies, and each violator is punished or not, up to the limit created by the sanctions constraint. That is, if there are eight or fewer violators, all get punished. If there are more than eight violations, then eight violators are chosen at random for punishment. A circle with a slash represents a sanction; a circle without a slash means an unpunished violation. (See figures 5 and 6.)

Then the violators adjust their propensities to violate, with those who got away with it becoming more likely to violate in the future (darker) and those who were punished becoming less likely to violate (lighter).

Once again, we have a "tipping" situation. If the distribution of initial propensities among the probationers is sufficiently low, then eight sanctions per round will be sufficient to punish a large enough fraction of those who violate to push the situation toward, and eventually to, its low-violation equilibrium.

Where the initial position is close to the tipping point, the outcome depends in part on chance. The initial position in figure 6 has the same distribution of propensities as that in figure 5.

But, by sheer randomness, the initial fluctuation in violation rates in figure 6 was up rather than down, starting the positive-feedback process working in the wrong direction. Once that had happened, the eventual outcome was nearly certain: the situation went to the opposite, high-violation equilibrium. Those are the only two stable states of the system.

An observer coming in after the two situations had gone to their respective extremes might wonder what it was about the figure 5 population that made it so well behaved, and what it was about the figure 6 population that made it so unruly. No doubt many hypotheses would be

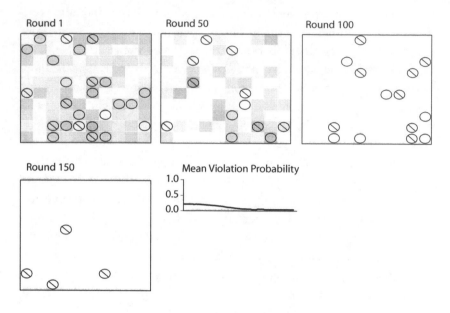

Figure 5. Tipping to the low-violation-rate equilibrium

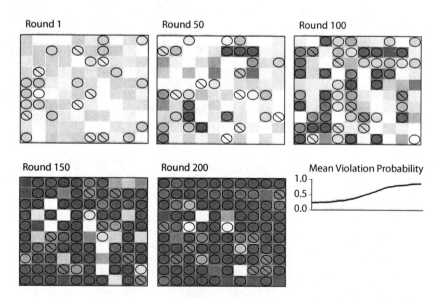

Figure 6. Tipping to the high-violation-rate equilibrium

offered, and much statistical work done, especially if the players in figure 5 are were white and those in figure 6 were black. But all that inquiry would be in vain: the difference would reflect merely the accident of history. Those searching for a deep explanation of the racial differences in offending rates that so starkly mark the American scene might do well to ponder this phenomenon. (See chapter 2 under the heading "The Uneven Impacts of Crime.")

Because both high violation rates and low violation rates are self-sustaining, the system is "path dependent": that is, historical accident can matter. It is one of the functions of policy-makers to arrange for the right historical accidents. Adding just a little bit of sanctions capacity at the very beginning, or doing something else to reduce those initial propensities to offend, could reliably tip this system toward its low-violation equilibrium. The managers of the sanctioning system in the figure 6 situation have good reason for regret, while the managers of the sanctioning system in the figure 5 situation are probably patting themselves on the back, for no good reason.

However, when the propensities to violate start out high and sanctions capacity low, the tendency toward the high-violation-rate equilibrium will be irresistible. High violation rates lead to small probabilities that any given violation will draw a sanction, due to enforcement swamping. If, say, there are forty violations in a round, then thirty-two violators will get away with it, meaning that many more of them will have the propensity to violate increased than will have it decreased.

Thus high violation rates lead to low sanctions risks, which in turn maintain the high violation rates, as in the low-sanctions-capacity situations displayed in the left-hand column of figure 7. The same level of sanctions capacity that was sometimes adequate for the population represented in figures 5 and 6 is nowhere nearly enough for the worse-behaved group on the left.

Simply adding sanctions capacity, even on a temporary basis, can drive the system to a low-violation state, which can then be maintained with sanctions capacity than was required to achieve it in the first place. But for that to work capacity must surpass some critical value, where the critical value depends on the initial distribution of propensities to violate, on how much an unpunished violation increases the future violation rate,

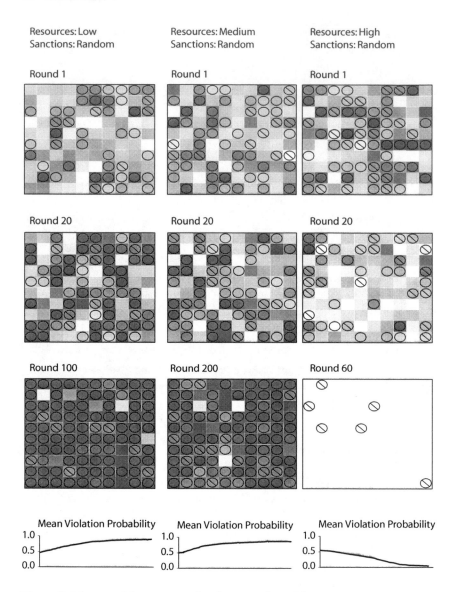

Figure 7. More punishment capacity, less actual punishment

and on how much a punished violation decreases it. Adding not enough capacity (as in the middle column above) is worse than useless: it multiplies penalties without much reducing violations.

But adding a sufficient amount of capacity (as shown in the right-hand column) can tip the situation into its low-violation equilibrium.

At the new equilibrium, there is sanctions capacity to spare: that is, fewer violations than potential sanctions. So the extra capacity is no longer needed, and could be made available to start the process of "tipping" another group of potential offenders toward high compliance. Indeed, the number of actual sanctions falls not just below the new, high sanctions capacity, but below the original low one.

As in the game-theoretic models and the two-player simulation, increasing the capacity to punish decreases the amount of sanction actually used, but, in this case, after a transition period.

The transition period: "Aye, there's the rub." The sanctions constraint is real, set by the resources at hand; a probation officer, unless she is Hermione Granger, cannot just use her Time-Turner to create more hours in the day. So unless a Judge Alm is present to simplify the reporting process, the temporary increase in sanctions capacity that would tip the system to its low-violation equilibrium may simply not be available.

Dynamic Concentration, Again

But, as in the game-theory analysis, it turns out that the same result can be reached within the existing sanctions-capacity constraint by abandoning equal-opportunity sanctioning and using instead what might be called "dynamic concentration": a variant of the alphabetical-order rule that kept Al, Bob, and Charlie in line with only a single available sanction.

Let the probation officer assign each probationer a number from one to 100; that might be done arbitrarily, by assigning the number one to the probationer occupying the top left square, two to the probationer on his right, ten to the top right square, eleven to the left-hand square in the second row, all the way down to 100 at bottom right. (In practice, it might be done on a less arbitrary basis, for example, by considering records of prior noncompliance or the seriousness of the underlying charges.)

Now the probationers in the first eight spaces *will never get away with anything*; no matter how many of them violate, and no matter what anyone else does, there will always be enough capacity to punish every violator among those first eight.* (See figure 8.) Thus their subjective probability

---

*The implausible assumption of infallibility on the part of the probation officer is not essential; the same results emerge, only a little more slowly, if we allow a modest-sized error rate.

Resources: Low
Sanctions: Sequential

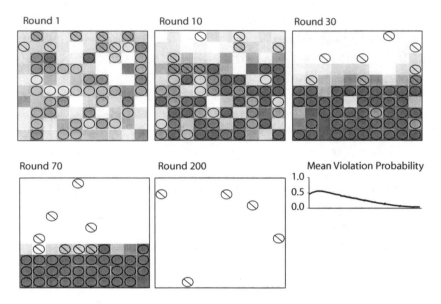

Figure 8. Dynamic concentration

estimates can only go up, and their propensity to violate can only go down. In the meantime, those at the other end of the priority list have the opposite experience: they never get punished, and their violation rates therefore go up.

But not for long. As the low-numbered clients become less and less prone to violate, the pressure starts to move to those just below them in the pecking order. That is the "dynamic" part of "dynamic concentration." The probation officer has not let up on the first group of eight; they still have priority. But once they mostly stop violating, they do not use much capacity, and the capacity they do not use then lands on those slightly further down the list. Those clients then come into compliance, and the pressure to comply moves to those still further down. At last, the situation reaches the same low-violation-rate equilibrium produced by additional enforcement capacity without ever actually adding capacity.

Thus the same initial conditions that led to the high-violation equilibrium under random sanctioning lead to the low-violation equilibrium under dynamic concentration. Once again, this has two benefits: fewer violations, and *fewer actual sanctions*. And it can be done within the original resource constraints. Dynamic concentration makes a little punishment go a long way.

That happy outcome depends on the numbers. Unlike the fairy tale about Al, Bob, and Charlie and the rest of the infinite list of offenders who could be controlled with a single threatened sanction, in a world of uncertainty there will always be some violations and therefore some use of actual sanctions, and at some point even the task of keeping a well-behaved group well behaved—though it requires much less capacity than making the transition from an ill-behaved group to a well-behaved group—will absorb all the available capacity to punish. Even using dynamic concentration, there is some maximum number of offenders who can be controlled by a given sanctions capacity. But that number is much larger than the number that can be effectively controlled by the same capacity when sanctions are handed out at random.

Of course these exercises in logic and simulation do not, by themselves, prove anything about the real world. But they do make sense of the H.O.P.E. results; indeed, the H.O.P.E. results are precisely what this model would have predicted.[*] To the extent that consistent sanctioning reduces offending rates while unpunished violations increase them, dynamic concentration turns out to be the deterrence version of the Miracle of the Loaves and Fishes.

LIMITS AND CAVEATS

The applicability of this model to any piece of the real world will depend on how closely reality matches its assumptions. Some are mere simplifications: a more complex model, to be fitted to real data, would have to include punishments of varying rather than uniform severity, heterogeneity among offenders (in personal crime rates and susceptibility to

---

[*]The H.O.P.E. strategy takes advantage of psychological effects as well as strategic calculations; it is transparently fair, and it encourages probationers to adopt the viewpoint that what happens to them depends on what they do rather than on random chance, a viewpoint conducive to any sort of effort to break bad habits (Rotter 1966).

deterrence), among offenses (in seriousness), the capacity of offenders to learn from the experience of others[3] and from warnings rather than always having to "find out the hard way," and the effects of incapacitation as well as deterrence. Incorporating those complexities will, in general, change the critical values and complicate the optimization problem without altering the qualitative effects of positive feedback and dynamic concentration.

However, one crucial assumption of the model is true only occasionally: that while the capacity to punish is limited, it is that capacity alone, and not the capacity to monitor behavior, that sets limits on the enforcement system. That assumption is workably true when it comes to controlling the drug use of probationers; tests are cheap, while hearings and jail and prison cells are expensive. In that case, when the rate of violation falls, so does the cost of maintaining any given probability of punishment for a violation. The same is true of open drug-market activity, precisely because of its openness.

In the more usual case, monitoring is expensive. Take, for example, driving under the influence (DUI). While it is likely true that intoxication reduces a potential offender's susceptibility to being deterred, it remains the case that when the probability of detection and punishment rises sufficiently high, the rate of DUI falls substantially. That has been demonstrated time and again by DUI crackdowns using roadblocks at which each driver is stopped, asked for identification, screened for signs of intoxication, and, where appropriate, asked to take a breath or blood test.

Those crackdowns consistently work. But they do not—cannot—last. Roadblocks are resource-intensive, and their cost does not depend very much on how many of the drivers screened are actually under the influence. Processing a drunken driver takes more time than screening a sober one, but since—even before the crackdown has had a chance to work—only a few percent of drivers on the road are drunk, most of the time of the officers is taken up by screening, a cost that does not fall with a falling violation rate. Even if every driver on the road is sober, the cost of maintaining the roadblock remains.

Typically, then, once the crackdown has done its work, the officers are reassigned to other tasks—perhaps a roadblock elsewhere—and, once the deterrent effect of the roadblock is lost, the rate of violation creeps back up toward its old level. In such cases, the strategy of dynamic concentration is not available, and the task of enforcement remains Sisyphean.

Of course, whether monitoring capacity is expensive is partly a technological question. The falling cost of position monitoring due to cellphone and mobile GPS technologies makes it possible to convert curfew enforcement from a drunk-driving-like problem of going out to offenders' homes to see if they are present to a drug-use-like problem of just acting on the information as it comes in.

The crucial difference between easy-to-observe and hard-to-observe behaviors leads to some apparently perverse policing strategies, such as the crackdown on squeegeeing in a city wracked with homicide and on turnstile-jumping in a transit system facing a serious robbery problem described in chapter 3. Because squeegeeing and turnstile-jumping were easy to observe, they were easy to deter at only transient cost; once concentrated enforcement had deterred New Yorkers from wiping the windshields of cars stopped in traffic and from trying to ride the subway without paying, the effort required to maintain that deterrence was trivial, and in fact lower than the cost of sporadic enforcement against widespread violations. That meant that, except in the short run, those "order-maintenance" activities did not detract from the resources available to deal with more serious crime, and any deterrence or incapacitation effects they generated against such crime came at little or no cost. Thus even quite modest "broken windows" effects (see chapter 6) on serious crime might be sufficient to justify the costs of the effort required to achieve them.

The other crucial assumption of the model is that offenders have limited or no capacity to coordinate their actions to frustrate dynamic-concentration effects. It is hard for buyers and sellers of illicit drugs to coordinate on a sudden shift in location; otherwise, drug crackdowns would be largely futile.*

The chief challenge, then, in applying dynamic concentration is to recognize, or create, the conditions under which it can operate.

---

*To take another example, there is an element of dynamic concentration in some counter-insurgency efforts, but the more capable the insurgents are of coordinating their actions the less successful such efforts will be.

Crime Despite Punishment

The conservative diagnosis of the crime problem—that we had, and have, too much crime because an inadequate enforcement and punishment mechanism means that crime pays—leads naturally to the prescription that we should continue building prisons until crime no longer pays.

Superficially, the low punishment-to-crime ratios of the 1970s—an expected punishment of less than five days per burglary, for example—supported that diagnosis. But if that were indeed the problem, it ought to have been solved by now. With a crime rate that is 30 percent lower now than it was in 1980 and an incarceration rate three and a half times as high, the punishment-to-offense ratios have quadrupled.* In this context, the question is not why crime has decreased, but why it has not decreased more.

But that original punishment-ratio analysis failed to take into account the gains from criminal activity by comparison with the risks of punishment it entails. Showing that crime had a seemingly low expected cost to the criminal in the form of punishment is not, by itself, enough to show that crime is the product of, or even that it is consistent with, rational choice. We need to weigh that expected cost against the expected gain. Doing so casts the problem in a different light.

In the case of burglary, we have some idea of the "take" from victims' reports. In 1974, the average burglary victim reported losing about $400 (equivalent to roughly $1600 in today's money). But on average the gain to the burglar (or burglars) would have been much smaller. Some of that loss reflected damage done in the course of the burglary rather than the property taken by the burglar; morever, stolen property, other than cash

---

*The growth of the illicit drug industry and of incarceration for drug offenses means that the punishment ratios for predatory crimes did not go up quite that much on average, and the increasing concentration of prison space on violent offenders means that incarceration for property offenses—other than residential burglary—has grown even more slowly. But a fourfold increase in punitiveness is about right.

and guns, brings much less when a burglar sells it to an acquaintance or to a "fence" than it cost the original purchaser. If we assign the burglar an average gain equal to 20 percent of the victim's loss, the $400 the average homeowner lost would translate into an average gain for the burglar of only about $80 (about $320 in today's money). Dividing that by the average punishment of four days, we get an average "wage" for burglary, per day spent behind bars, of about $20 in 1974 money, worth about $80 of today's money. By 2007, the prison-building boom plus the crime collapse of the late 1990s had brought the days-per-burglary figure up to sixteen days, while the "take" from a burglary had barely gone up at all in inflation-adjusted terms. Thus the burglar's "wage" had fallen by 75 percent, to about $22 per day of confinement. (See figure 9.)

When the terms are stated that bluntly, burglary does not appear to be an attractive proposition; it seems implausible that many of those who commit residential burglaries would accept a straight offer to spend a day in jail in return for $22, or sixteen days for $350, even if the money were paid up front, and even ignoring the other costs and risks attendant on housebreaking, such as getting shot by a homeowner.*

Admittedly, the calculation necessarily omits what UCLA sociologist Jack Katz refers to as "the existential pleasures of crime": the thrill of danger, the satisfaction of exercising power over someone else by invading his private space, the gratification of a shared enterprise (for group burglaries), and subsequent "bragging rights" among peers.[1] But it strains credulity to think that a flat-out offer of all those pleasures, plus $350, in return for spending the next sixteen days, or even the next four days, behind bars, would find many takers.

Thus, even in 1974, the conservative cry to make crime not pay was a demand for what already was the case. *Crime already didn't pay.* "The wages of sin," it has been said, "are well below the legal minimum," and burglary is far less attractive now than it was then, with about four times

---

*Since burglary is sometimes a group crime, the average risk of punishment for an individual committing a burglary is less than 16 days, but by the same token the reward is proportionally smaller. The ratio between average risk and average reward is unchanged. The calculation does not adjust for the proportion of burglaries committed by juveniles, and implicitly treats arrest, trial, a felony record, and probation and parole as not involving punishment at all; to that extent it understates just how bad a deal burglary actually is for someone subject to the jurisdiction of the adult courts.

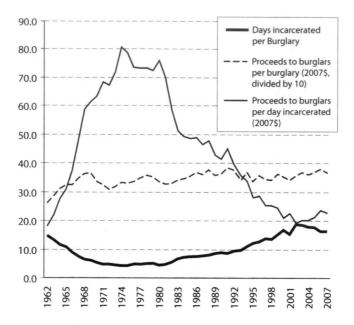

Figure 9. The falling wages of burglary

as many days behind bars per burglary for a financial gain that has barely budged in inflation-adjusted terms.

Perhaps the problem is that, among young men in the neighborhoods that produce most burglars, burglary (or retail drug dealing) is considered an honorable and manly activity, while the sorts of legitimate jobs that are available to those without much in the way of salable skills are considered demeaning and degrading. If so, then the key strategy for making crime not pay in the eyes of those who commit it might lie in changing their perceptions both about theft and drug dealing and about "flipping burgers." Or perhaps it is not the young men whose opinions need to be worked on, but the young women whose approval they desire.[2] Adding more prison cells does little to advance either project.

The statistics for retail drug dealing are, or ought to be, comparably daunting. A study of retail cocaine dealers in Washington, D.C., in the late 1980s found that they took in about $30 (in 1989 purchasing power) per hour of dealing (plus the cocaine they used but did not pay for).[3] In a year of full-time dealing, those dealers could expect to spend about three months, on average, behind bars. Given the risks of gunfire and of becoming addicted to crack, those dealers might not have been making an especially wise set of choices, as judged by an outside observer, but the monetary rewards of the trade were real enough.*

More recent studies, however, show that hourly earnings at the bottom level of the cocaine trade have fallen to roughly the minimum wage[4]; while the risks of violence have diminished since the late 1980s, the risk of imprisonment has risen substantially. Dealers' wages—and retail cocaine prices—have fallen sharply, even in the face of an increased threat of punishment.[5]

So, even for those with unattractive alternative uses for their time and energy, burglary and retail crack-dealing seem to be very poor career choices in purely economic terms: and much, much worse choices now then they once were. Yet burglary and dealing persist. No doubt some burglars and crack retailers, more skilled than others, face smaller-than-average risks for greater-than-average rewards. But that means that the rest of the burglars or crack dealers must face odds even worse than those computed above; the continued willingness to participate in burglary and retail drug dealing remains puzzling.

At least three candidate solutions to this puzzle—other than the possibility that some criminals are not ashamed to be criminals but would be ashamed to wear a McDonald's uniform—offer themselves: misperception of risks and rewards; non-utility-maximizing behavior in the face of uncertain outcomes; and the overvaluation (compared to rational-actor models) of the immediate future compared to the even modestly more distant future.

RISK PERCEPTION

One possible explanation for continued crime in the face of punishment is that offenders misperceive the risks they face and the rewards they can expect. Burglars, for example, might not know the average risk and reward of a burglary, or they might not know how the risks and rewards they would face as burglars compare with that average. There might,

---

*Many of the crack dealers in the sample had licit jobs paying $7–$9 per hour (Reuter, MacCoun, and Murphy 1995).

for example, be perceptual lag. The risks of burglary have been increasing steadily for a generation, but folk-wisdom among potential burglars might not have fully adjusted to the fact that the expected punishment for burglary is several times what it was a generation ago. Yet young, male residents of high-crime, high-incarceration neighborhoods surely know many burglars, including many who have been caught.

Like gamblers—for that matter, like most of us—burglars may tend to talk more about their successes than their failures, leading those who listen to them to overestimate the gains and underestimate the risks. Moreover, a burglar who is arrested and imprisoned is no longer around his neighborhood to talk about it, which may make instances of successful burglary more psychologically "available"[6] to potential burglars than instances of unsuccessful burglary.

Even if the risk-reward mix of the average burglary were well known among burglars, there are several well-established psychological phenomena that might lead someone contemplating burglary to think, falsely, that his individual odds were better than average.

The "optimistic biases" include the belief in luck, the illusion of control, and the self-confidence bias.[7] In the laboratory and in surveys, people on average tend to believe that luck favors them: in a situation they know to be purely chance, they take their own chances of winning to be higher than average. Moreover, they tend to think that they can exert some control over what are in fact chance events. The illusion of control matters in part because there is a widespread conviction that one's own skills are unusually sharp: 88 percent of drivers, asked to estimate the risks facing "the average driver" and the risks they personally face, will attribute to themselves less-than-average risk.[8] This last effect, formally referred to as "self-confidence bias," is sometimes called the "Lake Wobegon paradox," after Garrison Keillor's mythical village where "all the children are above average."

Even having been caught and punished before may be insufficient to disabuse someone of such optimistic biases. Since more than 90 percent of burglaries never lead to arrest, any actual arrest must necessarily be the product of unusual circumstances: some combination of random bad luck and poor planning or execution. Given the human predilection toward unjustified optimism, it might be easy for burglars to dismiss previous failures as unlikely to happen again, either because they resulted from random circumstances unlikely to recur or because they resulted from mistakes not to be repeated. The reflection that, given enough burglaries, either bad luck or a new mistake is a virtual certainty requires more statistical insight than the typical burglar may be able to summon.

The relative rarity of arrest could also contribute to perceptual lag; when the base probability is relatively low, it can be difficult to detect even a significant increase if all one has to go on are personal experience and word of mouth.

Nor is arrest the end of the story. Juvenile arrestees rarely face any substantial sanction; juveniles account for about a quarter of all burglaries—down from half in the 1980s—but less than 5 percent of those confined for burglary. Indeed, there is evidence that juveniles who have been arrested once are less afraid of subsequent arrests, and more likely to commit additional crimes, than those who have not been arrested: as if relatively mild consequences of the first arrest acted as a pleasant surprise. Lenity toward young adults and toward those facing a first adult felony conviction has similar effects: they suggest to someone beginning a burglary career that, even if he gets caught, the consequences are tolerable. By the time the punishments start to become substantial, the habit of burglary may be well established and noncriminal career options largely foreclosed.

On the other hand, misperceptions can work in both directions; offenders may overestimate some threats even as they underestimate others. In particular, very-low-probability threats tend to be overestimated, while moderate-probability threats are underestimated; in some experimental conditions, decision-makers will treat both a risk of one in a thousand and a risk of one in ten as if they were close to one in a hundred.[9]

The Valuation of Uncertainty

If the expected value of punishment for a burglary is greater than the expected value of the gain, and yet burglaries continue, that might be because of the variability concealed behind the expected-value calculation. It is not, after all, the case that each burglary yields $350 to the burglar and results in sixteen days' confinement. Both the yield and the punishment vary from incident to incident.

To start with, the typical burglary—as opposed to the average burglary—yields no punishment at all, because the offender is never caught. In recent years, there have been about one-seventh as many burglary arrests as burglaries known to the police, and half of all burglaries are never even reported. Nor does every arrest lead to a conviction, or every conviction to a sentence of confinement. For his average gain of about $350, a burglar faces, not sixteen predictable days behind bars, but something like one chance in forty of a prison term lasting an average of about two years. That is, for each two-year prison term served, the average burglar will enjoy about $14,000 in criminal "earnings." While it seems implausible that anyone would be willing to spend a day in jail for something less than $25, the offer of $14,000 now for spending two years in prison sometime later might well find takers.

That uncertainty can reduce the effectiveness of deterrent threats is far from a new idea. At least since the time of Beccaria* it has been a maxim of criminology that certainty of punishment is more important than severity in determining deterrent effectiveness. So perhaps it is the randomness of the punishment for burglary that keeps the activity attractive in the face of what would seem to be a net negative expected value.

But from the viewpoint of a rational actor, as economists understand that concept, that phenomenon is puzzling. Risk should in general decrease the attractiveness of an option rather than increasing it; therefore, uncertainty of punishment ought to make it more frightening, rather than less so. At least, that should be the case for monetary penalties; the diminishing marginal utility of income means that bigger losses are felt more sharply per dollar lost than smaller ones. The diminishing marginal utility of income leads, rationally, to what economists call risk aversion: the willingness to sacrifice some expected value in return for a reduction in uncertainty. That principle explains the existence of insurance markets. In order for rational burglars to accept a gamble whose expected value is negative because of the uncertainly involved, they would have to be the opposite of risk-averse: risk-seeking.

---

*Cesare Beccaria (1738–1794) can be said to have founded criminology with his book *Dei delitti e delle pene* ("On Crimes and Punishments," 1764/1986), which identifies swiftness, certainty, and severity as the three determinants of the deterrent efficacy of a threatened punishment and argues that severity is the least important of the three.

That might be the case. The prevalence of gambling, which is the opposite of insurance, seems to show that under some circumstances people voluntarily seek out risk, and it is not hard to see how "thrill-seeking" in the psychological sense—known to be a characteristic more common among offenders than among non-offenders[10]—might lead to risk-seeking in the economic sense.

Another possible explanation does not require assuming any subjective taste for risk. Perhaps some offenders' choices are influenced by the phenomena described by prospect theory[11]: perhaps, that is, they focus on whether each individual transaction produces a gain or a loss, thus overweighting both small gains and small losses relative to large ones. That behavior proves, in some laboratory conditions, to be much more prevalent than subjective thrill-seeking, and seems to be one explanation, for example, for the fact that most individuals' stock-market behavior does not in fact minimize risk for any given level of expected reward.

FIXED AND VARIABLE COSTS OF INCARCERATION

Or perhaps it is a mistake, descriptively, to treat prison time as a quantity that can be averaged out, as monetary losses can be averaged out: to assume that, before risk-preference is taken into account, a two-year sentence starts out being twice as bad as a one-year sentence.

Losing $100 twice ought, from a utility-maximizing perspective, to be the same as losing $200 once, and—again ignoring risk-preference—twice as bad as losing $100 only once; but are two one-year sentences the same as one two-year sentence, and twice as bad as one one-year sentence? It is not obvious that they are, considering both the fixed costs of arrest, incarceration, and the subsequent criminal record—costs that increase only slightly with the length of the term—and the psychological phenomena of acclimation and duration invariance (discussed below).[12] If so—if a two-year stretch behind bars is much less than twice as bad as a year behind bars, and much less than forty times as bad as sixteen days behind bars—then a burglary that a given offender would find not worth committing at the cost of sixteen days locked up might still seem worthwhile to him at the cost of one chance in forty of two years locked up, which is more or less the deal on offer to the average burglar.

The fixed costs of being incarcerated would give someone without a prior criminal record very strong reasons to prefer an even chance between two years locked up or going scot-free to the certainty of a year locked up. The embarrassment and stigma of arrest and trial, the disruption of family relationships, housing and employment arrangements, and other parts of the life routine, the subsequent difficulty of finding employment as an ex-convict, the stress of entering prison and the stress of leaving it to return to an uncertain future: all of these result from going to prison at all and vary relatively little with the length of the term.

The same is true, though to a lesser extent, for someone who does have a prior criminal history, or even prior experience of prison. Some of the fixed costs are already "sunk," but not all of them. Thus there are reasons to think that the deterrent impact of incarceration is subject to diminishing marginal returns at the intensive margin: that, for example, the second year of a two-year sentence packs less deterrent punch than the first year.

But while fixed-cost effects support the idea that certainty is more important than severity in determining the deterrent impact of punishment—the idea that, for any fixed amount of imprisonment for a given crime, the total deterrent effect would be increased by increasing the probability of incarceration while decreasing the average sentence length—there is a conceptual difficulty in using fixed costs to explain away the apparent irrationality of household burglary and similar crimes. Even ignoring those fixed costs and simply comparing a twenty-four-hour period spent behind bars to a twenty-four-hour period spent on the street, it is difficult to imagine many people accepting an offer to spend that period confined for a payment of $22. Or, to think about it a slightly different way, it is hard to imagine someone about to leave prison being willing to stay an extra day in return for a $22 payment. If the gain from a crime cannot cover the *variable* costs of incarceration, then the fixed costs simply stand as additional reasons not to commit the crime.

ACCLIMATION AND DURATION NEGLECT

Even on a day-to-day basis, all days in prison may not be equally aversive. Studies of self-reported happiness show that a wide range of people have astonishing capacities for acclimating themselves to what seem in prospect, or from the outside, like virtually intolerable conditions.[13] Quadriplegics, for example, report themselves as only moderately less happy than people with full use of their limbs once they have adjusted to their circumstances. Insofar as prisoners succeed in psychologically acclimating themselves to the prison environment, much of the aversive power of the prison experience may inhere in the first few days, weeks, or months.

Acclimation may be part of the explanation for another phenomenon, called by its discoverers "duration neglect" or "duration invariance."[14] It might seem logical that someone's overall evaluation of an experience, good or bad, would be something approximating the integral over time of the moment-to-moment evaluations: that is, to the average value of a moment during that experience multiplied by the duration of the experience. But that turns out not to be the case.

Whether people are asked to give a numerical rating of how good or bad an experience was, or instead asked, having experienced it once, to make a choice between experiencing it again and some fixed alternative, the answers they give turn out to be sensitive to the most intense moment of the experience and to its end, but only minimally sensitive to its duration.[15] In fact, adding an additional period of somewhat reduced, but still noticeable, unpleasantness at the end can actually reduce the overall recalled aversiveness of an unpleasant experience.[16]

The studies to date deal with durations measured in minutes or at most hours, not months or years; perhaps duration neglect is less prominent over longer time periods. But if the phenomenon does extend to periods of months or years, that would make sense of the incomplete success of the attempt to increase deterrence by increasing sentence lengths.

Duration neglect, even if it were present and virtually complete, would not utterly eliminate the deterrent effect of additional months in prison; the plea-bargaining process demonstrates that offenders do care about the length of their sentences in prospect. But duration neglect might mean that a former prisoner's memory of how bad a spell behind bars was, and consequently his willingness to repeat the behavior that produced that spell, might not vary much with sentence length. That would reduce both the "specific deterrent" value of the sentence—its effect on the future behavior of the person punished—and its "general deterrent" effect—on the behavior of other people. That provides one more reason to think that the total deterrent effect of a smaller number of longer sentences would be less than the effect of a larger number of smaller sentences amounting to the same aggregate of prisoner-days. If so, the expected-value calculation will tend to overestimate the deterrent effectiveness of our actual system of randomized severity. That may help explain why the explosive growth of total incarceration has not led to a larger decrease in crime.

TIMING

The punishment for any offense occurs later than the financial gain from committing it; that lag results not only from "the law's delay," but also from the randomness of arrest. Except for the unfortunates who get caught the very first time, burglars get to enjoy some of the gains from their activities before ever getting caught. Even when a burglary leads to arrest, the arrest may not lead to any time behind bars; that increases the average time between the stream of gains from burglary and the stream of losses. In addition, unlike a fine or corporal punishment, a term of confinement is by its nature extended in time. The second year of a two-year prison term starts a year after the sentence itself starts, and is thus that much more remote from the crime. The time lag between gain and loss requires an adjustment in the calculation of the balance between the gains from crimes such as burglary and the risks the criminal-justice system imposes on burglars.

Economists have a framework for thinking about the relative value of present and future gains, built around the idea that available money not spent now can be invested, while consumption out of resources not yet in hand requires borrowing at a cost in the form of interest. In this framework, the terms on which the actor can lend or borrow—the interest rates he can collect or must pay—create lower and upper bounds on the "discount rate" a rational actor uses in comparing present and future gains and losses, and all gains and losses ought to be discounted at the same rate.

In laboratory experiments, it is possible to measure something that looks like discounting behavior, and there is evidence that individuals with very high discount rates as measured by the experiments are, on average, more criminally active than those with lower rates. This remains true even controlling for background factors such as age, race, income, and education.[17] Whether that is the same phenomenon as the psychological trait of impulsiveness has yet to be determined. And it is possible that high behavioral discount rates and high rates of criminal activity are both the results of some common factor—such as stress or an unattractive set of options—rather than the discount rates "causing" the criminality.

There is evidence that personal discount rates go up under various forms of social stress, especially social exclusion, and with some forms of substance abuse.[18] This may reflect an evolutionarily supported mechanism that suspends concern for the future when the immediate present is sufficiently threatening. In social environments sufficiently unpredictable to discourage any sort of long-range planning, a radical improvidence and present-orientation can seem the only sensible stance to take.

Another line of laboratory studies has shown that, under appropriate conditions, most people (and other organisms) will demonstrate behavior inconsistent with any fixed discount rate, giving great weight to the present compared to even the near (and predictable) future.[19] When that happens, choices made by a given individual will not be consistent over time; decisions are taken that, in Schelling's phrase, are "deprecated in advance and predictably regretted in retrospect."[20] Procrastination, breaking a diet, and scratching a rash reflect such time-inconsistent behavior over different time-intervals, and the ubiquity of such behavior suggests that irrationality about the future is built fairly deeply into the normal human psyche. Sometimes these seem subjectively like choices; in other cases, temptation or fear seems to override the mechanism of rational choice entirely, in the phenomenon Aristotle called "akrasia," or "weakness of will."

That time-inconsistent discounting is a characteristic of the situation as well as the person is shown by the observation that, even in pencil-and-paper questionnaires, frequent heroin users make more present-oriented choices when asked questions about heroin (e.g., "Would you prefer a bag of heroin now or two bags tomorrow?") than about money ("Would you prefer $10 now or $20 tomorrow?").[21] Why some circumstances and decisions bring it out more than others remains an open question. George Loewenstein* points to pain, fear, hunger, addiction, and sexual desire

---

*Professor of economics and psychology at Carnegie Mellon University, and one of the founders of the new discipline of neuroeconomics.

among the "visceral influences" that defeat the attempt to make rational choices between present and future, though those factors seem to play relatively little role in procrastination, for example.[22]

Whether irrationally strong present-orientation is best described as discounting at a very high rate, as discounting hyperbolically, as giving in to visceral influences, as weakness of will, or as the victory of a present-oriented self in the context with a future-oriented self,[23] it weakens deterrence, perhaps fatally. Any crime-control effort organized around the threat of punishment, especially delayed punishment, has to reckon with the possibility that its threats may point too far into the future to have much impact on the decision-making of potential offenders.

The same conclusion follows if instead of imagining potential offenders as weighing risk against reward we think about adjusting behavior to the threat of punishment as a kind of learning process. In that context, the observation that delay reduces the efficacy of punishment is completely unsurprising. Cause-and-effect relationships are much more salient psychologically when the effect follows almost immediately on the cause: think about the difference between learning to type with a computer program that rings a bell whenever an error is made and learning to type with a computer program that provides a scoresheet on the completion of each exercise.

It is worth noting, though, that a study[24] by Daniel Nagin* and colleagues, the only attempt to measure directly the effect of delay, found the opposite of the effect discussed above. The study found that for one—perhaps atypical—group of offenders, college students facing jail time for driving under the influence, punishment is actually discounted *negatively*: the subjects of that study apparently wanted to "get it over with" and be able to resume normal life. Compared to burglars, college-student drunken drivers probably have more normal lives to resume; an overhanging prison term may be less of a disruption to an already disordered life. Moreover, the college students were dealing with sentences that they knew were going to be carried out, with timing the only unknown factor. Waiting for a punishment that is certain to occur may generate much more anxiety than arises when a punishment is not only delayed, but also uncertain. In the situation facing burglars, delay and uncertainty are so

---

*University professor of public policy and statistics at Carnegie Mellon University who is famous for studies of deterrence and developmental trajectories with regard to aggression.

intertwined that it may be hard to distinguish empirically between uncertainty effects and time-valuation effects.

DESIGNING PUNISHMENT REGIMES FOR IMPERFECTLY RATIONAL OFFENDERS

Does the recognition that criminals are not perfectly rational leave the project of deterrence in tatters? Advocates of the strong form of the "root causes" argument (see chapter 7) sometimes imply as much. They write as if an offender must either be perfectly rational or be so indifferent to consequences that his actions are only malleable in other ways. But that conclusion does not follow from its premise.

Instead of making the obviously false assumption that criminal behavior is always the result of expected utility maximization, we could make a much weaker assumption. Philip J. Cook* has introduced the idea of a "demand for criminal opportunities"[25]: the willingness to commit crime if the right circumstances offer themselves. If that demand is somewhat elastic to the socially established "price" (in the form of punishment), we are back in the world of common sense, where crimes, like other actions, are determined in part by their anticipated consequences. Other things being equal, we should expect the probability that someone will commit a crime is lower where the likely consequences are worse, compared to the alternative noncriminal pattern of actions. Thus, the threat of harsher, swifter, or more certain punishment will, in some instances, tip the balance away from crime.

Often, however, it is not possible to make someone worse off in the present—in order to deter whatever action led to punishment—without also making that person's future noncriminal prospects less attractive. The worse those prospects are, the more attractive any given criminal opportunity will be. Arresting and imprisoning burglars ought, other things being equal, to deter burglary. But if a burglar released from prison finds it impossible to get a licit-market job, the lack of attractive alternatives to burglary as a way of getting money may push him back toward his prior behavior pattern.

---

*Economist and public policy analyst at Duke University who has written extensively about crime, guns, and alcohol abuse.

Making the post-release consequences of conviction and incarceration worse may increase the deterrent effect of law enforcement, and advocates of "toughness on crime" embrace a range of disabilities for ex-convicts. But the results may easily be perverse, if the increased criminal activity of releasees as a result of having worse noncriminal opportunities turns out to be more important than decreased criminal activity as a result of enhanced deterrence.[26] That, along with the strong reasons to believe that offenders tend to be very present-oriented and therefore not especially sensitive to long-deferred threats, creates a strong reason to "front-load" the costs of arrest and conviction, leaving as little disability as possible at the point of release. Expungement—the process by which an ex-offender can have his criminal history erased on various conditions—reflects an attempt to implement such a strategy.

In locales of mass incarceration, where more than half of all men turning thirty have accumulated a felony conviction, very poor post-release prospects might even increase offense rates among those who have not yet been caught. If *ever* having a felony conviction ruins one's chances of licit employment, and if one is more likely than not to end up with at least one such conviction, then the cost of having one's first conviction this year rather than three years from now may not seem very high.[27] If, as seems likely, the post-release consequences of incarceration are largely the result of having been incarcerated at all rather than rising sharply with the length of incarceration, then the proposal for more and shorter prison terms to increase certainty of punishment at the expense of severity confronts a substantial disadvantage. That provides another reason to try to convert probation into a more effective substitute for incarceration. The importance of not impairing a released offender's legitimate opportunities is especially great in the case of juveniles; that makes sense of the rules sealing juvenile records at the point of adulthood.

Yet even leaving deterrence aside, there are two countervailing considerations.

First is the need of the criminal-justice system to identify habitual offenders in order to appropriately allocate scarce sanctions capacity. Similarly, potential employers, spouses, landlords, and housemates of ex-offenders may reasonably want to inform themselves about the risks they may be running. Most juvenile offenders do not turn into persistent adult criminals. But most persistent adult criminals were juvenile offenders. Hiring as a security guard a nineteen-year-old who committed an armed assault at age seventeen would seem grossly negligent on the part of an employer, and the employer might justly be held liable if the guard used unnecessary force. Yet under current rules that firm would have no way of knowing about that prior crime unless the juvenile had been tried as an adult.

Worse yet, the protection offered the guilty may come at the expense of their innocent neighbors; if there is no way of knowing whether a young adult job applicant has a recent criminal record, employers will be tempted to rely on proxy measures—race, age, neighborhood, accent, clothing style—to filter out such job applicants statistically. If so, the attempt to prevent employment discrimination against ex-offenders may have the side effect of increasing employment discrimination against those who demographically resemble many offenders, but have themselves resisted the temptation to offend, thus reducing one major advantage of maintaining a clean record. The awkward result might be to increase the rate of criminal participation in already high-crime neighborhoods.

Expungement faces the same problem. It makes sense because everyone benefits if offenders become ex-offenders, and it is easier to become an ex-offender if one has the employment and social opportunities to which a criminal history is a barrier. As mere punishment, post-conviction disability has very undesirable characteristics: it is diffuse, undramatic, extended in time, and largely without any value as incapacitation. But shielding criminal histories from scrutiny can damage both those who cannot access the information and those who have clean records despite sharing demographic characteristics with many offenders.

From an employer's viewpoint, knowledge of a job applicant's criminal past may be highly relevant to the problem of predicting how well that person will work if hired and what sort of risk he might pose to the firm, to coworkers, or to customers. The same is true if someone is considering a potential tenant or romantic partner. The losses to those who unsuspectingly hire, house, or date offenders who subsequently behave badly have to be weighed against the gains for the offenders and, potentially, for those whom they do not victimize because they have succeeded in getting their lives straightened out.

As with the sealing of juvenile records, expungement has a class of less obvious victims: those who are not themselves offenders despite having offender-like demographic profiles. A young white man from a prosperous low-crime neighborhood may benefit greatly from a policy that prevents his adolescent joy-riding, or a domestic assault committed when he was in college, from interfering with his job search: in the absence of evidence to the contrary, a potential employer is likely to assume that he is a non-offender. But a young man from a poor African American neighborhood faces a different problem. He may have a clean criminal history himself, but if potential employers reluctant to hire offenders cannot verify that he is not an offender, they may well resort to "statistical discrimination."

It would be utterly perverse to reduce the capacity of, for example, male African American high-school dropouts to earn an honest living, and thus their incentive to avoid criminal activity. Yet current policies may have just such effects; whether that is true, and to what extent, deserves some serious empirical investigation, and in the meantime we might want to be cautious about expanding expungement programs, and perhaps reconsider the wisdom of not allowing law-abiding poor young black men to demonstrate their law-abidingness to potential employers.

The argument for keeping a juvenile record sealed seems weaker yet after the first adult felony conviction; if the goal of sealing records was to give each juvenile a fresh start at adulthood, that purpose is no longer served once that fresh start has gone awry. In particular, a sentencing judge ought to know whether the eighteen-year-old he has to sentence for that person's first adult burglary conviction is literally a "first offender" or has simply continued into adulthood a well-established pattern of lawbreaking. Insofar as the project of selective incapacitation (see chapter 6) has merit, its promise is greatest with the youngest offenders, who have many of their most criminally active years still ahead of them. The repeated research finding that crime rates do not suddenly drop at the age of adult responsibility, sometimes interpreted as refuting the idea that consequences influence crime rates—at least for those around eighteen years of age—may reflect instead the fact that a first adult felony conviction, unless the underlying crime is a violent one, carries only a modest risk of a prison term.

Ideally, a juvenile offender attaining the birthday that makes him an adult under the laws of his state should be encouraged to reason, "If I go straight now, I can be all right. But from here on out I'm playing with the big boys, and likely to really get hurt if I keep at it." Current policies do not make that line of reasoning especially plausible.

SUMMING UP: THE LIMITS OF SEVERITY

The criminal-justice system as it now operates provides a level of expected punishment ample to deter any potential burglar, robber, or retail drug dealer who carefully calculates risk and reward in the manner of an economically rational actor. Therefore we should expect to find offending concentrated among those who heavily discount the future compared to the present, undervalue tiny risks of large disasters compared to high probabilities of small gains, and overestimate their luck and skill.

In that context, we should not expect that continuing to increase the severity of punishment will have much impact on crime, other than by the purely mechanical means of separating high-rate offenders from potential victims. If the use of brute force has passed the point of diminishing returns, we need to ask what we could use instead.

Designing Enforcement Strategies

Those who design and execute criminal-justice policies must allocate limited capacities to investigate, adjudicate, and punish, distributing these capacities across offense types, offenders, and locations. One goal of their decision-making and operations ought to be to minimize the sum of the suffering and economic loss caused by crime, including the suffering imposed by the enforcement and punishment machinery and the cost of running that machinery.

Of course, that is not and should not be the sole consideration; the demands of justice—justice to offenders, justice to actual and potential victims, and justice to their communities—will sometimes overrule the calculation of minimizing total damage. In a world constrained by political decision-making, by the iron laws of organizational behavior, by the norms of various professional communities, and by legal and constitutional limits, it will be impossible to carry out many policies that might be optimal in an unconstrained world. But insofar as minimizing total harm is a goal, then we should think carefully about how the crime-reducing effects of punishment are increased or decreased by different strategies.

Also, of course, punishment and the threat of punishment are not the only crime-control mechanisms available; anything that makes non-criminal options relatively more attractive—by creating better licit opportunity, or by fostering informal social control or more self-command[1] among potential offenders—will also tend to reduce crime. Still, it is reasonable to consider how the tools of coercion can best be used, before tackling the even more complicated questions of how to combine criminal-justice activities with other potentially crime-reducing policies and how to compare the two sets of policies in terms of their advantages and disadvantages.

The relevance of positive feedback and imperfect rationality to any given crime-control problem needs to be investigated rather than merely assumed. But the analytic framework set out in the preceding chapters, and the examples of H.O.P.E. probation, the squeegee crackdown, and the low-arrest crackdown that broke up High Point's open drug market, together point to three central ideas about how to maximize the crime-control effects of any given stock of enforcement resources: concentration, substitution of certainty and swiftness for severity, and the direct communication of deterrent threats. Those ideas play themselves out in complicated ways across the dizzying variety of criminal-justice operations. They all rest on the notion that the actions taken by criminal-justice agencies—arrest, prosecution, and incarceration—should be thought of as costs, not benefits.

Enforcement and punishment are costly in the literal sense of costing money, and are therefore limited in quantity at any given time. Once the prisons are full, every prisoner is taking up cell space that could be used by another; a police officer who has made one arrest is out of action for as long as the formalities of booking last and cannot make another arrest. Enforcement and punishment are also costly because they are inevitably painful to those arrested, prosecuted, and punished to their families and friends, and because they can cause anxiety and resentment even among those never arrested, prosecuted, or incarcerated; just being under potentially hostile observation is itself unpleasant. Although the punished often deserve the costs associated with the crime committed, their families and friends usually do not. In any case, even deserved suffering is still suffering, and even offenders are still persons whose suffering matters.

It is worth spending some amount of money and inflicting some amount of unpleasantness on offenders and their intimates, and on the rest of us, in order to avoid the suffering that crime would otherwise inflict on victims and to reduce the costs associated with potential victims' efforts to avoid victimization. But our willingness to spend money and inflict suffering should be limited: costs must be justified by benefits. In the presence of costs and constraints, "zero crime" is no more an appropriate target than "zero pollution" or "zero auto accidents."

How Does Punishment Reduce Crime?

Stepping back to first principles, punishment and the threat of punishment can reduce crime in (at least) four conceptually distinct ways.

- Incapacitation: Keeping offenders away from criminal opportunities: for example, by locking them up.
- Deterrence: Scaring potential offenders away from offending even when criminal opportunities are present. This can be subdivided into "general deterrence," the effect of the fear of punishment generated by the overall perceived pattern of punishment on the behavior of offenders generally, and "specific deterrence," the effect of a punishment as actually administered on that person's fear of punishment as he contemplates future offending.
- Rehabilitation: Improving offenders' noncriminal capacities and opportunities in order to make crime relatively less attractive and punishment more disadvantageous, or changing offenders' preferences, habits, and decision-making styles to make them less likely to offend when faced with any given combination of risks and rewards. Of course, there is no assurance that any particular punishment will tend to rehabilitate the person punished rather than exacerbating his tendency to break the rules.
- Norm reinforcement: Changing the level of disapproval of some offense in the minds of potential offenders and those whose good opinion they value. Drunk driving and spousal abuse, having gone from being joked about or even bragged about to being widely considered disgraceful over less than a generation, provide examples. More aggressive enforcement and stiffer sentences partly result from changes in social attitudes brought about by Mothers Against Drunk Driving and the feminist movement. But those policies not only reflected new attitudes; they helped drive them as well, through at least three different psychosocial mechanisms: cognitive dissonance (the social world is easier to understand if the vigor with which a given offense is investigated and punished more or less tracks the moral opprobrium attached to the offense); opinion conformity (tough enforcement and severe sentences suggest a majority view that the underlying act is seriously wrong, and people tend to adjust their opinions in the direction of the perceived majority); and behavioral conformity (if increased enforcement of some law leads to decreased, or even merely less flagrant, violation of that particular law, then that offense comes to seem less common and therefore more deviant). These effects will be less potent for crimes

committed largely within oppositional subcultures; in neighborhoods where drug dealing is rampant, stiffer sentences for dealing
may be taken as instances of injustice rather than as expressions of
a social consensus.

Incapacitation

Incapacitation is the simplest effect conceptually and the most mechanical in practice: by separating someone whose offense history suggests a
high severity-adjusted personal crime rate—known to criminologists by
the Greek letter lambda (λ)—from potential victims, incarceration can
prevent whatever crimes that person would have committed, in a way
that does not depend on behavioral assumptions about the person incarcerated. Not that incapacitation is utterly reliable: When some social
mechanism, such as the market for criminal labor, creates negative feedback—for instance, in an active drug market, where removing one dealer
creates a niche for another—incapacitation will not be effective. And if
incarceration delays the process of "aging out" of crime—for example, by
reducing the probability of getting married, which is a strong correlate of
crime desistance—then some of the reduced criminal activity due to incapacitation will be counterbalanced by increased criminal activity once
the offender is released.[*] The very large cohorts of people now emerging
from prison terms account for a substantial fraction of all crime, and the
growth of those cohorts due to increased incarceration levels may be one
reason crime seems to have stopped falling around 2004.

Incapacitation depends on incarceration, or on programs of noninstitu-
tional corrections—for example, continuous position monitoring—that
greatly reduce an offender's capacity to re-offend, or at least to re-offend
with impunity. But in the United States, correctional capacity is the
relatively scarce resource within the criminal-justice system: the police
currently arrest more offenders than the courts can process to felony convictions—leading to the process of "bargaining down" charges in return
for pleas—and the courts convict more felons than the prisons can hold.

---

[*] An exhaustive literature review by Daniel Nagin, Francis Cullen, and Cheryl Lero
Jonson (2009) finds that the average effect of incarceration on the offender's suggested criminal career is somewhere between zero and a modest increase in criminal activity.

So criminal-justice strategies focused on incapacitation, unless they are highly selective about whom they incapacitate, make profligate use of the scarcest resource in the system.

Whether incapacitation effects alone can justify keeping a given offender behind bars depends on how many crimes that person would commit if not imprisoned, how many of those crimes are committed instead by someone else—as when a new drug dealer steps in to fill the place of an incarcerated dealer, or a burglary ring recruits a new member to replace someone behind bars—and how serious those crimes would be. It has been known since the work of Jan and Marcia Chaiken* in the 1980s that offenders in prison—judging by their self-reports of the crimes they committed in the year before incarceration—are enormously heterogeneous, with no more than 10 percent of the imprisoned offenders accounting for more than half the total criminal activity of the group. The crime rate of the most active 20 percent of offenders average ten times the rate of the median prisoner.[2] Thus the prisoner with the median offense rate—who might be thought of as the typical prisoner—is a fairly low-frequency offender, but the average rate of all prisoners combined is much higher; the prisoner with the mean, as opposed to the median, offense rate is well worth holding on to.[†]

That observation raises an obvious question: Why not use estimated lambdas (personal crime rates) as guides to sentencing, trying to fill the prisons with as many high-rate serious offenders, and as few of the lightweights, as possible? To some extent, repeat-offender statutes and the use of criminal history in sentencing guidelines are intended to implement that idea—called "selective incapacitation"[3]—but they do a very poor

---

*The Chaikens, a husband-and-wife team, shook up the world of criminology with their pathbreaking *Varieties of Criminal Behavior* (1982), published when both were at RAND. They subsequently moved to Abt Associates and to LINC. Jan Chaiken served as director of the Bureau of Justice Statistics in the Clinton administration.

† Benefit-cost estimates of incarceration that rely on prisoner self-reports of offending in the year before going to prison need to be adjusted for two important effects. First, personal crime rates tend to go down with age, so a five-year sentence will not usually prevent five times the prisoner's pre-incarceration crime rate. Second, incarceration does not happen entirely at random; the year before incarceration is likely to have been an especially criminally active year for the prisoner, again making his pre-incarceration lambda an overestimate of his likely post-release lambda.

job of it. Unless adjusted for an offender's age, the *number* of (adult) felony convictions, or even arrests, is a very crude proxy for that offender's personal crime *rate*; by the time an offender is a "three-time loser," he is likely also over the hill in his career as a criminal. The median age of an adult felony offender is twenty-three, reflecting an age structure of offending very much like that of professional football. Yet almost two out of three inmates in California prisons are past the age of thirty, and half are older than thirty-five.[4] A study of prison releasees in Florida found that personal crime rates among a sample of people who had been incarcerated at some time fell by 3.2 percent per year, suggesting that a thirty-six-year-old prisoner would, if released, commit about 40 percent less crime than he was committing at his peak. So our prisons are filled with people who would otherwise be retired—or at least semi-retired—offenders, and repeat offenders statutes tend to make that situation worse.[5]

On the other hand, someone who racks up a second (nondrug) felony conviction in his first two years of adult criminal liability—in most states, that means before his twentieth birthday—is, statistically, a good target for a long prison term, since he seems to be committing serious offenses at a rapid rate and is still in his prime crime-committing years. But while no one with two felony convictions in two years is likely to be a Rotarian, only a minority among them will turn out to be truly high-rate serious offenders, because who gets arrested and convicted reflects, among other things, the skill of offenders. Some people with many arrests are what Jan and Marcia Chaiken call "low-rate losers,"[6] the Sad Sacks of criminality, who commit only a handful of offenses but get arrested for nearly all of them.

In addition to age and conviction history, the number of prior arrests, race, education, drug abuse history, employment history, family status, and housing status can all considerably improve the accuracy with which a judge can predict which offenders are worth sending away for a long stretch if the goal is simply to prevent the crimes they would otherwise commit. But some of those factors, easy enough to gather in a confidential interview after someone is already behind bars, are not available to the probation officer who prepares the pre-sentencing report for the judge. Others—race being the most obvious—cannot be used for ethical reasons: a system that intends to do justice as well as control crime should not treat misfortunes such as being unemployed, unmarried, uneducated, and homeless as if they were aggravating factors worthy of additional punishment. Sentencing based on the arrest count—which is potentially more valuable than the conviction count in predicting future offending—would amount to punishing someone for crimes of which he was never convicted and of which he is therefore, in law, innocent.

Juvenile criminal history is an especially accurate predictor of who, among a group of adult offenders, will turn out to be the most serious high-rate offenders. It makes its largest contribution when applied to younger adults, since adding in what may be a long juvenile history to a necessarily short adult history greatly improves the predictive power of any model.[7] The strong argument for sealing the juvenile criminal history at adulthood—to give someone who acted badly as a youngster the chance to go straight, unburdened by a criminal record that would deny him employment and educational opportunities—applies with much less force to preventing its use in sentencing once someone has begun to accumulate an adult felony record. It makes no sense to allow an eighteen-year-old whose career as a burglar or robber started at age thirteen and has continued steadily through his adolescence to claim "first offender" status for his most recent offense.

As the prison population grows, the relative scarcity of truly high-rate serious offenders among the run of ordinary felons makes selective incapacitation—thought of as trying to pick out those most worthy of long sentences, as opposed to picking out those too lightweight to be worth bothering with—a less and less promising strategy, just because more and more of the attractive targets will have already been sent away. If in fact long prison terms retard the aging-out process, that again leads to diminishing returns.[8]

So, while selective incapacitation has obvious appeal in principle, real-world constraints on the gathering and use of information greatly limit its potential contribution to crime control. Even a thoroughgoing application of the principle has been estimated to yield no more than a 6 percent reduction in crime[9]: far from trivial, but equally far from the optimistic claims originally made for the idea. Most of the potential gains come not from imposing extraordinarily long sentences on high-rate serious offenders, but from cutting back on the sentences of those whose age and criminal history suggest that they are not, in terms of incapacitation, worth the prison space they occupy.

Deterrence

The sentencing rule suggested by selective incapacitation is the opposite of the sentencing rule suggested by the analysis of deterrence in the face of imperfectly rational offenders. For perfectly rational, risk-averse offenders, assuming that the unpleasantness of a prison term grows in direct proportion to its length, handing out a few very long sentences, more or less at random, would maximize the deterrent effect. But to the extent that offenders are present-oriented, reckless, and overconfident, swiftness and certainty of punishment will be more important than severity in shaping offense rates. If severity means a long prison term, then by definition only a small portion of a severe sentence happens quickly. Even for a group of economically rational (but not omniscient) offenders, estimating the expected value of the punishment for some crime demands more cognitive resources than estimating the likelihood of punishment and how quickly it follows the offense.

Severity, at least in the form of lengthy prison and jail stays, is the enemy of certainty and swiftness. That competition is partly mechanical: for any given total amount of punishment, there is an inverse relationship between the average severity (of nonzero punishments) and their frequency. One twenty-year sentence uses up as much cell space, over time, as forty six-month sentences. But severity also defeats swiftness because a more severe punishment will be more fiercely resisted, slowing the process and increasing the delay between crime and punishment, except for those held pending trial. As to certainty, an arrestee who might well plead guilty to a lesser offense expecting a short term might decide to "roll the dice" with a jury trial if facing a long term, with the possible result of being acquitted and suffering no punishment at all. A judge faced with a probation officer's request to revoke a noncompliant probationer's probation term and send him to prison is more likely to say, "Let's give him one more chance," than the same judge confronted with a request to send the same probationer to jail for a weekend, and the probationer's defense lawyer is more likely to insist on a full-dress evidentiary hearing.

Thus long prison terms require special justification either in terms of justice or in the form of evidence that the offender involved poses a substantially greater risk of serious re-offending (greater either in probability or in severity of offense) than the average of the much larger number of offenders who could otherwise occupy the same cell space.

Deterrence, when it can be made to do the job, is preferable to incapacitation because it uses threatened, rather than actual, punishment, thus
economizing on the capacity to punish and also reducing the pain inflicted
on offenders and their families and friends. That is even more emphat-
ically the case for the underutilized approach of providing positive incentives for good behavior, and for other measures leading to rehabilitation.

Some additional deterrent value might be squeezed out of existing
capacity by making confinement more aversive to those confined. That
might well be consistent with making it less horrible, threatening, and
destructive of the inmate's future well-being and social and employment
prospects, and thus more rehabilitative as well as more deterrent. An
orderly, quiet prison where inmates spent much of their time working or
studying alone might be less congenial to many offenders than the current combination of noise, violence, idleness, and sociability, which has
a strong resemblance to many inmates' pre-incarceration social settings.
It is important to reflect that offenders may not have the same tastes
as policy-makers, or as the author and readers of the present volume,
perhaps especially as to noise and interpersonal conflict: a prison that
resembled a Benedictine monastery rather than an urban street corner
might seem more unpleasant to most actual inmates, even if in prospect
it seems far less horrible to you or me. It may be possible to design prison
stays that will be shorter and less damaging to offenders' well-being and
future prospects, but which will also be recalled by them, and communicated by them to others, as more unpleasant and therefore more to be
avoided. Especially for a juvenile, a forty-hour sentence served in solitary
with no radio or television might be highly unpleasant without being at
all damaging to the juvenile's future, and at the same time so undramatic
as to deprive him of bragging rights.

Still, the big problem is that most offenses do not result in arrest, and
a substantial number of offenses that do result in arrest, and even conviction, lead to no substantial punishment. Both delays in the adjudication
process (in cases where the offender is released while awaiting trial) and
the fact that prison terms are extended in time make it the case that the
formal part of punishment for crime—as opposed to the nominally nonpunitive processes of arrest and pretrial confinement—mostly happens at
some considerable distance in time from the offense. And the system is so

unpredictable that it helps foster the kind of superstitious thinking that is one source of optimistic bias, as well as the rage that comes from being punished seemingly at the whim of officials rather than as a predictable result of one's own actions.

INCREASING DETERRENCE BY INCREASING CERTAINTY

Since uncertainty, delay, and inaccurate perception all limit the effectiveness of deterrent threats, designers of criminal-justice policies should look for ways of increasing the probability of some nontrivial punishment for each offense, to reduce the time-gap between offense and punishment, and make the risks of crime to criminals easier for them to perceive. All of that, of course, is easier said than done.

Consider first increasing the probability of punishment.

Any given stock of incarceration capacity can be spread over more offenders by spreading it more thinly, reducing the average sentence length and thus increasing the probability that any given offense leads to some time behind bars. That gain in deterrence might come at some cost in incapacitation if those released earlier are more criminally active than those who replace them. If shorter average sentences also meant fewer and shorter trials, there might be some gain in immediacy of punishment as well. Against this must be weighed the risk that increasing the number of people who pass through the prison system will also increase the number of career criminals by increasing the number of people with stunted licit opportunities, and decrease the fearsomeness of the threat of incarceration by making it seem routine. That is already a major problem in high-crime neighborhoods.

Or we could increase the probability of punishment without reducing severity by simply adding prison and jail cells. Since there are already more people convicted than the corrections system has space to hold, more space could be converted directly into a higher probability of punishment. The continued prison-building boom, combined with the crime bust, has increased both the probability of incarceration for any given offense and the average length of a prison term. But do we really want to further increase the scale of incarceration?

The biggest and cheapest opportunity to increase the probability that an offense results in a punishment the offender cares about is to transform probation from a mere legal status—a placeholder for an absent punishment—into something substantial. About twice as many offenders are given probation each year as are sent to either prison or jail. At any one time, the U.S. criminal-justice system manages—or fails to manage—about four million probationers.[10]

The sheer number of probationers, compared to the modest size of the probation workforce, means that most offenders find probation only a mild inconvenience. The nationwide budget for probation supervision is about $5 billion, or about $1000 per client per year, representing about 13 percent of the total corrections budget.[11]

Probation departments also enforce other "alternative" sanctions: forcing offenders to pay money—whether called a fine, a court fee, or a victim restitution payment—requiring them to do unpaid and sometimes onerous work ("community service"), or imposing mandatory treatment for substance abuse, assaultive behavior, or predatory sexual conduct. The weakness of the probation system—its failure to enforce the mandates the courts impose on probationers—weakens the value of all those alternatives and thus makes them seem to judges and prosecutors less attractive competitors with prison terms. Fines and restitution payments have proven difficult to collect; moreover, they risk creating perverse incentives, inducing those who must pay them to return to crime to secure the requisite funds. "Community service" has also proven harder in practice than it seems in concept, partly due to the difficulty of finding appropriate assignments and partly due to the difficulty of getting unpaid workers to show up as assigned and to work diligently without a convincing threat of consequences for failure to appear. "Drug diversion" programs, in which offenders with drug problems are spared jail time on condition of going through a course of treatment for substance abuse, suffer from very low compliance rates; typically, fewer than half of those who enter finish the prescribed course.

Probation, fines, community service, and drug diversion all have something in common: they involve the voluntary—albeit unwilling—compliance of the person punished. The offender always has the option of ignoring the rules: not paying the fines, skipping work, or dropping out of treatment. Since offenders tend to be less averse to breaking rules than the population at large, none of these alternatives to incarceration will be very effective unless noncompliance leads to some unwelcome consequence. That means that there needs to be an enforcement mechanism that detects violations, apprehends violators, adjudicates the fact of the violation, assigns a sanction, and administers it: the probation system.

With probation officers now typically trying to supervise 150 "clients" each, enforcement of alternative punishments is often merely nominal.[12] Thus theoretically mandatory restrictions, payments, work-tasks, and treatment are, in effect, voluntary, and savvy probationers know it. Consequently, those mandates are poorly complied with, reducing whatever value they might have in deterrence, incapacitation, or rehabilitation. A broken probation system means that the only practical alternative to incarceration is, in effect, nothing. Reducing the share of incarceration in the total punishment system therefore requires improving the capacity of probation departments to enforce rules.

That underlines the importance of the H.O.P.E. program's demonstration that probation terms can be enforced without either greatly expanding probation resources or sending many probationers to jail. The combination of a greater likelihood of detection given a violation, greater likelihood of punishment given a detected violation, and lower punishment intensity—probation modification rather than revocation, meaning days rather than months or years behind bars—holds out the promise of making the entire range of substitute punishments effective alternatives to incarceration. The greater the capacity to deliver real punishment and control without incarceration, the fewer people need to be kept behind bars to maintain any given level of deterrence and incapacitation.

There are already twice as many probationers as there are prison and jail inmates, so a change in probation would be a fundamental change in the entire system. And since the budget for probation supervision is less than 15 percent of the corrections budget, an improvement in probation supervision that allowed even a modest reduction in the population behind bars could easily pay for itself while also improving public safety. (See below, "Sketch of a Cost-Benefit Analysis.")

With a H.O.P.E.-like sanctioning process in place, the main limit on the capacity of community-corrections institutions to punish past crimes and prevent future ones is the capacity to monitor offender behavior.

Drug testing monitors a narrow but important slice of behavior, and does so relatively cheaply. The capacity to continuously monitor an offender's whereabouts could make a much more profound impact: on offenders' lives, on the number of people behind bars, and on the crime rate.

It is now possible to manufacture a unit consisting of a GPS receiver and a transmitter that reports continuously on the position of that receiver (for example, via the cellular telephone system), and to mount that unit on an anklet that cannot be removed without breaking it and with a sensor to detect if the anklet were broken. By requiring an offender on probation or parole to wear such a device, continuously recording his location, and comparing those locations against crimes reported to the police—via the 911 system, which is automated and geo-coded in most large jurisdictions—it would be possible to deter future crimes by making it virtually impossible for that offender to commit most kinds of crime without being detected.

Cell-phone companies are now selling position-monitoring services to enable parents to locate their children for about $10 per month; a system to monitor offenders would be more technically challenging—for example, requiring tamper-evident anklets for security and GPS rather than cell-phone technology to increase precision—and therefore more expensive, but still dirt-cheap by comparison with the cost of incarceration.

Just the capacity to tie probationers and parolees to the scenes of new crimes would be valuable. Police departments ought to be interested in using that capacity, and in responding promptly when the system signals that the band on the anklet has been broken, just as police respond promptly when a prisoner escapes from prison or jail. Add to that a probation or parole department prepared to create and enforce time-and-place restrictions—curfews, restraining orders, requirements to show up as scheduled for work, "community service," or treatment—and suddenly position monitoring becomes a genuine alternative to incarceration, a kind of "outpatient incarceration," that would deliver deterrence and incapacitation without the room-and-board bill and without the pains, or the risks, the "hardening" effects of time behind bars.

Ex-offenders have difficulty finding jobs: partly because employers think, not unreasonably, that they might be unreliable as workers, and at risk for re-offending on the job. A combination of drug testing and position monitoring could change that calculation from the employer's viewpoint, much to the potential benefit of former offenders trying to "go straight."

Compared to routine probation, such a system would represent a great tightening of social control and an increase in effective punishment capacity; it would amount to a prison without walls. But compared to current "inpatient" incarceration, it would reflect a great loosening and a great reduction in punishment actually inflicted, especially if it proved to be able to keep prisoners from returning to prison. What fraction of those currently in prison or jail could be adequately punished and prevented from committing future crimes by having their drug use monitored and their whereabouts monitored 24/7? Without actually developing and testing such a system, it is impossible to guess. Could that fraction be as high as one-half? Higher? (Recall that the median prisoner is already a fairly low-rate offender, even without the additional incapacitation due to position monitoring.) Discovering the answer to that question ought to be the first priority for anyone interested in shrinking both crime and incarceration.

A system that monitored drug use and location would have the advantage of allowing offenders to in effect identify themselves as low risk by complying with the rules or as high risk by defying them, thus replacing attempts by judges, probation officers, and parole boards to use statistical "risk assessment" tools to judge which offenders need to be confined and which it would be safe to let out. Angela Hawken* calls this approach "behavioral triage," and it has much to recommend it, both operationally and morally.

POLICING

Policing is the most prominent aspect of the criminal-justice system in the public mind, and the most popular. Hiring more police is a popular crime-control measure. At first blush, this seems hard to fathom. As noted, police forces already make more arrests than the courts can process,

*Hawken, an economist, is professor of public policy at Pepperdine University and has conducted studies both of California's "Proposition 36" diversion program and of the H.O.P.E. program.

and the courts convict more offenders than the corrections system can effectively punish or monitor; it is not immediately obvious why adding more police should be effective, any more than adding more raw materials can expand the output of a factory already working at full capacity.* And police are expensive; policing accounts for more than half of the total criminal-justice budget.

But there are good theoretical reasons to think that in this instance the public instinct is correct, and the empirical results, while admittedly ambiguous, seem to agree. In a world of imperfectly rational offenders, police presence might reduce the level of criminal activity even if it had no effect on the total level of formal punishment, simply because the sight of a police car or an officer walking a beat represents a visible threat.† Anything that increases the risk of arrest as perceived by potential offenders will tend to reduce the frequency of crime, and thus of incarceration, regardless of whether offenders currently under- or overestimate that risk. The effect will be magnified by the positive feedback from lowered offending rates to higher actual per-crime arrest rates because the stock of police attention is being spread over fewer offenses. William Stuntz argues that one source of over-incarceration in African American neighborhoods is under-policing.[13]

"Broken Windows"

One version of the idea that police can reduce crime by changing offenders' perceptions goes under the name "broken windows." The term, first coined by James Q. Wilson and George Kelling†† in a famous magazine article[14] and expanded on in a subsequent book by Kelling and Cather-

---

*This analogy is imprecise, because increasing the number of arrests allows prosecutors and courts to be more selective about whom to prosecute and punish, and also makes it easier to pick out serious high-rate offenders from the rest by making an offender's arrest record a somewhat better sample of his total criminal activity. Still, those are second-order effects.

† Even an arrest that never leads to a conviction is unpleasant for the person arrested. Unlike formal punishment, it happens almost immediately.

†† George Kelling, professor of criminology at Rutgers University, has been central in developing a new body of theory about police work and a new approach to practice centered on the ideas that communities do most of the actual work of crime control and that dealing with incidents does not equal solving problems.

ine Coles,[15] is a prominent catchphrase in both public and professional discussions about crime, both as a description of how events can unfold and as a remedial strategy. The focus of the broken-windows analysis and strategy is on minor "public-order" offenses, and even on behaviors, such as a rowdy group of young men hanging out on a street corner, that do not amount to offenses at all. The slogan that generally accompanies "broken windows" is "zero tolerance." Both as analysis and as prescription, "broken windows" is so ambiguous that disputes about "whether broken windows (as an analysis) is right" or "whether broken windows (as a strategy) works"—like the parallel questions about "zero tolerance"—are often confused because the disputants are working with different meanings for the same phrase.

The basic "broken windows" idea is that bad behaviors cluster. Visibly neglected property, such as a house with a broken window not promptly repaired, is often the target of mischief. Repairing the first broken window can discourage vandals from breaking the other windows. An already litter-strewn park is likely to attract more additional litter than a neatly kept park.[16] It also seems natural to think that physical conditions influence other sorts of behavior, and not just behavior that contributes to those conditions. An ill-tended park, or a street where many houses have broken windows, might encourage more public drinking or public urination or shouting rude things at passers-by than a neatly kept park or a street with well-maintained houses. By the same token, disorderly behavior may tend to be self-reinforcing, even without physical conditions as an intermediate; the presence of a rowdy crowd on one street corner might easily encourage forming a similar crowd on a nearby street corner. These are all matters of common-sense observation, and surely they must be valid to some extent: more so in some circumstances than in others.

The enforcement idea that comes out of this is that influencing seemingly minor forms of disorderly behavior can make a significant difference to the quality of neighborhood life. Wilson and Kelling observe that a police-community meeting about "crime" is often dominated by complaints about public drinking, not by complaints about armed robbery. Not only is a disorderly neighborhood less pleasant to live in (for those with a taste for peace and quiet), but neighbors and strangers alike are likely to take cues from the behavioral and physical environment in deciding how dangerous a place is. Thus insofar as the fear of crime is a

problem in its own right, police work that concentrates on order maintenance can help manage that problem even if it does not change the actual
rate of serious crime.

None of that should be very controversial as analysis, though there
is legitimate debate about the priority that fear reduction should have
compared to other police work goals and about how to trade off the good
of order maintenance against its costs in the form of intrusive police behavior: for example, stopping people not suspected of any crime for brief
interviews, which may include pat-downs for the nominal purpose of protecting the officers against any weapons the subject might be carrying.
Those debates carry an ideological edge as a result of the ethnic, class,
and age differences in what is perceived as "disorder" and the fact that
the intrusions created by order-maintenance policing will inevitably be
concentrated on poorer, younger, and lower-status individuals.

The more controversial "broken-windows" claim is that offenders, as
well as other people, use the visible level of physical and behavioral disorder as a clue to how safe it might be to commit a crime in a given location.
The positive-feedback "enforcement swamping" analysis (see chapter 4)
provides a rationale for that claim. Since it is safer to commit both serious
crimes and petty infractions where the ratio of police to crime is low, and
if high-violation places also tend to be high-disorder places, then a mug-
ger might use physical and behavioral signs of disorder to select the safest
environment in which to practice his trade.

If that analysis is right, then, by helping residents maintain neighborhood order, police might actually reduce serious crime in that neighborhood. A recent experimental study provides some evidence for the claim
that physical signs of disorder can increase some forms of law breaking.[17]

The strong "broken windows" claim that order maintenance prevents
serious crime might easily be false, or true only to a slight extent or under
limited conditions, even if the weak "broken windows" claim that order maintenance reduces the fear of crime were true. And while reducing
fear is an independently valuable goal, obviously a level of intrusion and
resource expenditure that could be justified to produce an actual crime
reduction might not be justified if the only benefit is fear reduction.

In the minds of some politicians, pundits, and police, the natural implication of "broken windows" is "zero tolerance": making every detected

infraction the occasion for an arrest. The positive-feedback analysis does not support that idea; attempting to enforce every rule can too easily lead to such dispersion of attention as to result in effective enforcement of none of them. What the positive-feedback idea does support is the idea of *targeted* zero tolerance: deciding, and announcing, precisely what behaviors will not be tolerated in what areas, and then delivering on those commitments.

As a result, there is no straightforward way to test the strong "broken windows" claim by looking at places where the police have proclaimed zero tolerance for disorder and measuring whether serious crime has fallen in those areas. That such tests have had generally negative findings[18] may show as much about the difficulty of measuring police behavior and the variability in the skill of police management as about the underlying idea. Order-maintenance policing done in some ways under some circumstances might reduce serious crime, while worse-designed efforts in less appropriate settings might be futile or even crime-increasing.

What looks like order-maintenance police work might also reduce serious crime through mechanisms unrelated to "broken windows": deterrence and incapacitation. When the New York City Transit police cracked down on riders who jumped the turnstiles to evade paying the fare, they wound up confiscating many guns and arresting substantial numbers of serious offenders wanted on bench warrants. No doubt that helped reduce serious crime, but that success proves nothing about the "broken windows" hypothesis. Similarly, aggressive stop-and-frisk activity by the police can discourage gun-carrying, apprehend fugitives, and advertise to potential offenders that the level of police resources in the target neighborhood is high. All of those things will tend to reduce crime—at some cost in money, liberty, and police-community relations—but again not through the "broken windows" mechanism of making the neighborhood more orderly and thus less inviting as a place to offend.

The "collective efficacy" or "collective social capital" of a neighborhood—roughly speaking, the ability of the neighborhood as a whole to get residents and visitors to act in a "public-spirited," rather than a purely selfish, manner—is clearly an important contributor to crime control.[19] Whenever as order-maintenance policing or a drug-market crackdown increases the collective efficacy of the neighborhood, we would expect it to help reduce crime, perhaps with a time-lag. On the other hand, the feeling of being under siege from intrusive policing might easily have the opposite effect. From this perspective, the "community organizing" prelude to an enforcement push—the work to make the push acceptable to the neighborhood—may have value far beyond making a particular operation possible and avoiding a political backlash.[20] Insofar as the neighborhood leadership comes to "own" the result, the result may be an increase in collective efficacy not just from a reduction in disorder, but also from changed social relationships. These effects are not easily captured by econometric methods.

Arrests as Informal Punishment

Aside from the "advertising" effects of police presence, arrests themselves—and the consequent confinement before arraignment or awaiting trial—constitute a form of punishment. Indeed, they are the only part of the corrections process that occurs in close time-proximity to actual offending, and they are enormous in volume compared to any other form of punishment. Each year, there are 13.7 million arrests in the United States, but no more than a quarter that many prison and jail terms imposed. Pre-arraignment confinement is inevitably brief, measured in hours or a few days; pretrial confinement can be much longer, but in the aggregate these two forms of pre-conviction detention amount to no more than 20 percent of the total; the other 80 percent of cell time is served after conviction.

However, if probability and immediacy trump severity in generating deterrence, then arrest and its immediate consequences have a deterrent importance far greater than the 20 percent figure would suggest.

From the viewpoint of legal theory, this is disturbing, even shocking. As a legal matter, nothing that happens before a finding of guilt is "punishment." Punishment is not for the innocent, and every arrestee is, legally, presumed innocent unless and until he pleads guilty or is found guilty.

But, partly by design, the actual handling of accused offenders before trial is often extremely unpleasant. Handcuffing, for example—nominally a security measure—is deliberately made both humiliating and uncomfortable, and it is applied routinely to arrestees who obviously pose no real risk of flight or resistance. Pre-arraignment holding facilities and the sections of jails reserved for the population awaiting trial—facilities that hold the presumptively innocent—are frequently dirtier, more uncomfortable, and more dangerous than the prisons to which the convicted are sent. The fact that courts in most jurisdictions are closed for the weekend converts a Friday arrest into a three-day jail sentence without trial, and some police officers make strategic use of that fact. The handcuffs and the jail cell certainly feel like punishment to the person subjected to them, and there is no reason to think that the theoretically nonpunitive nature of pre-conviction unpleasantness robs it of its deterrent efficacy.

Officially, these facts are deprecated when they are not merely denied. Yet the analysis above suggests that these swift unofficial punishments may carry with them a large portion of the total deterrent effectiveness of the criminal-justice process. Thinking of arrest as merely the prelude to trial—more typically, to a guilty plea—and formal punishment may be a mistake: arrest alone may be an important deterrent.

Insofar as that is the case, the high attrition rate from arrest to incarceration may be less of a problem than it seems at first blush. Increasing the number of police or their arrest activity may have little impact on the distribution of prison and jail terms, but might still help reduce crime insofar as arrest and its immediate consequences are doing much of the work of deterrence.

Another, more unpleasant implication is that reforms designed to bring enforcement practice more closely into alignment with legal theory—by treating arrestees as considerately as we would if we truly presumed them to be innocent—might have unwanted side effects in the form of higher crime rates, unless accompanied by offsetting changes in other parts of the system.

Still, evidence on the crime-reducing efficacy of merely adding more police officers is mixed. How those additional officers are used seems to matter a great deal. Most police departments use arrests as a measure of how much work is being done. "Prosecutable felony arrests" is often a part of a department's formal or informal officer-appraisal system. From the viewpoint of an individual officer—especially in departments where overtime pay is available for the hours an officer spends in the booking process—and that officer's immediate supervisor, an arrest looks like a benefit.

Compared to officers aimlessly cruising the streets, arrests—even when the rest of the system is at capacity so that the arrest simply further crowds the lockups, jails, and courts—contribute something to crime control. But from a resource-management perspective the arrest itself is a cost, not a benefit: it uses scarce resources that cannot be used for other activity, or for a different arrest. And of course arrest imposes costs on the person arrested; in neighborhoods with very high arrest rates, it may contribute to police-community tensions that exacerbate crime and make it more difficult for the police to obtain the information they need to identify and arrest criminals and prepare prosecutable cases against them.

In departments that use arrest counts as part of their internal scoring system and of the presentation of their results to the public, officers and their supervisors have no incentive to economize on arrest. In a department run that way, a low-arrest crackdown on the model of High Point might look, from an organizational viewpoint, like a drop-off in officer productivity. The CompStat process,[21] which started in New York under Commissioner William Bratton and has spread in various forms to several other departments since, makes crime reduction, rather than the arrest count, the central performance measure. That in itself constitutes an important reform.

Still, CompStat is no panacea. The efficacy of the CompStat management model depends on several factors, including the skill and ruthlessness of the command staff implementing it, the existence of a repertoire of crime-reducing tactics for local commanders to implement, and basic competence at the patrol-officer and sergeant level. CompStat is part of a management approach, not a substitute for a strategy. The question, "Does CompStat work?" makes about as much sense as the question, "Does surgery work?"

Direct Communication

Policing presents many opportunities for the direct communication of deterrent threats. "Zero tolerance" is merely a slogan; but by deciding and communicating what specific activities will not be tolerated in which specific locations, and then enforcing those decisions, police can make explicit threats do much of the deterrent work that would otherwise have to be done by arrest. Again, the police and most potential offenders actually have a common interest in avoiding arrest if deterrence can do the job instead.

Many police departments keep a list of high-rate serious offenders, and target the people on that list for surveillance with the goal of putting them in prison as quickly as possible for as long as possible. These "major violator" or "ten percent" lists are often formally assembled according to agreed-on criteria, and shared with prosecutors, usually with the understanding that the prosecutors will cooperate by refusing to plea-bargain with those offenders or to accept their testimony against others in lieu of all-out prosecution. Both in New York and in Los Angeles, prosecutable arrests of targeted offenders are a significant focus of the CompStat process.

With the people on the "major violator" list, the police are primarily playing a zero-sum game of "cops and robbers," though, even for those offenders knowledge of their targeted status might reduce offending and keep some of them out of prison. Yet the crime-control benefits of major-violator programs can be enhanced by using them as directly communicated threats to offenders not yet on those lists. The process that assembles the major-violators list can easily assemble a second list of those offenders who barely failed to make the cut: the "junior varsity" or "B Team." By calling those offenders in and explicitly warning them that one more offense will be enough to promote them to the "A Team," with a strong probability of a long prison sentence to follow shortly thereafter, police can make what is fundamentally an incapacitation-oriented program do substantial deterrent work.

Direct communication can also be applied to offenders under a particularly heavy punitive threat as a result of their prior criminal histories. The federal Armed Career Criminal (ACC) statute, for example, imposes draconian penalties on any weapons possession by any offender with two prior violent felony convictions. But in the years just after its passage, almost no one eligible for ACC sentencing seemed to know that the law existed, which must have vitiated any deterrent effect. Merely sending postcards to the list of ACC-eligible offenders might have saved a substantial amount of gunplay and a large number of prisoner-years of incarceration.

Boston's Ceasefire project, which ended, for the two years it was in operation, what had been an intractable problem of fatal shootings among members of the city's youth gangs, employed a different version of direct communication.[22] In that case, the focus was on groups rather than individuals; the "sets" of young men who constituted the gang-violence problem were called in for meetings *as groups*, and warned that any gunplay engaged in by any member of the group would lead to a full crackdown on the whole group. The goal was to induce the groups themselves to exercise control over their members' violence, with group members and leaders restraining one another rather than encouraging and praising the most violence-prone. Once the threat of a crackdown had been carried out on two groups, all the rest, without ceasing their usual array of other criminal activity, promptly stopped shooting at one another.[*]

The police also have a central role to play in making probation effective. In any H.O.P.E.-style probation-enforcement program, some probationers who break the rules will not voluntarily show up to be sanctioned. When that happens, the judge issues a bench warrant: an order to the police to pick up the absconder and bring him to court. But police traditionally have given warrant service low priority. Without warrant service, the project of providing immediate and consistent sanctions falls apart.

A strong case can be made for upgrading the importance of warrant service generally, as absconding is a strong correlate of high-rate serious offending, and such an upgrade was a significant part of the Bratton reforms in New York City. But even where a department cannot or does not make warrant service an across-the-board priority, probationers subject to a H.O.P.E.-style program must be arrested when warrants are issued, or the program will collapse. By showing when such a program starts that defiance leads to prompt arrest, police can, with a modest investment of resources, force that part of the system into a high-compliance equilibrium, which, once established, costs little to maintain.

PROSECUTION

Thinking about criminal-justice operations in terms of their efficacy as crime-control efforts has especially profound implications for prosecution. Prosecutors play an important role in setting the punishment-price attached to different offenses, by different offenders, at different times and places. In the interest of crime control, they ought to use that power strategically, which does not come naturally to a profession that historically has focused on getting the "right" outcome in each individual case rather

---

[*]Conceptually, Ceasefire was an ancestor of the High Point low-arrest market crackdown (see chapter 3).

than thinking systematically about how to use its powers to create public safety.

Prosecutors and defense counsel cooperate to speed cases through the system via plea and sentence bargaining. But the adversarial nature of the courtroom process encourages prosecutors to think of their job as securing a conviction on the most serious sustainable charge and achieving the maximum sentence legally possible, up to some maximum set by office policy and the individual prosecutor's notion of justice. But where prison cells are scarce, this is profoundly misguided; a sentence, like an arrest, is a cost, and eats up scarce resources that have opportunity costs in terms of crimes not prevented. For a defendant who would be released pending trial, a shorter sentence as a result of a plea bargain reached at arraignment may have as much or more deterrent value as a longer sentence imposed after a deferred plea bargain or a trial. Accordingly, many prosecutors' offices have formal or informal policies of "best deal first."

Insofar as police employ strategies of concentration and direct communication, they need the cooperation of prosecutors' offices. Sometimes that means prosecuting to the hilt a charge that would otherwise be disposed of quickly for a modest sentence or none at all, when that offense is the target of a focused zero-tolerance policy. Sometimes it means the opposite: being willing *not* to prosecute drug dealers who have been scared out of business by a High Point-style low-arrest crackdown. Decentralizing prosecution in large jurisdictions and allowing each local office some discretion in setting charging and plea policies has the potential to improve the prosecutorial contribution to crime control by fitting strategies to local circumstances. But it also risks exacerbating the problem of unequal justice by inflicting harsher punishments in less crime-ridden neighborhoods, which will tend to accentuate the already extreme differences in victimization rates from area to area, between rich and poor, and between African Americans and others.

CRIME-CONTROL DECISION-MAKING IN AN ERA OF MASS INCARCERATION

There are two quite different ways of reasoning about the decision whether to maintain the current rate of growth of incarceration, slow it or stop it, or begin instead to shrink the prison system. One asks what

economists call the "marginal" question: if we imagine adding or sub-
tracting a single prisoner from the pool, how do the costs and benefits of
holding him compare with the costs and benefits of releasing him? The
other asks the question of scale: what are the broad impacts of having
quadrupled the rate of incarceration over the past thirty years, and what
would the consequences be of substantially reversing that change?

Those who have begun to study what they call "mass incarceration"
as a phenomenon in its own right have assembled a long list of its macro
consequences, all of them bad. This reflects in part the predisposition of
those who have opened this line of inquiry, but it is not easy to imagine
any desirable impact of the scale change on its own. In particular, there is
good reason to think that the prisoner-by-prisoner calculation overstates
the crime-control benefits of mass incarceration, even over and above the
"diminishing returns" issue.*

Some of the crime-control benefits claimed for incarceration depend
centrally on attitudes. The stigma of being, and having been, incarcerated, and the desire to spare one's family the reflected stigma that will
result from one's going to prison, forms part of the deterrent value of
the threat of prison. Yet the intensity of that stigma must be in part
a function of its rarity. When incarceration becomes a routine incident
in the life of a young adult male, as is now the case in many high-crime
neighborhoods, that stigma will tend to diminish, though it would require heroic feats of measurement to determine how much. If so, every
additional prison sentence diminishes the deterrent value of prison for
the entire population of potential offenders. In the worst of all possible
worlds, the stigma as experienced by the offender will fall more quickly
than the stigma as perceived by important outsiders, especially employers, thus increasing the perverse aftereffects of incarceration without en-
hancing its deterrent value.

By the same argument, the capacity of a prison term to reinforce the
sense that the underlying offense was a grave one, and thereby to

---

*Selectivity creates diminishing returns. Since police, judges, and prosecutors all at-
tempt to give priority for incarceration to those likely to commit the most crimes if not
incarcerated, each additional prisoner is likely to be somewhat less criminally active than
average. If that is so, imprisoning twice as many individuals should not be expected to incapacitate twice as much crime.

increase the moral onus on those who commit it, must also diminish as prison terms become less extraordinary. That ought to be especially true of offenses for which large numbers of people have been incarcerated: does sending one more crack retailer to prison really have any influence on attitudes toward crack dealing?

An especially perverse effect of mass incarceration is to increase the power of prison-based gangs, and of the street gangs with which they are affiliated. For inmates in prisons dominated by rival ethnic gangs—and the rate of gang infestation seems to have grown along with, perhaps in part because of, the growth of the population size and the strain that this put on the capacity of institutions and their staff to control inmates—getting along with the gang leadership of one's own ethnicity is more or less a necessity. The leadership of those prison gangs often overlaps with the leadership of the street gangs in the neighborhoods that produce large numbers of prisoners. When that is the case, a young man on the outside facing a high probability of going to prison sometime in the next few years might well consider the promise of protection "inside" among the major benefits of joining a gang, or at least remaining on friendly terms with one, on the "outside." In effect, the streets of high-crime, high-incarceration neighborhoods can become extensions of the prison yard.[23]

Among poor African Americans in particular, the impacts of disproportionate incarceration are likely to grow with the scale of total incarceration. Even those who never go to prison themselves are likely to suffer what might be called "statistical stigma," leading to "statistical discrimination."[24] Anything that reduces the opportunity to pursue a successful licit career makes participation in crime that much more attractive. Moreover, high incarceration rates contribute to the sense that African Americans are being deliberately victimized by the larger society, a perception that may help fuel criminogenic rage directly and make it much more difficult to mobilize community resources in support of law-enforcement efforts.[*]

Mass incarceration has other costs besides these potentially crime-increasing effects. By greatly shifting the sex ratio among reproductive-age residents of high-incarceration neighborhoods, mass incarceration can

[*] See David Kennedy's account of the need to overcome this barrier in the course of the drug-market crackdown in High Point (Kennedy 2009, ch. 9.).

influence courting patterns in ways that disadvantage women and may contribute to a growing number of children born not just outside wedlock, but with little or no expectation of paternal contributions, either personal or financial, to the child's upbringing.

If a high-crime neighborhood were an independent jurisdiction, its law-abiding residents probably would not want to maintain current high incarceration rates, especially not the very high lifetime prevalence for males.[25] Such a neighborhood might want to "define deviancy down," even at the expense of somewhat higher crime and disorder, and especially by reducing the rate of incarceration for non-predatory, "transactional" crimes, rather than face a circumstance where as many as half of all young men spend time behind bars. In particular, the neighborhood leadership would want to reduce the lifetime prevalence of incarceration, and would want to focus on reducing that prevalence for each new birth cohort. Incorporating those considerations into the decision-making processes of criminal-justice agencies when those neighborhoods are part of wider political units represents a set of difficult problems: conceptual, operational, and political.

The more seriously we take "mass incarceration" as a problem in its own right, the greater the premium on all the means of crime control that do not involve incarceration, even when the simple "marginal-prisoner" analysis would suggest that those alternative strategies prevent fewer crimes per million dollars spent than simply crowding more prisoners into the cellblocks. Adding more police could improve the terms of the trade-off between incarceration and crime. So could spending more money on social-service programs with demonstrated crime-reduction capacity. Most of all, anything that makes community corrections a more effective alternative to imprisonment ought to be eagerly grasped at by those who look with horror at having 1 percent of the country's adult population behind bars.

SKETCH OF A COST-BENEFIT ANALYSIS

How do the three main categories of criminal-justice expenditure—on policing, on incarceration, and on community corrections—stack up against one another as ways of spending public dollars to reduce crime?

Any attempt to answer that question must necessarily elide the differences within each of those categories; some police activities are more useful than others, some prisoners more worth confining than others, some probation programs more successful than others. Still, though the aggregate numbers do not tell us everything, they can tell us something.

John Donohue,[*] summarizing and re-analyzing a large literature, estimates[26] that the elasticity of crime to incarceration is about −0.2: that is, a 10 percent increase in incarceration would be expected to lead to about a 2 percent reduction in crime. That estimate is closer to the top than the bottom of the range of figures reported by Steven Leavitt[†] and Thomas J. Miles.[27] Both reviews cite the work of William Spelman,[††] who gives a range of between −0.2 and −0.4.[28] If the true number were in this range, and restricting our attention to the costs and benefits to taxpayers and actual and potential crime victims while ignoring the costs to offenders, the gain would exceed the cost. If the total cost of crime is something like $1 trillion per year, the value of a 2 percent reduction is $20 billion per year, while a 10 percent increase in the $50 billion incarceration budget would cost only $5 billion. Thus the argument that we "can't afford" to build more prisons seems dubious.

But there are reasons to think the actual effect of incarceration on crime might be smaller. The prison population has grown even as the crime rate has fallen, implying that today's prisoners are less criminally active when not in prison than were prisoners at the time when most of the empirical work on the topic was performed. And, assuming that the criminal-justice system does some sorting by personal crime rate in making incarceration decisions, further expansion is likely to come among offenders still less active than those already behind bars: the average offender in prison has ten to fifty times the personal crime rate of the average

[*]John J. Donohue, III, is an economist, criminologist, and professor at Yale Law School, and one of the leading scholars in the empirical study of the effects on crime levels of various public policies, from gun control to incarceration to abortion.

[†]Steven Leavitt, professor of economics at the University of Chicago, and the coauthor of *Freakonomics*, worked with Donohue on the abortion study and has done pathbreaking econometric work trying to measure the impact on crime of the level of police activity.

[††]William Spelman, policy analyst and criminologist at the LBJ School at the University of Texas, has done some of the most influential research about the impact of incarceration on crime.

offender not in prison.[29] If instead greater incarceration were achieved by handing out longer sentences, that would push up the age distribution of prisoners, and thus push down the average number of crimes prevented per prisoner-year.

In terms of deterrence, Nagin suggests that "time served in prison reduces responsiveness to future punishment."[30] If so, current incarceration makes future incarceration less effective. Further expanding incarceration would also be expected to reduce the stigma associated with having been to prison[31] and thus the incentive for those who have never been imprisoned to avoid that first prison term. These arguments provide theoretical support for recent statistical evidence that as incarceration grows, its effect on crime falls.[32] Bert Useem and Anne Morrison Piehl* calculate that a 10 percent increase in incarceration from current levels would likely bring a reduction in crime of only 1/2 of 1 percent, and that in high-incarceration states adding still more prisoners tends, on balance, to *increase* crime.[33]

All in all, then, adding to the prison population is not as attractive a bargain for taxpayers and crime victims as the crude numbers might suggest. And if we count in the costs to prisoners and those who care about them, it starts to look like a very bad bargain indeed.

Leavitt estimates the elasticity of crime to policing to be substantially larger, somewhere between −0.3 and −1.0: that is, adding 10 percent to the police force would be expected to reduce crime by between 3 percent and 10 percent. If the actual number were in the middle of that range, at 6.5 percent, that would represent a benefit of about $65 billion per year.

The policing budget is more than twice the incarceration budget, so the $5 billion that buys a 10 percent increase in incarceration would buy only a 4 percent increase in policing. Even so, that would generate about $25 billion in crime-reduction benefits, roughly as much as spending that same money on incarceration would produce using Donohue's elasticity figure. And the suffering inflicted on offenders and those who care about

---

*Useem is a sociologist at Purdue University; Piehl, an economist at Rutgers who worked with political scientist John DiIulio of Princeton University and the University of Pennsylvania on the replication (with improvements) of the Chaiken and Chaiken study of crime rates of prison inmates, has subsequently done a number of studies of the effect of incarceration on crime.

them would be much less. Overall, then, adding to the police budget looks like a better way to spend crime-control dollars than further expanding incarceration.

With probationers accounting for 15 percent of felony arrests,[34] and with the total probation budget at only about $5 billion per year, improving probation might be a highly cost-effective way to control crime. If the elasticity of crime to probation spending were as small as −0.2, so that doubling the probation budget yielded as little as a 20 percent reduction in crime by probationers, that would still represent a 3 percent reduction in total crime: a $30 billion benefit for a $5 billion cost, which, like added police spending, would be at least partly offset by reduced incarceration expenditures. Adding in the smaller, but more criminally active, population of parolees, people who were under community-corrections supervision at the time of the offense of which they were most recently convicted constitute 44 percent of prison inmates.[35]

H.O.P.E., which costs about twice as much as routine probation supervision (with most of that extra spending going for drug treatment services), has shown an elasticity closer to −1.0. Doubling the budget, it has reduced felony arrests among its clients by more than 50 percent, compared to the randomly selected control group. A 50 percent reduction in crime by probationers would be a 7.5 percent reduction in total crime: $75 billion in benefits for $5 billion in costs. And, if the crime reduction were really that big, the program would more than pay for itself in reduced incarceration costs, as H.O.P.E. has in fact done.

True, experiments with "intensively supervised" probation (ISP) in the 1980s yielded very disappointing results.[36] Perhaps what was needed was not more supervision but faster and more predictable sanctions. On the probation-services side, recent efforts focused on job placement seem to work much better.[37] And the H.O.P.E. results, if the program can be generalized, would make probation reform a spectacularly cost-effective approach to crime control compared to either incarceration or policing.

It is possible that a H.O.P.E.-plus-position-monitoring "outpatient incarceration," applied to those currently in prison and to serious offenders being released on parole, would have even more dramatic results. It might prevent a substantial amount of crime, could easily save money with even a small reduction in recidivism rates, and could rescue some of the people who now cycle in and out of prison from doing what has been called "a life sentence on the installment plan." But there is no point in pretending to do a benefit-cost calculation on a program that does not yet exist.

Again, these crude aggregate calculations hide much crucial detail. How new money gets used is as important as where it gets used. It is possible to add money to probation with no apparent benefit; the results of the ISP program make it seem unlikely that simply reducing caseloads by adding probation officers would do much to reduce crime. Conversely, holding a persistent high-rate violent offender in prison can be terrifically cost-effective, as would spending a larger police budget on some of David Kennedy's "pulling levers" strategies. But precisely because the probation budget is tiny, the potential gains from adding even $1 billion to it—if that money actually goes to something useful—are substantial.

Putting Crime Control First

Judges, legislators, elected chief executives and their staffs, and budget bureaus all make decisions that shape the world of criminal-justice operations. They do so under their own sets of political and institutional incentives, pressures, and habits, and their own ideas, formed in part by professional norms, about justice and about the public interest in reducing crime. In a system with not merely so many moving parts but so many independently directed moving parts, optimal performance from the perspective of minimizing total social cost is not to be expected. But since all involved will agree that less crime and less cost are to be preferred, other things being equal, to more crime and more cost, it is not unreasonable to hope that strategic thinking and the calculation of benefits and costs will have some role in shaping the choices they make.

Crime Control without Punishment

Since punishment is costly to inflict and painful to undergo—painful both for the person punished and for those who care about him—why not shift the emphasis of the crime-control effort from punishment, and the associated activities carried out by the agencies of criminal justice, to ways of reducing crime that do not involve hurting people? The epic political defeat suffered over the past generation by the advocates of "soft" rather than "tough" approaches to crime control should not make us forget that this is a perfectly straightforward, common-sense question to ask. Given a choice between two equally effective crime-control programs, we should prefer the less costly, in all the ways that a program can be costly. Economizing on the infliction of suffering is as obvious a requirement of rational policy-making as economizing on the expenditure of public funds. If, instead of imposing suffering as a side-cost, nonpunitive programs could reduce crime while producing side-benefits such as more employment, less homelessness, and more resilient children, so much the better.

Crime accompanies social disadvantage, both among perpetrators and victims. In addition, since most crime, as argued above, does not actually pay, crime is more likely to be committed by people with defective decision-making styles or inadequate self-command. That suggests that reducing disadvantage and improving the capacity of individuals to make and carry out sensible decisions in their own interest ought to reduce crime. Since social disadvantage and bad decision-making are also correlated, to the extent that anything helps with one of those problems it is likely to help with the other. Thus if we can make some people less poor, less discriminated against, better educated, and less prone to self-defeating behavior, we should expect to reduce crime in the process. And, since crime is a cause as well as a consequence of disadvantage, reducing crime will tend at the same time to help cure the conditions that foster crime.

THE TWO "ROOT CAUSES" CLAIMS

It is not difficult, looking at crime-ridden neighborhoods, to observe many other problems, from litter to noise to housing abandonment to poor air quality, any one of which might be improved by spending money. Why not, then, start our crime-control effort there, and why not spend some of the money we now spend on police and prisons on the programs that might help make police and prisons less necessary? This is what might be called the "weak form" of the claim that we should give priority to social programs over criminal-justice operations. There is, moreover, an argument from justice: insofar as different social conditions would have led to lower levels of criminal behavior, criminals alone do not bear the moral onus of crime.

The weak-form "root causes" argument has, perhaps, had less persuasive power than its merits would entitle it to because of its confusion with the much less plausible strong form of that claim. It is sometimes said that bad social conditions make crime inevitable and render punitive crime-control efforts futile and perverse. Crime, it is said, cannot be addressed without addressing its "root causes." That stronger claim has surface plausibility and some remaining political resonance, but lacks for anything resembling evidence. The crime collapse of the 1994–2004 period—not notably a period of improved conditions (other than reduced crime) for the disadvantaged or of heavy spending on public programs in aid of the poor—seems to contradict the strong-form "root-causes" argument.* Philip J. Cook writes: "The 1990s experience—the large across-the-board reduction in crime without much progress in the socio-economic fundamentals—is hopeful, in a way. It creates the possibility that crime rates can change dramatically, independently of changes in the fundamental socioeconomic conditions. Thus crime is not only volatile but also potentially malleable, with policies more feasible and immediate than those required to 'reshape society.'"

---

*The tight low-wage labor market during the 1996–2000 boom should have been expected to reduce crime, but the crime decline started before the boom and continued into the following bust; the 2002–2008 recovery failed to improve wages or employment opportunities at the bottom of the income scale.

COST-EFFECTIVENESS AND TARGETING

One simple answer to the reasonable question, "Why not spend money on programs rather than prisons?" is relative cost. By comparison with education or health care, criminal-justice operations are fairly cheap in dollar terms. If we abolished prisons and jails entirely, or cut the police budget in half, and spent all of the money saved on public elementary and secondary education, the savings could finance about a 10 percent budget boost for the schools. Whether a budget increase of that amount, as spent by actually existing school systems, would make any measurable impact on educational outcomes remains a topic of hot scholarly debate; the truth might vary from jurisdiction to jurisdiction. But no one would assert that the resulting improvement would be sufficient to substantially reduce crime. If we think instead about more plausible cuts in criminal-justice budgets, the increase in education budgets those cuts could pay for is somewhere down in the rounding error.

Arithmetically, the well-worn argument that drug enforcement should shrink and the savings transferred to drug treatment is more plausible. Drug enforcement and the resulting incarceration have total budget costs several times total public spending on drug treatment.[1] Even so, it is not obvious that an increase in drug treatment should be financed specifically from a cut in drug law enforcement. Another candidate to finance the increase in drug treatment programs ought to be the rest of the health-care system.

Even the public share of health-care spending—about half of the total—is five times the entire criminal-justice budget. Indeed, drug enforcement is a large enterprise and drug treatment a small one. But that is not because the criminal-justice sector is well financed compared to the health-care sector. Rather, the criminal-justice system spends a large proportion of its small budget on arresting and imprisoning drug dealers, while the health-care sector spends only a negligible fraction of its much larger budget on treating people with drug abuse disorders. Indeed, the share of drug treatment in health-care spending is almost certainly smaller than would be dictated by health considerations alone. Given that the drug-treatment effort ought to grow, why should that growth come at the expense of law enforcement rather than being reallocated from other parts of the health-care system?

The unit costs in the criminal-justice system are high. A year of a police officer's services costs about twice what a schoolteacher-year costs. The cost of maintaining a prisoner is about three times the cost of teaching a high-school student. But there are four times as many schoolteachers as there are cops, and eight times as many high-school students as there are jail or prison inmates.

The criminal-justice system is much more tightly focused than are other social services. Every child needs an education. All of us need health care. But few become persistent offenders. Thus criminal-justice actions, expensive as they are, benefit from greater "target efficiency": compared to generalized social programs, even those aimed at high-crime demographic groups, they deliver more of their effects where the problem is, rather than where it is not.*

If we knew in advance which children will grow into high-rate, serious offenders, it would be worth spending very large amounts of money (compared, for example, to current per-pupil spending in public elementary and high schools) to divert them from the criminal careers they would otherwise follow.[2] But that would require both good predictive models— not just good enough to be interesting social science, but good enough to allow accurate individual-level targeting—and effective interventions, and we would still have to ask whether the disadvantages of labeling some children as potential offenders might not outweigh the benefits.

It is not enough to know that some intervention works as a pilot project, faithfully implemented by, or under the watchful eyes of, its inventor, and benefiting from the placebo-like Hawthorne effect that sometimes makes observation alone an apparently effective intervention. For example, both bilingual education and the post-Sputnik revolution in teaching arithmetic known as "the New Math" worked well at pilot scale but poorly at mass scale, at least in part for lack of adequately skilled teachers. We need programs that work when implemented by the staff

---

*Once someone has begun to interact with the criminal-justice system, the targeting problem gets easier, even as the prospects for diverting that person from crime get dimmer. That is the logic of rehabilitation efforts within the corrections system. How to square the circle by making punishment both aversive (for deterrent purposes) and beneficial to the punished (for rehabilitative purposes)—a problem noticed no later than the time of Plato (*Republic* I 335 b–d)—remains largely unsolved in practice, though in principle any painful form of self-improvement could combine aversiveness with benefit.

actually available, and at a scale large enough to make a measurable impact on the problem.

The same is true, of course, for criminal-justice programs. Crime is a mass-market phenomenon that cannot usefully be addressed with boutique programs. We now have "proof of concept" for several innovations, but that does not prove that it is possible to fit those innovations into the routine processes of police, prosecutors, courts, and community and institutional corrections agencies nationwide.

Managing Social Programs for Crime-Control Benefits

The politics of crime control are complicated. Arguing that we ought to have social programs instead of criminal-justice spending is a commonplace among liberal thinkers. But when it gets down to brass tacks, social programs are not usually designed, sold, or evaluated according to their crime-control benefits. (The Job Corps is a big exception, with most of the measured benefits coming in the form of reduced lawbreaking while participants are in the Job Corps camps, far from opportunities for income-producing crime.[3]) Crime also figures in evaluations of some drug treatment programs[4] and some pre-school programs. Generally, these studies do not include all the costs of crime; some use only public-sector costs of, for example, arrest and incarceration, and most of the rest use only direct victimization costs rather than making full estimates of the willingness-to-pay for crime reduction.[5]

One reason: Social-service advocates do not want the beneficiaries of their programs to be thought of as criminals, or even potential criminals, both to avoid stigmatizing program participants and to avoid reminding voters that the recipients of those services include the criminals those same voters hate and fear; advocates for programs aimed at poor children seem especially reluctant to portray the people served by those programs as potential criminals. By the same token, evaluations of the effectiveness of social-service interventions as crime control routinely ignore their non-crime-control benefits.

And while paying more attention to crime-control benefits might expand the political constituency behind some social programs, reduced crime will rarely be the central benefit of a successful social program. If crime can be prevented by making those who might otherwise engage in it better off generally—for example, improving their success in school or in the job market—most of its beneficial impacts will be on the well-being of the individuals served, rather than on potential crime victims. The savings from keeping people out of prison and jail may be a substantial proportion of fiscal benefits flowing back to the government, and some programs with large crime-prevention effects may be cost-justified on that basis alone, but it is hard to incorporate future and uncertain cost offsets into annual budget processes.

Thus crime-control benefits of most social programs are side-benefits. Inventing new social programs specifically for crime control may sometimes be the right thing to do, but more commonly the best course of action will be to increase the size of some program as measured by the number of participants, make it more intensive by spending more money on each participant, or simply to make some shift in the program's operations, perhaps without spending any more money, in a way that reduces crime.

Some changes in non-criminal-justice program operations would substantially reduce crime at modest cost, but the officials who run those programs, not being charged with crime-control responsibilities or evaluated by their contribution to crime control, have little incentive to take advantage of those opportunities. The demand that social-service agencies measure the results of their efforts is surely a sound one in principle, but in practice the measurement systems often neglect important categories of social benefit, including reductions in crime. For instance, the "welfare reform" transition in income-support programs for low-income families with children included holding welfare caseworkers and their superiors accountable for the rate at which their clients (mostly women) found and held jobs: no doubt an important objective, and one worth measuring and managing. But children of poor single mothers are also a high-risk population for future criminal activity, and surely there are things their mothers—and their caseworkers—can do to influence that risk, with results that should be measurable by the time the children reach their mid-teens. Yet the scoring system for welfare offices does not usually include reducing the number of contacts between clients' children and the police.

Conversely, criminal-justice agencies routinely neglect opportunities to contribute to the control of social problems other than crime: most obviously, the chance to use the prisons, and especially the jails, as places to conduct health education, screening for disease (especially infectious disease and mental-health disorders), and treatment. The sickest part of the (non-elderly) population flows through the correctional institutions, and yet the standard of health care—again, especially in the jails— is appalling. No one expects the sheriff to solve the syphilis problem or control the spread of multiple-drug-resistant tuberculosis, and so jail inmates come in sick and go out sicker, spreading disease back to the general population.

EDUCATIONAL MANAGEMENT

One clear, and largely ignored, opportunity to reduce crime without punishing anyone is changing the hours of schooling for middle-school and high-school pupils. Juvenile crime peaks between the end of the school day and the time adults get home from work. If the school day started later, and ended when the workday ends, there would be much less opportunity for residential burglary by juveniles during the school year. That change would also improve educational and health outcomes, since making adolescents get up at 7 or 7:30 to get to school runs against their natural circadian rhythms, leading them to, for example, fall asleep in class.[6] Yet changing hours would inconvenience the adults in the system; teachers would wind up commuting at the evening rush hour, rather than before it, and parents would find it harder to get their kids off to school before themselves leaving for work. So the change is not made. Perhaps it should not be made; perhaps the burdens on schools and families outweigh the educational and crime-control benefits of shifting school hours. But that such a change has never been the subject of serious debate, while arcane questions of pedagogical technique have become political shibboleths, testifies to the low standing of crime control among the objectives of educational policy.

Keeping later hours is not the only potential contribution of K–12 education to crime control. Pupil-on-pupil violence and extortion—concealed under the rather benign-sounding label of "bullying"—is a substantial crime problem in its own right: or at least it would be so considered if adults rather than children were being beaten up and shaken down on a daily basis. It is also a potent generator of future crime, both by the bullies who get away with it and by the victims who learn that violence is not only rewarded but necessary for self-protection.

There is much social-psychological speculation about why children join gangs; a need for belonging on the part of children without strong parental ties is frequently mentioned. A simpler explanation could be offered. Perhaps adolescents join gangs in part for the same reason prison inmates do: for self-defense. Gangs offer a substitute for the security against victimization that the state is supposed to provide.

Part of the blame falls on the police, who do not treat assault and extortion among children as requiring investigation and arrest. Imagine the response if a fourth-grader called 911 and complained that a sixth-grader had stolen his lunch money; among adults, that would be called "robbery" and treated as a serious crime, but after all, "boys will be boys." The U.S. practice in this regard is not universal; police in France and Japan, for example, are said to treat juvenile-on-juvenile aggression as crime, calling for arrest. But part of the blame falls on school authorities; much of the aggression takes place either at school or in travel to and from school.

Some "bullying prevention" programs, combining attempts to change norms by persuasion with the use of the school discipline system to repress aggression, are demonstrably successful.[7] But since cracking down on bullying is only peripherally related to the reading-score improvements on which principals' jobs now depend, the research results mostly remain on the shelf.

Well-designed and well-executed programs to persuade schoolchildren to avoid drug abuse and conduct their sexual lives more responsibly—admittedly, a minority of all such programs—have measurable, albeit modest, beneficial effects.[8] There exist similar programs aimed at reducing some forms of criminal activity, notably gang membership; how effective they are remains an open question. It is possible, though not demonstrated, that more generalized efforts to improve pupils' impulse control and increase their capacity to make sensible decisions might reduce the prevalence of criminal activity, perhaps even among those who otherwise would become persistent high-rate serious offenders.

Yet current efforts to impose "accountability" for educational outcomes on the schools do not include juvenile arrests in their outcome measures. On the one hand, that seems natural and appropriate; educational efforts are measured by cognitive outcomes. But on the other hand, it reinforces the idea that crime control is primarily the business of the agencies of criminal justice, and that if other social-service agencies deliver crime-control benefits, that is merely a pleasant side effect, not something they should aim at directly. Since most schools do not currently aim to reduce crime among their pupils, and since their efficacy at doing so is not currently measured, we have no idea how successful they might be if they were encouraged to try.

One tantalizingly encouraging result comes from the "good behavior game."[9] The "game," which makes classroom deportment into a competitive team sport, is taught in a teacher-training program aimed at first-grade teachers, with the goal of improving their capacity to maintain order in their own classrooms. In pilot-scale implementations supervised by the developers of the game, students whose teachers were randomly assigned to receive the training had markedly fewer encounters with the law than otherwise similar students whose teachers were not so trained. Despite the sterling reputation of the inventors of the program, and the utterly trivial cost of the intervention, this result lay largely dormant for two decades after it was first published. It is only now being subjected to large-scale trials.

If there were in fact a national crime-control budget, as opposed to many agency budgets at all levels of government made largely independently of one another, and if that national budget were allocated rationally, a large-scale experiment on the classroom-management game would be high on the priority list. The most likely result would be failure; few programs successful at the pilot level turn out to scale up effectively. But if the program turned out to work even if not administered by its inventors, national-scale implementation would have very large benefits for very modest costs. Presumably the benefits would not be limited to crime control, since better-managed classrooms are no doubt more conducive to learning, but the crime-control benefits alone might easily justify the costs of the program.

One reason such programs do not get much attention in the debate over crime control is that their effects are slow to arrive. The peak age for committing serious crimes is twenty-three. A program aimed at eight-year-olds will yield no crime-control benefits at all for several years, and most of the prevented crime will (not) occur fifteen years later. Thus early childhood programs are no part of the answer to the question, "How can we reduce crime next year?" The sheer impatience of citizens and politicians demanding that Something Be Done About Crime right this minute has in it an ironic echo of the inability of many criminals to take the future fully into account in deciding whether to commit a crime today. The lag between efforts and results also complicates accountability; it will be hard to focus the attention of an elementary-school principal, worried about being fired if reading scores do not go up next year, on the crime reductions a decade hence that might be produced by improving her teachers' classroom-management skills.

Perinatal and Early Childhood Intervention

Since much of a child's behavioral repertoire and social coping capacity develops before kindergarten age,[10] substantial crime-control effects might be available from programs aimed at children under the age of five, especially children whose neighborhood and family situation makes them higher-than-average risks for becoming criminally active. The famous Perry Preschool Project appears to have largely failed in its attempt to raise the measured IQs of participants, but the effects on criminal behavior seem to* have been profound.[11]

Even at very high per-participant costs—about $20,000 per pupil in today's money—Perry-like programs in high-crime neighborhoods look like very good investments: if the claimed results were close to accurate, and if the program could be made to perform nearly as well at full scale as it seems to have done as a pilot project. Alas, although the Perry Preschool Project is often cited in support of the Head Start program, it was in fact much more resource-intensive, and there is only scant evidence that Head Start as currently delivered reduces crime.[12] Then again, since crime control is not among Head Start's announced objectives, any crime-control benefits might well have been overlooked in the evaluation literature.

---

*"Seem to" because the original evaluation had significant methodological flaws, and— surprisingly—the program has not been formally replicated.

The earliest possible intervention with at-risk children starts before they are born. In a well-evaluated experiment in upstate New York, nurse home visitation for expectant mothers whose demographic profiles put their children at high risk of poor outcomes reduced the arrests among the children of those mothers by 69 percent compared to the matched control group.[13] If that result is even close to correct, nurse home visitation focused on high-risk mothers is surely cost-effective as crime control—compared, for example, with prison-building—even ignoring all its other benefits and cost savings. Again, whether a national program could match the effects of the pilot program remains to be demonstrated, but given the size of the potential benefits the failure to date to conduct a large-scale trial is, or at least ought to be, striking.

The benefits of nurse home visitation are especially marked among low-income families; they are not obviously worth the cost as applied to higher-income families. That has made even liberal elected officials wary about pressing for universal nurse home visitation. One obvious targeting approach, less crude than reliance on demographics alone, would be to make a nurse home visit part of routine prenatal care, at least for a firstborn, and to have the nurse use the first visit to decide how much additional help that family might need.

Of course, children have fathers as well as mothers, and the correlation between absent fathers and criminal activity by the children, especially but not only the boys, is remarkably strong.[14] (Alas, having a male other than the biological father living in the home seems to confer little if any benefit.) It is hard to imagine what sort of public program might change the rate at which fathers abandon their children. For those fathers who do stay, it is possible that successfully encouraging better fathering might be as effective a crime-control measure, or even more so, as encouraging better mothering through nurse home visits. It might be possible to encourage better fathering by changing norms, providing incentives, or inculcating skills. But if there has been any concerted effort to do so, the evaluation literature remains unaware of it. That does not, of course, prove that promoting better fathering is impossible; it might instead argue for intensive research and development devoted to figuring out how to do it.

The attention of public agencies tends to focus on the collection of child-support payments from absent fathers, even from those with little or no income that could be used to make the payments* as opposed to the true "deadbeat dads" who could pay but will not. Collecting child support from an absent father can benefit the child, the mother, and the taxpayer (by replacing public income-support payments). But there is little reason to think that money alone, even supposing that it is collected and is spent on the child, reduces criminality. (Child-support enforcement might reduce crime by discouraging fatherhood among those men disinclined to support and care for their children, thus preventing the birth of some children who would, if born, be fatherless, but that seems a rather indirect approach.)

HEALTH CARE

The health-care system, which spends several times as much money each year as the criminal-justice system, has many opportunities to contribute to crime control. Few of those opportunities are currently exploited, because crime control is not part of the professional ethic of health-care providers, and that fact is reflected both in their training and in the ways that health care is evaluated and paid for.

Pediatricians are often listened to more respectfully both by their young patients and by the patients' parents than are many other authority figures; as physicians, they have both greater professional prestige and a less adversarial relationship with young men who carry guns than do police. Starting on a life of crime has demonstrably bad long-term health consequences. But a pediatric history and physical is even less likely to inquire about whether the patient is engaging in theft or assault, or about gang activity, than it is to inquire about the patient's use of alcohol and other mind-altering chemicals. The inquiry might be uncomfortable for both sides, and is not now considered part of the physician's job. It is hard to know how much impact pediatricians could make on juvenile crime (and thus on adult crime later on) if they tried, because they mostly never try. The HEADSSS assessment (Home, Education, Activities, Drugs, Safety, Sexuality, Suicide), which is accepted, but not

---

*Such men are sometimes called "turnips," as in, "You can't squeeze blood out of a turnip."

universal, practice, might include questions about crime and gangs under the "Activities" or "Safety" headings.[15]

Hospital trauma centers treat the victims of gunshot wounds. Many, though of course not all, such victims—especially in gang-ridden cities—are themselves perpetrators of violence; it has been said, with only slight exaggeration, that the difference between the victim and the perpetrator of a gang homicide is who fired first. When the victim's friends gather at his bedside, often the talk is of retaliation; gunshot victims have been known to check themselves out against medical advice in order to take revenge. Yet there is no consensus among trauma-center medical and nursing staff about whether preventing retaliatory violence is part of their professional mission, or whether instead the medical task is done when the patient is able to walk out of the hospital.

Of course, physicians should not confuse their role with that of preachers, or sit in moral judgment on their patients' behavior. Their job is protecting life and restoring health, not ethical uplift. Still, physicians treating infectious disease have no difficulty with the idea that preventing the current patient from spreading the illness is part of their professional responsibility. Why should reducing the "contagiousness" of gunshot wounds not have equal standing as a medical task?

Part of the answer is that how to prevent someone with chickenpox or syphilis from transmitting that disease to someone else is part of the physician's professional expertise; it does not take four years of medical school to know that shooting people is generally bad practice. Another part is that while protecting the health of her current patient is obviously the job of the physician, protecting the health of those not currently patients is less obviously so: it would be grossly improper for a physician treating a tobacco-company executive to try to protect the public health by urging his patient to change corporate practices.

But even ignoring the risk that retaliatory gunfire poses to the community, it poses a deadly risk to the person who engages in it: the death rates for active gang members in some cities, for example, resemble those of combat troops during the Vietnam War.[16] So if a trauma-center physician were in fact capable of persuading some proportion of his gunshot-wound patients not to retaliate, she would make a substantial contribution to their life expectancies by doing so. And yet preventing retaliatory violence is nowhere near the top of the agenda of the typical urban trauma center.

MENTAL HEALTH CARE

The mental-health sector is an exception to this rule. For complicated reasons, mental health is starved for funds compared to other parts of the system,[17] but especially at the community-clinic level mental health-care providers are aware that their clients' behavioral problems can get them in trouble with the law, and often try to do something about it. (Providers of mental health care reasonably feel a greater license to try to influence their patients' behavior than do most providers of care for somatic disease.) The character disorders aside—by definition, much criminal behavior reflects an antisocial personality—the "Axis I" mental-health diagnoses, especially schizophrenia, depression, and bipolar disorder, are strongly correlated with offending. They play an especially large role in creating the repeated incidents of disorderly and aggressive conduct which constitute one important facet of the "crime problem" as perceived by ordinary citizens and which chew up a substantial proportion of police and jail resources.

It is a commonplace that the jails have largely replaced the state mental hospitals as housing for the chronically mentally ill[18]; the Los Angeles County Jail has been described as the largest mental-health facility in the nation. And it is another commonplace that the failure of the states to spend the money they saved by closing down the mental hospitals to build and operate community mental-health clinics have contributed both to crime and to homelessness.* But since most mentally ill people are not active offenders, simply expanding the community mental health system has low target efficiency as a crime-control program.

However, it is not hard to identify the minority of the chronically mentally ill who do have repeated contacts with the criminal-justice system. And it turns out that the frequency of those interactions, and the costs borne by police and jails, can be greatly reduced by reaching out to that population with mental-health services, and following up by sending providers to them (for example, to make sure that they are taking their medications) rather than simply hoping that they will present themselves for treatment and then comply with it.[19]

---

*However, the claim that the rise in incarceration reflects primarily a transfer from locked wards to cellblocks (Harcourt 2006) does not fit the data very well (Raphael and Stoll 2007, 45–54).

Since these clients are extremely expensive to public budgets while untreated, the cost of treating them is easily offset by the resulting savings. The protocols for what is now called Assertive Community Therapy (formerly "Aggressive Community Therapy," maintaining its acronym ACT while adopting a less threatening-sounding label) are well worked out, and its results robustly demonstrated.[20]

ACT is hard to manage because it requires coordination between police and probation agencies on the one side and mental-health providers on the other, across very substantial cultural and organizational barriers. Criminal-justice agencies do not have budgets to fund the mental-health side of such programs, though they could on balance save money by doing so, and community providers of mental health care, who have more walk-in patients than they can well serve, frequently decide that ACT is not the best use of their scarce funds. But the fact that ACT programs exist at all suggests that it is not impossible to apply health-care resources to the crime-control problem.

PUBLIC HEALTH

While disease prevention, especially at the social level, has a distinctly secondary role in the professional lives of most physicians, it is the central task and competence of the public-health community. Public-health physicians have in fact analyzed gunshot wounds in terms of infectious disease, even going so far as to consider guns as "vectors." This has led to some remarkably unpersuasive contributions to the literature on gun control,[21] but only rarely to measurable reductions in the frequency or lethality of violence. An important exception is "CeaseFire,"* which uses what have become the standard techniques of public-health "social marketing" campaigns to address lethal violence. "CeaseFire" tries to change attitudes toward violence in the Chicago neighborhoods where violence is most prevalent, pairing this with services targeted to gang members willing to leave "the life." An evaluation shows homicide reductions greater than 50 percent in target neighborhoods, with matched "control"

---

*Not to be confused with the largely enforcement-oriented "CeaseFire" gang-violence intervention applied in Boston (Kennedy, Braga, Piehl, and Waring 2001).

neighborhoods showing much smaller changes over the same time periods.[22] So far, however, the program is more discussed than imitated, and has drawn most of its support from foundation grants rather than public-sector budgets, even though the cost of drastically reducing violence in an entire neighborhood using these techniques is less than the cost of keeping a single murderer in prison for thirty years.

But if one asks precisely which public agencies ought to be financing such work, there is no obvious answer. Police departments enforce laws. Public health agencies prevent disease. Changing attitudes toward violence does not fall clearly within the purview of either set of agencies. And so programs that prevent crime and save lives fall between stools. It will probably be necessary for chief elected officials—mayors, county executives, and governors—their budget bureaus, and state and local legislative bodies to close the public management gap.

That same observation applies to most of the other nonpunitive means of crime control. Preventing burglary is not the school board's job; preventing homicide is not the job of the hospital that houses the trauma center; encouraging law-abiding behavior by the children of families receiving public assistance is not the job of the welfare bureau. Where the means are within the control of one set of agencies but the end—reducing crime—is the charge of another set of agencies, it is only at the top of the governmental pyramid that the requisite decisions can be made and carried out.

LEAD AND OTHER ENVIRONMENTAL INSULTS

Even environmental protection can turn out to have important crime-control implications. If there is lead in the atmosphere—for example, from burning leaded gasoline in automobiles—there will be lead in the soil. Children play outdoors, get their hands dirty, and put their hands in their mouths. Amazingly small quantities of lead can make permanent changes in developing brains.* Today's American children gained about

---

*A young child's body might contain three liters of blood; concentrations of lead in blood as low as 10 micrograms per deciliter—less than a third of a milligram total—create measurable and lasting cognitive damage.

half a standard deviation in IQ compared to children of the Baby Boom generation as a result of decisions taken in the 1980s to remove lead from gasoline.[23]

Not only does lowering IQ have a strong statistical effect on crime—directly through poor decision-making and indirectly through increased risk of failure at school and in the labor market—but lead has substantial additional behavioral impacts, increasing impulsivity and reducing self-command.[24] Given the decrease in lead exposure among children since the 1980s and the estimated effects of lead on crime, reduced lead exposure could easily explain a very large proportion—certainly more than half—of the crime decrease of the 1994–2004 period. A careful statistical study relating local changes in lead exposure to local crime rates estimates the fraction of the crime decline due to lead reduction as greater than 90 percent.[25] That represents benefits worth hundreds of billions of dollars per year, several percent of Gross Domestic Product, a figure more than an order of magnitude greater than the total cost of switching from leaded to unleaded gasoline.[26] The behavioral impacts of lead exposure were known when that decision was made. And yet the very careful benefit-cost analysis that led to the decision to phase out lead gasoline[27] never mentions reduced crime among the estimated benefits; after all, the Environmental Protection Agency does not have crime control as part of its legislated mission.

The great remaining source of lead exposure among children is the lead paint that remains in many houses and apartment buildings built before 1960.[28] De-leading dwellings has long been on the environmental agenda, but the costs are substantial—the total national bill to eliminate the remaining lead has been estimated at some $30 billion—and are largely borne not by taxpayers but by the owners of the affected housing units, who are naturally reluctant to spend thousands or even tens of thousands of dollars per unit to eliminate a problem they cannot even see.[29] The benefits of eliminating that risk—to the children, to their families, and to public budgets for programs such as special education—greatly exceed the costs on any reasonable calculation, but the decision to act has yet to be made.

Here again, the crime-control benefits are barely mentioned. But eliminating lead exposure from lead paint would, it has been estimated, lead to roughly a 5 percent reduction in crime.[30] If that estimate is close to right, the *annual* crime-control benefits would be greater than the total one-time cost of lead elimination: that is, the rate of return on that investment would be greater than 100 percent per year. Even ignoring all the other benefits of protecting children from lead, very few criminal-justice programs can claim to be even nearly so cost-effective in reducing crime. But an office-seeker who promised to fight crime by scraping the lead paint from old houses would find it hard to get a respectful hearing for the idea; it simply does not sound like a serious crime-control measure when compared to much more expensive and less effective measures such as building yet more prisons.

Do the high levels of noise in poor urban neighborhoods contribute to crime? It would be surprising if they did not, given how much mental-health damage chronic noise exposure is known to cause.[31] But while there are many studies on crime, and a substantial number of studies on the effects of environmental noise, there seems to have been no study of the link (if any) between the two.

OTHER PROGRAMS

Examples of non-criminal-justice programs claimed to reduce crime could be multiplied: some with sound research support, others more speculative. Providing summer jobs for poor adolescents might reasonably be expected to reduce their criminal activity, since the jobs compete with crime for time and energy and increase the opportunity cost of time spent locked up. Indeed, crime control is an often-cited benefit of such programs. But there is no convincing evidence-backed estimate of the extent of those benefits or about how jobs programs could be designed and targeted for maximum effect. The same is true of recreation programs. Conservatives had a fine time poking fun at liberal proposals to include funds for "midnight basketball" programs in the 1994 crime bill; indeed, the model program that won a White House award as one of the first President Bush's "thousand points of light" turned out to have no data to back its claim to having reduced crime.[32] Yet the absence of evidence is not evidence of absence; the simple fact is that no one knows whether such programs have crime-control benefits, and if so how those benefits stack up against their costs. It would be cheap to find out with some controlled experiments.

The literature on managing low-income housing pays considerable attention to the important problem of providing security against crime for the tenants, but little or no attention to the broader problem of encouraging tenants to raise law-abiding children. Surely housing managers have some capacity to influence these outcomes, but no one has asked them to try.

While there is no good reason to think that shifting public budgets overall away from law enforcement and toward social-service programs would make us safer, there are opportunities to reduce crime at modest cost scattered across the social landscape. Finding and exploiting those opportunities is central, not peripheral, to the task of crime control. The problem is first to identify programs that work and give them greater priority than they now have on the agendas of public and private agencies that do not have crime control as a primary mission, and then to monitor those effects to see that they are being carried out competently. Alas, managing offenders is easier than managing officials.

Guns and Gun Control

Firearms are used by some people to damage themselves and to threaten or damage others. Otherwise, there would be no such topic as firearms policy. Firearms are also used for recreation and, more urgently, for self-defense. Otherwise, firearms policy would be easy.

VARIETIES OF GUN CONTROL

Speaking crudely, there are three approaches to reducing crimes committed with guns; these might be called broad acquisition policies, tailored acquisition policies, and use policies. Broad acquisition policies aim to reduce the prevalence of gun possession. Tailored acquisition policies aim at reducing access to firearms, and especially handguns, specifically by those whose personal characteristics and histories suggest a higher-than-average risk of misuse, or reducing access (broadly) to narrowly tailored classes of weapons. Use policies try to discourage carrying guns and using them to threaten, wound, or kill among those who have managed to acquire them, licitly or otherwise.

Reducing the number of guns and gun holders—the broad acquisition approach—seems the obvious strategy: if the problem is guns, the solution must be fewer guns. Criminologist Franklin Zimring* at the University of California, Berkeley, has argued strongly that the link between the prevalence of guns and the prevalence of gun crimes will not be easily broken.[1]

But that obvious strategy has two equally obvious problems attached: there are many, many guns out there, and some of their owners are pow-

---

*Franklin Zimring, professor of law at Boalt Hall, has produced an amazingly long shelf of books (most often with his collaborator Gordon Hawkins) covering virtually the whole range of topics in crime-control policy.

erfully attached to those guns and politically organized to defend their right "to keep and bear arms."

To this political problem there corresponds the policy-analytic argument that guns do good as well as evil, especially if one is prepared—in keeping with the usual practice in measuring economic welfare—to count as a benefit a gun owner's willingness-to-pay for whatever psychological benefits gun possession may confer as well as its practical benefits in self-defense or crime deterrence.

Thus tailored acquisition strategies and use strategies have operational as well as political advantages over broad acquisition and use strategies. To the extent that the benefits sought from broad acquisition strategies could be obtained instead with a set of gun-control measures that allowed the apparently non-dangerous majority to buy, keep, and even carry firearms with only minimal regulatory inconvenience, the political obstacles to reducing firearms violence, and the social costs of doing so, would be markedly reduced.

It is widely agreed that criminals, children, and the dangerously insane should not be allowed to have guns; the controversy surrounds just how to define those categories and just what rules are required to effectively reduce the access of gun-ineligible persons to firearms. Bans on the private ownership of machine guns, sawed-off shotguns, hand grenades, and weapons of mass destruction are relatively uncontroversial examples of tailoring by weapon class; controversial examples include high-caliber weapons, armor-piercing bullets, and weapons that can pass unnoticed through metal detectors. (Bans on cheap handguns, variously called "junk guns" or "Saturday-night specials," are probably better thought of as attempts to reduce the number of those with access to weapons by raising the minimum price of being armed. Attempts to disguise them as safety measures are unconvincing.)

The most controversial recent example of tailoring by weapons class was the congressional ban on "assault weapons," passed in 1994 and allowed to expire in 2004. That provision did not, as written, make much technical sense, being limited to a list of named weapons, but experts say that there would be no technical difficulty in defining a class of high-lethality, high-fire-rate, high-magazine-capacity, and relatively concealable long guns that are not actually used either in hunting or in target shooting.

While neither the passage nor the expiration of the ban was associated with any measurable change in crime, that fact does not quite prove that the ban was irrelevant. It is true that very few homicides are currently committed with "assault weapons" (however defined), but it is also true that criminals equipped with such weapons are in some ways more dangerous than criminals not so equipped. While having only a finite list of weapons, rather than a set of criteria, reduces the value of an "assault weapons" ban, it is not clear that it reduces that value to zero. Insofar as the measure is valuable, its value is largely prophylactic, which makes any sort of quantitative assessment extremely hard: what did *not* happen is hard to measure. Now that the ban has been repealed, we may find out that repeal was a mistake; Miami police report an upsurge of assault-weapons crimes, including the deaths of two officers in 2007.[2]

Politically, the significance of the "assault weapons" ban was massively misrepresented by proponents, who succeeded in duping more than a few reporters. Fully automatic weapons of the kind used in the military, which fire a burst of rounds as long as the trigger is held down, are already virtually illegal: they are classified as "machine guns," and a machine-gun license is extremely hard to get. The dispute was over certain kinds of "semi-automatic" weapons, which automatically reload when fired but require a separate trigger-pull for each round. It is not surprising that gun-rights advocates were outraged by the misrepresentation, or that some gun owners were angry and contemptuous at the prospect of being ordered around by people they regarded as technical illiterates.

Allowing the mothers of juvenile gun-possessors living at home to invite the police to search the children's rooms, with the promise that any gun found will be confiscated but that the child will not be arrested[3] takes some guns out of dangerous hands without at all inconveniencing those legally entitled to be armed. The same is true of programs that offer cash rewards for anonymous tips leading to the confiscation of illegally possessed weapons[4]; in addition to confiscating some guns, they discourage brandishing by creating a risk the brandisher would otherwise not face. Threatening to mount strong enforcement efforts against any gang one of whose members shoots someone, on the model of Boston's "Ceasefire" operation,[5] can be thought of as a group-level use-reduction policy. Other use-oriented policies include sentence enhancements for being armed in the commission of a crime (not very effective), and attempts to identify and arrest those who are carrying weapons that they have no legal right to possess.

Concealed-carry laws are another use-oriented policy. Most states, even where gun acquisition is largely unregulated except by federal law, require some sort of permit to carry a concealed weapon. In some of them, those permits are issued only at the discretion of local law-enforcement officials, and in some subdivisions those permits are, by law, policy, or practice, extremely hard to obtain. Other states have what are called "shall-issue" laws, allowing anyone who may lawfully possess a handgun the right to a permit to carry it concealed, sometimes subject to a requirement to take a gun-safety course.

Claims by pro-gun researchers that "shall-issue" laws reduced crime have not stood up well to reanalysis by less partisan scholars.[6] But those reanalyses have failed to provide any convincing evidence that "shall-issue" laws noticeably *increase* crime.[7] Moreover, gun crime by concealed-carry permit-holders seems to be vanishingly rare. That suggests that a loosening of concealed-carry laws—for example, allowing those with permits from one state to carry concealed weapons anywhere in the country—which would greatly please gun-rights advocates, would do little, if any, harm. "More guns, less crime"[8] was never a very plausible claim; but if the weaker claim "more guns, no more crime" is true, then the case for the discretionary concealed-carry permit seems hard to make.

ARE GUNS A "PUBLIC HEALTH" ISSUE?

From a policy analyst's perspective, the basic question about guns is how firearms policies—including enforcement and other administrative practices as well as statutes—can influence the frequency of injuries and threats of various kinds, and with what benefits and side effects,[9] including, of course, the forgone benefits of whatever non-harmful gun uses the laws prevent, such as the "defensive gun uses" about whose frequency there has been vigorous—not to say acrimonious—debate.[10]

That question is not precisely the same as the public-health inquiry that looks only at morbidity and mortality and how to prevent them, ignoring non-health costs and eliding the distinctions among criminal violence, intentional self-injury, and accident. In most public-health analysis, each death incurred or prevented, or at least each quality-adjusted life year lost or saved, is treated as equally important, and, by omission, every value but longevity and health is treated as of no importance at all.

There is more at stake in firearms policy than reducing the body count. Intentional self-injury (suicide, suicide attempt, or suicide gesture), intentional injury to others (assault), and unintentional injury (what we used to call accident) are different kinds of events for purposes of policy-making, even if they look the same to the trauma surgeon. Victimization is an insult as well as an injury. Being robbed or threatened with a gun, or hearing gunshots outside one's window, are all damaging experiences even if there is no physical wound.

There are both moral and practical arguments for giving greater weight to crimes—committed with guns or prevented by armed self-defense—than to self-inflicted and unintentional injuries. Morally, the role of public authority in defending us from one another seems more obvious, and is certainly more widely agreed to, than its role in defending us from ourselves, and can often be done at less cost to personal liberty and autonomy.

Practically, crime causes fear, and induces costly avoidance efforts, in those who may never become its victims in any direct sense. No one ever moved out of a neighborhood because the suicide rate had gotten out of hand. That is not to say that preventing impulsive suicides and other forms of intentional or unintentional self-injury is not a legitimate public concern, only that preventing firearms assault deserves a higher priority than the death toll alone would justify. Since gun accidents and suicides are more broadly dispersed in the population than are gun crimes, a focus on crime prevention will tend to push gun policy away from broad acquisition policies and toward tailored acquisition and use policies.

GUNS AND CRIME

Compared to other advanced democracies, the United States does not have an especially high level of crime, or even of violent crime. It does have a startlingly high level—about five times the Western European/ Canadian/Australian average—of homicide. It also has an astoundingly high level of private gun—especially handgun—ownership, and the difference in gun homicide rates, linked to differences in the lethality of robbery, residential burglary, and aggravated assault, accounts for much of the difference in overall homicide rates.

A robbery or assault committed with a gun is much more likely to turn into a fatality than the same crime committed unarmed, or with a knife or club. Even within the United States, a robbery in Chicago, where the police put a very high priority on enforcing the gun laws and have managed to somewhat reduce the prevalence of gun-carrying in the criminally active population, is noticeably less likely to result in a death than a robbery committed in another big city.[11] That suggests that if the prevalence of gun-carrying among American offenders resembled the prevalence of gun-carrying among, say, English offenders, the American homicide rate would be closer to the English rate. And one reason so many American criminals are armed is that so many Americans are armed: the country has about one firearm per adult, not counting those carried by police officers or members of the armed services. This line of thinking has led many scholars and citizens to believe that reducing the sheer number of handguns in private hands would yield substantial crime-control benefits.

If every gun, regardless of its owner, had the same probability of being used in a homicide, then it would follow that reducing the number of guns by some fraction would produce an equivalent reduction in homicide. If, at the other extreme, all of the homicide risk were concentrated among a relatively small and identifiable group of dangerous gun-owners, then only policies designed to make it harder for that dangerous population to acquire guns or riskier for them to carry guns would matter.[12] (Consider the analogous problem of preventing motor vehicle fatalities: we could do that either by reducing total miles driven or by getting dangerous drivers off the road, and the right mix of those two policies depends on what fraction of fatalities are caused by identifiably dangerous drivers.)

Half a century ago, when the typical homicide was a husband shooting his wife or vice versa, there was a strong prima facie case for general gun-prevalence reduction: it seemed logical, given the risks of spousal homicide, that a household with a handgun in it would, just for that person, be a riskier place to live than a household without one. But as the share of domestic homicides declines, which it has been doing steadily since the 1960s, and the share of gang homicides increases, the fraction of gun-using killers with serious criminal records also increases. Consequently, the direct relevance of reducing handgun prevalence falls, except insofar

as reducing general prevalence has the side effect of reducing gun ownership and gun carrying among the identifiably dangerous part of the population: for example, by making it less likely that a burglar will be able to
steal a handgun.

This may be a case where the benefits of a small change are less than
proportional to the benefits of a large change. Getting the prevalence of
handgun ownership in the United States down to Western European or
Canadian levels would probably have a big impact on the homicide rate,
but no politically, operationally, or legally feasible strategy holds out any
serious promise of doing so. Local gun-ban ordinances, for example, have
negligible effects on rates of gun crime.[13] The same was true of the passage
of the Brady Law.[14]

We might, with mighty effort against strong political resistance, manage to reduce the prevalence of handgun possession by 10 percent. Current studies suggest that such a reduction would be expected to shrink
the number of homicides by no more than 3 percent, with no measurable effect on other crimes.[15] Under current U.S. conditions, the project
of substantially reducing violent crime by reducing the sheer number of
guns may be a case of "you can't get there from here."[16]

GUN POLICY FOR CRIME CONTROL

What remains are policies to make it harder for people who should not be
trusted with guns to acquire weapons, policies to make it riskier for those
same people to carry weapons even if they can get them, and perhaps limits on certain highly lethal or easily concealed weapons.

People with prior convictions for a felony or for domestic assault, or
people subject to domestic-violence restraining orders—those most likely
to use guns to commit crimes—are already forbidden to possess firearms.
The Gun Control Act of 1968, which defines classes of people ineligible
to possess firearms, as amended by the Brady Law requiring background
checks for gun purchasers, is a primary example of a law intended to implement a narrow acquisition strategy. So far, the Brady Law's impact on
crime has been unspectacular. It is possible that adding a few more categories—those convicted of more than one violent misdemeanor (such
as simple assault) and those with records of violent crime as juveniles—

might be useful, and perhaps not very controversial. The quantitative research to support such a step—showing what fraction of gun crimes are committed by people not now ineligible to possess firearms but who would be ineligible if the restriction were extended in various ways—has yet to be done.

One major limit on the efficacy of the Brady Law as an enforcement mechanism for the prohibitions in the Gun Control Act is the loophole that law leaves for private gun transactions: about a third of the total. A licensed dealer—"federal firearms licensee," or FFL—must verify that his customer is eligible to purchase a gun by checking the customer against a national database of ineligibles. That was the innovation of the Brady Law. But no such requirement attaches to someone who gives a gun as a present or sells a gun in a private transaction; about 40 percent of handguns are acquired in those ways. Private sales go on at gun shows, among other places, but there is no "gun show loophole" in the law, and promising to close that nonexistent loophole makes gun-control advocates seem ignorant to gun owners. People always resent being bossed around, but they resent it more when the orders are being issued by those who know less than they do about the subject.

Penalties for evasion of the rules by FFLs—especially selling to "straw purchasers," people themselves eligible to buy who intend to transfer the guns to others not eligible—and for deliberate sales to ineligible purchasers by non-FFLs, are so slight that many U.S. Attorney's offices regard the cases as not worth prosecuting. Moreover, legislative limits on the use of information technology by the Bureau of Alcohol, Tobacco, Firearms, and Explosives (BATFE, still often referred to as simply ATF) make gun-trafficking cases artificially difficult to investigate. Under the Clinton administration, "crime-gun tracing"—the process of following the paper trail on a weapon used in a crime back to its last lawfully recorded sale—was developed into a powerful tool both for analyzing weapons-acquisition patterns and for identifying "scofflaw" gun dealers.[17] It is plausible, though not yet shown to be true, that improving gun tracing, removing the limits on BATFE data-processing, toughening sentences for gun trafficking and giving those cases higher priority for prosecution, and requiring private gun sellers to have licensed dealers perform Brady background checks on purchasers could increase the difficulty of acquiring guns for criminal use enough to noticeably reduce violent crime.

The development of portable and aimable magnetometers could discourage gun carrying by those ineligible to possess guns.[18] In the absence of such a technical solution, anything that increases the rate at which high-risk individuals are "frisked" by the police—whether incident to a stop or incident to an arrest—also increases the risk of carrying, and there is some evidence that gun-oriented police patrol can substantially reduce violent crime.[19] For example, one unexpected side effect of the crackdown on turnstile-jumping in the New York City subways was the seizure of a large number of guns from turnstile-jumping arrestees, and a consequent shrinkage in the rate of gun-carrying among them.

All this suggests a rather modest "gun control" agenda:

- Raising penalties for "gun trafficking," not just to increase deterrence by threatening more severity but to encourage investigation and prosecution.
- Aggressive efforts to identify gun traffickers at the local level by encouraging those convicted of unlawful gun possession to "cooperate" against whoever sold them their weapons in return for a reduced sentence. (Given the risk of receiving false information about a crime that leaves no physical trace, such cases ought to be brought only when there are at least three gun possessors who independently identify the same source, or where someone identified as a source makes an illegal sale to an undercover officer.)
- Bounties for information leading to the seizure of an unlawfully possessed weapon.
- Enforcement efforts aimed at discouraging gun use by street gangs, such as Boston's Ceasefire program.
- Making it easier to take a gun used in a crime—or ideally even a bullet or shell casing found at a crime scene—and trace that weapon back to its last lawful seller and purchaser. This involves both freeing federal investigators from legislative limits on their use of information technology and developing better means of using a recovered bullet or shell casing to identify the gun that fired it.
- Requiring a background check for each private gun sale. (This could be provided, for a fee, by licensed gun dealers.)
- Enabling police to spot people carrying a gun in public, and permitting them to ask anyone carrying a weapon to identify himself.

That requires the development both of portable metal-detectors and of the capacity to check a name and date of birth in real time against a database of concealed-carry permits.

- A narrowly targeted ban on high-lethality rapid-fire weapons not suitable for hunting or target shooting.
- If it turned out to be useful, extending the current firearms-possession ban to repeat misdemeanor assailants and those with violent juvenile histories.
- Insofar as guns made and sold in the United States are currently being illegally exported to Mexico for the use of criminal gangs there, tightened laws and toughened law enforcement here might help save lives there.

That about covers the range of gun-control efforts that would be useful in reducing violent crime. That list does not include two proposals dear to the hearts of some gun-control groups:

- *Gun registration.* If we can trace a crime gun back to its last lawful owner, there is no need to keep an ownership list. If we can prevent ineligible persons from acquiring guns, there is no need for a permit process.
- *Tight controls on carrying concealed weapons.* In the absence of evidence that liberalized carrying laws create crime, there seems to be no strong argument for maintaining a discretionary permit process.

The list also omits some of the favored policies of the gun-rights groups, such as draconian sentences for gun possession by those with violent histories or those engaged in dealing drugs.

GUN POLICY AND THE CULTURE WARS

The "gun rights" versus "gun control" issue is intertwined with a broader set of issues—abortion, birth control, gay rights, drugs, pornography, the teaching of evolution, prayer in schools, race relations—known collectively as "the culture wars," pitting "Red" (conservative) against "Blue" (liberal) values, opinions, and ways of life. While much of the culture wars involve the struggle of the Red population to enlist the help of the state in suppressing what it takes to be culturally threatening practices such as the use of illicit drugs, pornography, and homosexual conduct, in the case of guns it is the Blue team that is trying to suppress something taken as central to the Red way of life. That gives the gun-control issue all of the nastiness inseparable from "identity politics."

Anyone who has spent time with "gun control" (i.e., broad acquisition policy) advocates can testify that many of them share a strong hostility to guns, gun ownership, and gun owners, a hostility that resembles the hostility of "drug warriors" toward illicit drugs and those who use them. These fervent gun controllers see the desire to own a gun as rooted in psychopathology, which is the way drug warriors see the desire to use illicit drugs: opponents of "gun control" are frequently referred to as "gun nuts." The "gun controllers" are simply impatient with the notion that any positive value should be assigned to anything having to do with guns. Some still hold, at least in private, what used to be the standard "liberal" position on the gun question (embraced, for example, by Governor Michael Dukakis in the 1988 presidential contest): that there is no reason for anyone to have a handgun other than in connection with police or military duty, and that private handgun ownership ought ideally to be abolished.

Many of my coastal urban and suburban friends are like me: they may not disapprove of target-shooting, but they really don't *get* hunting on an emotional level (I suspect that much hunting is actually a "guy" form of nature-meditation). They (we) think having guns for self-protection is sort of weird and primitive, and regard the "armed citizenry against tyranny" stuff as utterly crazy. Having guns around makes them (us) very uncomfortable.

There is nothing wrong with having a visceral aversion to guns. The problem is that many people who feel that way are willing to write their prejudices into law, using largely spurious claims about crime control as a justification.

It is hardly surprising that such a campaign should have excited fear and hatred in a portion of the Red population, especially given the strong Blue tint of much of the gun-control movement. Long guns for hunting and handguns for self-defense powerfully symbolize the virtue of self-reliance, and do so in a specifically masculine way. It is a fact of human life, as Orwell pointed out,[20] that we all depend on people with weapons to defend us from other people who might want to kill us or take our stuff. But dependency has always been problematic in American culture. A rifle means being able to feed yourself. A handgun means being able to defend yourself. It should not surprise us that perceived threats to such basic notions of personal autonomy are strongly resisted.

The belief that every measure of gun control is merely a step on the road to gun confiscation, carefully fostered by organizations such as the National Rifle Association (NRA), greatly complicates the task of making policies that will reduce the rate of gun assaults and homicides. And some of the more extreme rhetoric issuing from "gun rights" groups—about gun control as part of a plot to disarm the citizenry and pave the way for New World Order tyranny—fully justifies the "gun nut" label. When the late Charlton Heston said, in perfect seriousness, that the Second Amendment is more important than the First Amendment because "the right to keep and bear arms is the one right that allows 'rights' to exist at all"[21]—and was elected to high office in the National Rifle Association rather than being laughed at—he testified to the depth of rage and fear felt even within the mainstream gun-rights movement.

That sort of gun-nuttery is part of the identity politics of rural white males, especially in the South and the Mountain West. And gun-nuttery partly grows out of the opposite sort of identity politics embodied by anti-gun nuttery: before the assassination of John F. Kennedy sparked a political movement for gun control, the NRA was still largely a collection of hunters rather than an arm of the Republican National Committee. It is as hard to talk sense about the actual effects of gun availability on crime to someone from the Brady Campaign as it is to talk sense about the actual effects of drug policy to someone from the Parents' Resource Institute for Drug Education. All they know is that Guns Are Bad, and that it is essential to make everyone else understand that Guns Are Bad. It is not really surprising that people who have other reasons for being strongly attached to their guns react badly to such disrespect, combined with a desire to make their hobby illegal; compare NRA literature with literature from the Drug Policy Alliance.

As Lincoln summed up the even older debate over alcohol, the question is whether we are dealing with the use of a bad thing or the misuse of an otherwise good thing.[22] In that context, the recent Supreme Court decision[23] in *D.C. v. Heller*—holding that the Second Amendment right to "keep and bear arms" is a right of each individual that cannot be restricted to members of an organized militia—might make practically relevant gun-control policies easier to enact and enforce by taking the prospect of confiscation off the table. Without the confiscation issue, gun-rights advocates may have a harder time stirring fervent opposition to sensible measures designed to reduce the prevalence of crime committed with firearms.[24] The NRA slogan that we need, not more gun laws, but enforcement of the laws we have is substantially correct. However, we are not, in fact, enforcing the laws we now have—laws that forbid criminals to obtain or possess guns—and we are failing to do so for structural reasons, not as a result of the whims or inadequate commitment of officials.

A Political Bargain?

The combination of tightening the Gun Control Act eligibility criteria, closing the private-sale loophole, and more intensive crime-gun tracing and enforcement against scofflaw dealers could, in combination, provide all the crime-control benefits that would be provided by a much more politically controversial national gun registry. A package of legislation combining those tightening measures with a national "shall-issue" law and permission for someone licensed in one state to possess a weapon or to carry a concealed weapon to do so in any state might be able to command a legislative majority and to result in both more freedom and convenience for gun owners and less violent crime.

Drug Policy for Crime Control

Discussions about crime control inevitably turn to the subject of drugs. No one doubts that drugs and policies to control them are linked to nondrug crime: to all the varieties of theft, assault, and offenses against public order. But the precise nature of those links remains obscure, and what best to do about them remains controversial.

That is true partly because making seriously informed conjectures about the effects of alternative drug policies is exceptionally difficult,* but largely because the political forces around drug control put a premium on ideology and symbolic politics rather than on outcomes; facts and analyses are more likely to be crafted to fit policies than vice versa. Asked whether research could influence drug policy, John Carnevale, a former director of research for the Office of National Drug Control Policy (the "drug czar's" office) responded, "Yes. Especially bad research."

Both sides in the war about the war on drugs—the "drug warriors" and the "drug policy reformers" (called "anti-prohibitionists" by themselves and legalization advocates by their opponents)—tend to treat the question of which drugs should be prohibited for nonmedical use as the central question of drug policy. Not so. The details—enforcement practices, sentencing patterns, treatment policies, attempts to suppress substance abuse by those under criminal-justice supervision—matter as much or more than the broad question of legal availability versus prohibition in determining how much damage is done, and in particular how much nondrug crime is caused, by drug abuse, drug dealing, and drug enforcement.

---

*The best study of comparative drug control policies and their outcomes is Robert Mac-Coun and Peter Reuter's *Drug War Heresies* (2001); for an American-focused view, see David Boyum and Peter Reuter, *An Analytic Assessment of U.S. Drug Policy* (2005). An older and longer document is the present author's *Against Excess* (1992a).

THE DRUGS-CRIME CONNECTIONS

Active criminals are disproportionately substance abusers. Data from arrestee drug testing (before that program was foolishly discontinued) showed that in virtually every big city half or more of felony arrestees—even excluding those arrested on drug charges—had taken one or more illicit drugs in the days before their arrest.[1] A majority of state and federal prisoners report that they were under the influence of drugs or alcohol, or both, at the time of their current offense.[2]

Statistics about crime related to drug dealing are harder to come by, but scholarly studies echo newspaper headlines about "drive-by shootings" in attributing changes in homicide rates to the rise and fall of open markets for illicit drugs and the patterns of weapons acquisition, carrying, and use associated with them.[3]

These facts are often offered as proof of the need for vigorous enforcement of the drug laws. If drug trafficking is inherently violent, and if illicit drug use catalyzes criminal and other delinquent behavior—both in the short term, as intoxication makes potential offenders more present-oriented and reckless and therefore less deterrable, and in the longer term through the impacts of substance abuse on the character, social connections, and non-criminal opportunities of those who engage in it—then it would seem to follow that enforcement efforts to suppress drug-selling and drug-taking will tend to reduce crime.[4]

But that argument can be turned on its head. Arguably it is drug policy, and not drug abuse, that is principally responsible for the observed drugs-crime connection.[5] Drug laws and their enforcement make illicit drugs more expensive. Since many heavy users of those drugs commit crimes to finance their habits, those higher prices may increase, rather than decreasing, nondrug crime. As to violent crime among dealers, that is even more obviously attributable to the laws rather than the chemicals; when alcohol was an illicit drug, alcohol dealers settled their differences with firearms, just as cocaine dealers do today. But two contemporary liquor-store owners are no more likely to shoot one another than are two grocers. On this view, drug laws, being criminogenic, should be repealed, or at least drug law enforcement should be radically cut back and reformed, and the problems of drug abuse addressed in ways designed to minimize individual and social harm rather than the rate of drug consumption.

Neither argument is valid in its pure and undifferentiated form. By creating black markets, prohibition can cause crime, but so too can intoxication and addiction, even when the underlying drug is legal. Thus, the answer to the question, "Does crime result from drugs, or from the drug laws?" is "Both." The right question, from a crime-control perspective, is "What set of drug laws, enforcement practices, and other policies would cause the least crime?" And even if it were true for some drug that some form of legalization would reduce crime, it would not follow that minimizing enforcement against what remains an illicit market would be a good second-best, any more than the arguments for prohibition logically entail all-out enforcement of the drug laws.

The crime-minimizing set of drug policies might not be the best set of policies, all things considered. On the one hand, making abusable drugs more easily available will tend to lead to more abuse and addiction, with predictable costs not only to those who get into trouble with drugs but their families, friends, and neighbors. Against that public-health concern must be set the equally predictable losses to those people who would otherwise use banned or tightly restricted drugs for harmless pleasure or other benefit, and the basic liberal principle that argues for as much scope as possible for individual choice.[6]

For cannabis, the most widely used illicit drug and the one that generates more arrests than all the others combined, there is at least a reasonable case for ending the ban. That would wipe out an illicit market worth some $10 billion per year, eliminate about 1 million annual arrests, and free about 30,000 prison and jail cells now occupied by cannabis offenders—mostly dealers—to hold more dangerous criminals. It would also tend to make the millions of otherwise law-abiding pot-smokers less ambivalent in their attitudes toward the police, and toward the law.

But the examples of alcohol and tobacco, and of gambling, give warning of the likely consequences of creating an industry around yet another habit-forming activity. The minority of users who develop substance-abuse disorders—under illicit conditions, about one cannabis smoker in ten—will account for the bulk of cannabis sold; in the case of alcohol, those who average at least four drinks per day year-round account for half of total sales. Thus the primary business of a licit cannabis industry would be creating and maintaining addiction, and the firms in that newly legal industry would make every attempt to lower taxes, weaken regulations, and promote the (over)use of their product. One way to prevent that would be to allow individuals to cultivate and use cannabis themselves, to give it away, and to form small consumer-owned cooperatives that did not advertise, while maintaining the ban on commercial production and marketing.

It is far less straightforward—some would say impossible—to design a set of taxes and regulations that would eliminate the much larger and more violent market in cocaine, especially crack, without a large increase in the number of people suffering from cocaine addiction, even if such a step were politically thinkable.* Thus from the standpoint of practical crime control the debate about cocaine legalization—and cocaine accounts for about half of the total dollar volume in the illicit drug markets—is largely a distraction from the work at hand.

Even the narrower problem of designing drug policies to minimize nondrug crime is complicated enough, with causal chains that loop, evidence that remains stubbornly ambiguous, and policies whose effects, even as to their direction, may depend on difficult-to-predict details of implementation.

More obviously, the crime-control costs and benefits of various drug policies are likely to vary sharply from drug to drug, even among those currently illicit, in somewhat complicated patterns. Only by exploring the myriad ways in which drugs and drug policy might logically cause or prevent predatory criminal behavior, and reviewing what (often scant) evidence there is about the existence, signs, and sizes of those logically possible effects, is it possible to rough out an analysis of what drug policies would minimize nondrug crime.

That inquiry needs to start by distinguishing drug law violations from predatory crime. Since law-enforcement and criminal-justice agencies exist in large part to control predatory crime and disorder, it seems natural to think that all of their activities, including drug enforcement, contribute to crime and disorder reduction, and that therefore drug law enforcement

---

*The present author addressed the problem of designing a post-prohibition regime for cocaine some fifteen years ago (Kleiman 1992b), and concluded that the design criteria— eliminating the illicit market and the associated violence and incarceration without allowing an explosion of crack abuse—could not both be satisfied. That argument may have been wrong, but it has not been answered; an effort by a group of drug-policy reformers to design a post-prohibition regime ended without publishing such a design.

is crime-reducing. But that is not always the case. Even for drugs whose users steal to support their drug consumption or whose dealers engage in violence, enforcement will sometimes make those problems worse rather than better. Moreover, since drug law enforcement competes with other activities for the resources and attention of criminal-justice agencies, the crime-control gains from drug enforcement need to be weighed against the losses from reducing the level of police, prosecution, and corrections capacity available to attack predatory crime and disorder directly.

ALCOHOL POLICY

An observer from Mars would find the treatment of alcohol in the American drug-policy debate hard to understand. The heavy burden of alcohol-related crime is used by opponents of the current drug laws to argue that prohibiting other drugs while allowing alcohol to be marketed aggressively is irrational. They have some facts to back them up: according to surveys of jail and state prison inmates, more crimes, and especially violent crimes, are committed under the influence of alcohol than under the influence of all illicit drugs combined.

Logically, though, observing that the one legal addictive intoxicant does more damage than all the illegal addictive intoxicants makes it more difficult, not easier, to believe that legalization tends to minimize aggregate harm.

Drug-war "hawks" and drug-war "doves" tend to tacitly agree that no change should be made in current policies toward alcohol. Since those policies seem to be producing miserable results—there are four persons meeting clinical criteria for alcohol abuse or dependency for every one person meeting those criteria for any other drug[7]—this agreement seems, on reflection, very strange, especially since there are clear opportunities to change alcohol policies in ways that would unambiguously reduce crime and other alcohol-related harms.[8]

Alcohol consumption, and especially consumption by heavy drinkers, who spend a large proportion of their personal budgets on drinking, is responsive to price.[9] At present, the federal and state tax burden on the average drink is only about 10 cents, roughly one-tenth of the total price. The effect on alcohol-related crime (including domestic violence and child abuse) of raising that tax to a dollar a drink would likely be substantial, even allowing for the risk of developing illicit markets in untaxed alcohol: the safety and convenience of legal alcohol, and drinkers' loyalty to legal brands, would tend to keep such markets small. Even a doubling of the tax would probably reduce the homicide rate by several percent, while imposing no substantial tax burden on any but problem drinkers; someone who averages two drinks a day year-round would pay additional taxes of less than $4 per month.[10]

A more radical step would be to make alcohol less available to those likely to commit crimes under its influence, as evidenced by prior convictions. Like the current age limit, a ban on drinking by those previously convicted of alcohol-related offenses—in effect, a selective, rather than a blanket, prohibition—would have to be enforced primarily by regulations on sellers rather than by legal threats aimed at buyers.[11] The crime-control benefits might be substantial. That such a relatively modest step remains well outside the bounds of political discussion, let alone political feasibility, reflects the extent to which practical efficacy continues to bow to the symbolic politics of the culture wars in framing policy toward alcohol and other drugs.

DRUG LAW ENFORCEMENT

Drug dealing is a transactional crime, in which buyers and sellers seek one another out; this contrasts with predatory crimes, whose victims seek to avoid their victimizers. When the perpetrator of a predatory crime is imprisoned, both deterrence and incapacitation effects will tend to result in a lower incidence of that crime, if we hold constant the precautions taken by potential victims.[12] There is nothing about deterring or incapacitating one predatory victimizer that encourages another to take his place, unless the supply of victims is for some reason so limited that predators must compete with one another in seeking them. For example, it seems unlikely that the incarceration or retirement of one house burglar would lead to offsetting increases in burglary by others; burglars do not have to compete for a limited supply of targets.

But when law enforcement puts a purveyor of a forbidden commodity out of business, either directly by imprisoning him or indirectly through the threat of punishment, the result is to create a market niche for a new supplier or for the expansion of effort (e.g., hours of work) by an existing supplier.[13] So too with the seizure of drugs; as long as there are retail dealers ready to sell them and customers ready to buy them, the drugs themselves can be replaced, at a price. Thus while imprisoning a burglar directly prevents burglary, taking drugs and drug dealers off the streets does not directly prevent drug selling in anything like the same fashion. So filling a prison cell with a drug dealer (or, more rarely, a drug user) rather than a burglar or robber will tend to increase the rate of predatory crime—unless the dealer or user in question is also a high-rate predatory criminal—while not markedly decreasing the extent of drug dealing or drug abuse. That will not be true when the incarceration delivers on the threat that underlies a low-arrest drug market crackdown on the High Point model described in chapter 3, and it might not be true if the cutback in drug enforcement and incarceration were sufficiently radical, but it seems quite plausible that if the number of drug dealers in prison were halved the level of drug abuse would not change measurably.

The transactional nature of drug dealing also means that there is usually no complaining witness. That forces drug enforcement to rely on unusually intrusive investigative techniques: the use of undercover officers who pretend to be dealers or buyers, the employment of criminal informants who are themselves active participants in the trade, wiretapping, and dangerous and frightening "dynamic entry" raids on suspected dealers' living quarters, sometimes with fatal results to innocent victims of police error, in what has been called "an epidemic of isolated incidents."*

Drug enforcement can influence both the money prices of drugs and the nonmonetary costs and risks of drug acquisition. Those costs and risks include the time, effort, and know-how it takes to find a seller and the dangers incident to drug purchase: robbery, being sold poor-quality or adulterated drugs, and arrest for possession. The result of all this on crime is conceptually complex and empirically obscure. Reducing availability unambiguously tends to reduce nondrug crimes by users and dealers.[14] Raising price might increase or decrease such crimes, depending

---

*The phrase is from Balko (2006), which set out a wealth of supporting detail.

on how much consumption falls as prices rise. It now seems likely that most illicit drugs are elastically demanded, suggesting that higher prices might mean less crime. Unfortunately, the experience of the past quarter-century casts grave doubt on the capacity of drug enforcement to raise prices; cocaine prices, for example, have fallen by more than two-thirds (in inflation-adjusted dollars) even as the ratio of arrests and prisoners to tons of cocaine sold has multiplied tenfold or more.[15]

Enforcement can also influence how the drug business is carried on in ways that change the impact of the illicit drug trade on nondrug crime. It can do so by selectively winnowing out those dealers whose conduct, beyond delivering illicit drugs, creates the most noxious social side effects. Furthermore, enforcement can reduce nondrug crime by influencing the incentives facing the remaining market participants, and in particular the risks they face from enforcement itself: arrest, conviction, prison time, and asset seizure. Since these risks are the most important costs of selling illicit drugs, there is every reason to hope that making them vary systematically with the behavior of dealers and dealing organizations could significantly change that behavior.

If enforcement and sentencing were focused, and known to be focused, on the most violent organizations rather than the largest, most visible, or most vulnerable organizations, a dealer would have to weigh the benefits of violence—reducing enforcement vulnerability (by intimidating witnesses) and creating bargaining leverage vis-à-vis employees, suppliers, customers, and competitors—against the disadvantage of moving himself up on the list of enforcement targets. Moreover, those organizations and individuals most prone to violence would be taken out of the trade by enforcement action at a higher rate than their less violent rivals, exerting a kind of Darwinian pressure favoring more peaceful drug dealing.

Dealing organizations, and the markets they create and inhabit, also differ in flagrancy. At one extreme is highly discreet hand-to-hand selling to a limited customer base in a private, multiuse setting such as a dealer's apartment or, in a more recent style, door-to-door delivery based on orders placed by text messaging. At the other extreme is dealing in the open or in dedicated drug locations such as crack houses. Flagrancy is of concern not only because it increases the availability of drugs to those not—or not yet—deeply knowledgeable about how to acquire them or strongly committed to their acquisition, but also because flagrant dealing is linked to violent crime. Flagrant dealers face greater risk of robbery than discreet dealers, which creates stronger incentives for them to become armed. Flagrant dealing also creates the sort of disorderly conditions that not only directly diminish neighborhood quality of life, but can also attract serious criminal behavior to the area by creating the (partially self-fulfilling) impression that the risks of arrest and punishment for offenses committed there are low. Open drug markets are perhaps the ultimate "broken windows" (see chapter 6).

That analysis suggests that enforcement agencies ought to focus their attention on those flagrant forms of dealing that create the most criminogenic disorder, and to consider carefully the extent to which they want to crack down on the more discreet dealing styles facilitated by new communications technology; a dealer who makes home deliveries creates less disorder than a dealer standing on a street corner or sitting in a crack house. Insofar as the two styles of dealing compete, making the less obnoxious style less risky in terms of enforcement will discourage the use of the more obnoxious style, while cracking down on the text-message, home-delivery dealers will help keep the crack houses and street-corner markets in business.

Flagrant dealing, precisely because of its flagrancy, is vulnerable to enforcement pressure. But, due to the replacement effect, an established retail market can sustain itself in the face of even relatively high levels of arrest. A sustained crackdown can break up a market, but as the Pressure Point experience demonstrates, a crackdown using mass arrests imposes more strain on the criminal-justice system than it can routinely bear. Low-arrest crackdowns of the kind used in High Point (see chapter 3) offer the promise of greatly shrinking flagrant dealing at sustainable cost in enforcement, adjudication, and incarceration.

Controlling Intoxicated Behavior

Much of the social damage caused by drug users occurs while they are intoxicated. As noted earlier, a majority of jail and state prison inmates report that they were under the influence when they committed their current offense. Even allowing for the possibility that those who commit crimes while intoxicated are more likely to be arrested than people committing the same crimes while sober, it seems that something like half of all crimes are committed under the influence of alcohol or other drugs.

While some of the crimes committed under the influence would surely have been committed even if the offender had remained sober, some of them would not. Being drunk or high clouds judgment and diminishes self-control. For some individuals, in certain circumstances, the ambient-level punishment risk is a sufficient deterrent to crime when they are sober but inadequate when they are intoxicated.

The taxation and regulation of alcohol, and the prohibition of other drugs with the attendant enforcement effort, all aim at reducing the frequency of intoxication. So do the "demand-side" prevention, treatment, and control efforts discussed below. But intoxication and intoxicated behavior can also be targeted directly, for example, by laws forbidding being intoxicated in public or forbidding engaging in otherwise licit conduct, such as driving or carrying a weapon, while under the influence.

PREVENTION

"Prevention" is a conventional term in the discussion of drug abuse control policy, but it is also a misleading one. Prevention properly refers to a set of purposes: reducing the rate at which young people start to use drugs or the proportion—always a minority—of those who initiate who go on to substance abuse problems. By that standard, drug law enforcement is part of the prevention effort, though how successful it is remains an open question. But as conventionally used in the policy debate, "prevention" refers to a set of programs—school-based, community-based, and mass-media—aimed at persuading nonusers not to initiate nonmedical use of some or all psychoactives and persuading young people to defer their initiation until they are older.

By contrast with supply-reduction programs, which have crime-increasing as well as crime-decreasing effects, even modestly successful prevention programs are unambiguously beneficial in reducing crime. They offer the benefit of reduced drug use and reduced drug dealing without any of the unwanted side effects of enforcement.

That is the good news about prevention. The bad news is that few prevention programs have demonstrated that they can consistently reduce

the number of their subjects who use drugs. In addition, the positive results that have accompanied some pilot programs have often proven difficult to replicate in other settings.[16] Results from the top tier of programs
are significant, though not spectacular: reductions of about 25 percent
in rates of early initiation. Since even the best programs cost relatively
little, these modest gains, if they were to carry over into reductions in
heavy, chronic use of alcohol, cocaine, methamphetamine, opiates, and
cannabis, would make prevention highly cost-effective as a means of reducing substance abuse and, presumably, crime as well. But no existing
prevention program has been shown to achieve dramatic changes; the
programs are cost-effective not because they are effective, but because
they do not cost much.[17]

Another potential target for prevention efforts would be the prevention of drug dealing.[18] Again, the crime-control benefits of such prevention efforts, were they successful, could be immediate and substantial.
The risks of dealing are much greater than the risks of initiating drug use,
and may be underestimated by potential dealers, who may also grossly
overestimate its rewards.

Drug-Abuse Treatment

From a crime-control perspective, successful treatment of drug-involved
offenders is, like prevention, an unequivocal help. The criminal activity of
addict-offenders seems to rise and fall in step with their drug consumption,
and importantly, the relationship holds whether reductions in drug use are
unassisted or are the product of formalized treatment, and whether participation in treatment is voluntary or coerced.[19] A treatment-induced reduction in demand does not bring with it the side effects of an enforcement-
induced reduction. In addition, many drug-involved offenders sell drugs
in addition to using them, and some may exit the drug trade if they gain
control over their own habits. Thus treatment can have supply-reduction
as well as demand-reduction benefits, though those benefits, like the
supply-side benefits of drug law enforcement, will be blunted by replacement effects. The reduction in criminal activity during drug treatment
seems to be large enough that on cost-benefit grounds it can justify treatment costs even if treatment had no effect on post-treatment behavior.[20]

Most estimates of drug treatment effectiveness are based on simplistic pre-post comparisons, or worse, comparisons of treatment completers with treatment drop-outs. That means they are likely to be overestimates, because the analyses fail to adjust for selection effects—treatment entrants and completers are more interested in quitting than average, and might have done so without treatment—and regression toward the mean.* But even making generous allowance for those methodological problems, the finding that treatment on average generates at least short-term benefits is fairly robust.

Expanding the number of criminally active drug users in treatment could shrink both the drug markets and the crime rate without using up scarce prison capacity. Thus the inadequate availability and poor quality of substance-abuse treatment—attributable at least in part to the reluctance of public and private health insurance to finance treatment for substance abuse and dependency on the same terms as treatment for other disorders—constitutes an important missed crime-control opportunity. But the "treatment gap"—the difference between the number of people in "need" of treatment by clinical criteria and those actually receiving treatment—is at least as much an effect of deficient demand as it is of deficient supply, as demonstrated by the high drop-out rates from even nominally "mandatory" treatment programs.

Conversely, it is not the case that everyone suffering from substance-abuse disorder needs treatment; about two-thirds of those who meet clinical criteria for a diagnosis of abuse or dependency today will no longer meet those criteria three years from now, and only a few will have had any formal treatment in the meantime.[21] Raising that figure from two-thirds to three-quarters would greatly reduce the total damage done by substance abuse, and there is no reason to think that two-thirds is any sort of natural upper limit. The campaign against cigarette smoking demonstrates the potential power of concerted efforts to encourage "spontaneous desistance," but there has been no comparable effort directed at users of illicit drugs other than cannabis.

---

*People tend to enter treatment when their problems are unusually bad, so their behavior would be more likely to improve than to worsen even if the intervention itself had no effect.

Compared not only to no treatment but also to other forms of treatment, opiate-substitution therapy dramatically reduces crime among those who receive it. Unlike most treatment modalities, substitution has little trouble attracting and retaining clients. Yet only about one-eighth of U.S. heroin addicts are currently enrolled in substitution-therapy programs, which remain crippled by excessive regulation (less so for buprenorphine than for methadone) and discriminated against in drug-diversion programs. The result is unnecessary crime.

Parity for substance abuse in health insurance and managed care plans, better funding for drug treatment for those without health insurance, improvement in medical education regarding substance abuse, and relaxation of the regulations that limit opiate maintenance would all reduce nondrug crime.

Contrary to the promises of treatment advocates, though, expanding treatment availability is no magic bullet. We can no more treat our way out of our current drug problems than we can arrest and imprison our way out of them. Drug abusers who remain in treatment almost invariably reduce their drug use, and those who had been criminally active reduce their personal crime rates as well. But most people with drug problems are reluctant to seek treatment, and most of those who enter treatment programs quit before receiving much benefit from them. Substitution therapy is the major exception, but there is no substitution therapy for either alcohol or stimulants.

DIVERSION PROGRAMS AND DRUG COURTS

While many drug-involved offenders will not seek out treatment voluntarily, perhaps some of them can be induced to enter and remain in treatment if the alternative is jail or prison. This is the thought behind the set of programs referred to as "drug diversion" and its variant, the "drug court." In either case, a defendant, either before or after conviction, is offered the chance to avoid incarceration—and often to have the case expunged from his criminal record—if he will undergo a prescribed course of treatment. As a means of incapacitation, drug treatment is by far more cost-effective than incarceration, reducing the rate of criminal activity among participants during the treatment period by much more than half, at perhaps a seventh of the cost of a prison cell.[22]

Both diversion programs and drug courts rely on the threat of incarceration as a lever to secure treatment entry, retention, and compliance. Some such programs are limited to those charged with drug offenses, but others—sensibly, from a crime-control perspective—engage drug-involved offenders arrested for other offenses as well. Alas, compliance rates in diversion programs tend to be low; fewer than one-third of those mandated to treatment complete it, with a substantial proportion (as much as a third) never even entering.[23] Probation departments tend to be quite lax in enforcing the mandate to enter treatment, making most "mandatory" treatment voluntary in practice.

Most offenders eligible for diversion programs have low enough personal rates of nondrug crime that they would not have been worth locking up in any case, so diversion programs can justify themselves simply by freeing prison and jail space for more "deserving" prisoners. But a small fraction of diversion clients are quite dangerous, and in California it turns out that high personal nondrug arrest rates (five arrests in thirty months) are a very strong predictor of subsequent serious nondrug crime. Imprisoning the 1.6 percent of Proposition 36 clients who had five or more arrests in the thirty months prior to their current arrest—instead of offering them treatment—would have eliminated more than a quarter of the total crimes committed while on Proposition 36 release.[24]

Compliance is somewhat better in drug courts, which leverage the power of a judge—over both offenders and other agencies inside and outside the criminal-justice system—to make the treatment mandate real. While outcome evaluations have been mixed, there seems little doubt that some drug courts are performing quite well and saving money.[25] Certainly drug-court judges tend to be passionate advocates of their program.

The question of whether drug courts can be scaled up enough to make a measurable dent in crime remains open; with fewer than 100,000 drug court slots to serve at least two million drug-involved offenders,[26] drug courts have not yet reached the relevant scale. Their capacity to grow is limited both by the number of judges interested in playing the nontraditional role of a drug-court judge and by the profligate use drug courts make of scarce treatment resources. Moreover, most though not all drug courts screen out potential clients with significant nondrug criminal histories, improving their measured success rates but reducing their potential contribution to crime control.

Diversion, then, is often better than incarceration, and the treatment drug court is often better than diversion, especially for offenders with serious drug problems and nontrivial rates of predatory crime. But, at least in the current institutional environment, neither of them seems capable of making a major dent in the problem of drug-involved offenders.

If H.O.P.E.-style testing-and-sanctions programs spread, they might change the situation drastically. An ideal diversion system might consist of three tiers following the principle of "behavioral triage" (see chapter 6): use the offenders' behavior rather than expert evaluation to determine the level of supervision. To start with, drug offenders could be put on low-resource, virtually unsupervised diversion with no treatment mandate; in effect, their sentence would be an order to abstain from illicit drugs and submit to sporadic testing to verify that abstinence. Those who failed to comply—who missed tests or tested positive—could then be transferred to a H.O.P.E.-style program, still without any treatment mandate but with frequent tests and quick and consistent sanctions for failure to comply. Those who repeatedly failed even under that level of compulsion might then be moved into drug courts, with mandated treatment backed by judicial supervision.

Behavioral triage would economize on treatment and supervision resources by reserving formal treatment for those unable to remain abstinent without it. The same three-tiered system could be used for other probationers and parolees, focusing on compliance with other probation terms. Since most people with expensive illicit drug habits—who collectively account for the bulk of hard-drug use—are criminally active,[27] any program that substantially reduces illicit drug use among offenders supervised in the community has more potential to reduce the volume of the illicit trade, and thereby on the side effects it generates, including the need for drug law enforcement and related imprisonment, than any feasible program of enforcement, prevention, or voluntary treatment.

What Could Go Wrong?

Imagine that it is ten years from now; a number of the ideas in this book have been tried, with results somewhere between disappointing and disastrous. What went wrong? I can think of several possibilities; others, of course, I have not yet thought of.

MISAPPLICATIONS OF DYNAMIC CONCENTRATION

The project of arranging for swift and certain sanctions for selected combinations of offense, offender, and location, in hopes that the additional cost of doing so will be largely or entirely transient because the rates at which the targeted offenses are committed will fall, depends for its success on ease of detection. As long as there are more offenses being detected than the system can punish, dynamic concentration (see chapter 4) makes sense. But if the limiting factor is detection rather than adjudication and punishment, and if it is not possible to greatly reduce detection costs, then the project falls to the ground. Under those circumstances, it remains possible to reduce offense rates using swift and certain punishment and direct communication of deterrent threats, but that process will be costly, and the cost of maintaining lowered violation rates will remain high even in the face of reduced offending.

Drunken driving provides an example. Drunk drivers do respond to the threat of punishment, even though their very drunkenness may reduce their responsiveness. Establishing a "checkpoint"—a place where police stop cars and scan their drivers for signs of intoxication—along any stretch of road reliably reduces the frequency of drunken driving on that road during whatever hours the checkpoint operates, as soon as word gets out. At first blush, this might seem a good application of dynamic concentration: set up checkpoints on whatever roads have the most drunken driving at the hours when the rate is highest, advertise them in advance, watch the rate of drunken driving on those roads plummet, and then move on to the next-worst group of locations.

The problem with that plan is the "moving on" part. Drivers can see whether a checkpoint is in operation: no checkpoint, no deterrence. And even if all the drunken drivers who would otherwise go past a given point have been scared into temporary sobriety—or into taking a taxi-cab, drinking at home, or finding another route to a bar—the checkpoint still has to be staffed. The officers running one checkpoint cannot run another at the same time. So one checkpoint team cannot control several drunk-driving hot spots at the same time, and successful deterrence does not generate free resources to be used elsewhere.

Contrast that with a probation officer enforcing a "no illicit drugs" rule: drug testing is cheap compared to writing up violation reports, hav-ing hearings, and using jail cells, especially if probationers who achieve consistent records of testing "clean" are rewarded with reduced testing frequency. If testing a group of probationers with a credible threat of swift and certain sanctions succeeds in reducing their drug use as much as H.O.P.E. has reduced the methamphetamine use of its clients in Hono-lulu, maintaining that low level requires much less effort than achieving it in the first place. Once the first target group has been brought into high compliance, the probation officers involved can start putting pres-sure on an additional group, *without ever relaxing the pressure on the first group*.

The bad news is that most predatory—as opposed to transactional or public-order—offenses are hard to observe. There is no direct analogy of a drug crackdown for controlling burglary. That helps explain the at-tractiveness of certain "broken windows" strategies that focus on easily visible forms of offending; they can actually save resources.

However, it is still the case, especially with small-dollar theft and mi-nor assault, that the police make more arrests than the prosecutors and the courts can handle, and that the courts convict more offenders than the jails and prisons can hold. That leaves some scope for the application of dynamic concentration, either by identifying a group of high-rate of-fenders to be warned first and relentlessly prosecuted if they fail to heed the warning or by selecting particular neighborhoods for concentrated prosecution. But no police department can expect to make automobile break-ins disappear the way the police in High Point made open crack dealing in the West End disappear.

FAILURES OF DETERRENCE

Some offenders will turn out to be more refractory, even to swift and consistent punishment and direct warnings, than this analysis assumes will be typical. Perhaps they are mentally ill. Perhaps they do not find occupying a cell for a while especially aversive, which is likelier to be true if their alternative to a cell is sleeping under a highway overpass. Or perhaps they simply resent the system's attempts to control them enough to continue to violate, as if in protest. If the number of such highly refractory offenders is small, punishing them consistently is somewhat costly to the system—and of course painful to them—but not crippling. The higher the share of refractory offenders in any group, the greater the cost of bringing the whole group's behavior under control, because such offenders put heavy demand on scarce sanctions capacity. The enforcement-swamping effect means that an offender with given characteristics is likely to offend more frequently if other offenders subject to the same control effort are refractory.

And while it is true that a successful testing-and-sanctions program will reduce aggregate incarceration among those exposed to it by reducing their rearrest rates as well as their risks of finally having their probation revoked, it is equally true that an unsuccessful program could instead increase aggregate incarceration, especially if the short jail stays incurred for violations either caused probationers to lose their licit jobs or disrupted their attempts to build stable residential and family patterns.

No one knows, for example, what a H.O.P.E.-like program would do if applied to a group of crack-using probationers in Los Angeles or Washington, D.C.: they differ in many ways from methamphetamine users in Honolulu or heroin users in Lansing. If the violation rates start high and stay high despite consistent sanctioning, that will limit the number of drug-using probationers who can be controlled by a given number of probation officers and judges, with a given number of jail-cell days to hand out. If the violation rate turned out to be much higher in practice than it was assumed to be for purposes of program design, the effort might collapse of its own weight as the system proved incapable of actually delivering the promised sanctions to all who have earned them. Yes, it would be possible to just keep adding resources—if they could be found—but it might turn out that the game was not worth the candle.

Analysis can point to circumstances where some version of dynamic concentration *might* work, but there is no way to know whether a dynamic-concentration program *will* work in a given situation other than by trying it out; part of the uncertainty involves the behavior of officials, which may be less predictable than the behavior of offenders. The cost of the effort, and the risk of a failure to deliver, can be minimized by starting small and expanding slowly. That allows the program to develop a reputation for relentlessness, thus increasing the credibility of warnings given to those added to that group. As the Maryland experience demonstrates,* however, that approach may conflict with the needs of the political and managerial actors whose support the program requires: in particular, the need to be seen to be doing something substantial rather than something trivial.

FAILURES OF DELIVERY

Most programs do not work if they are not actually implemented. The structure of the criminal-justice process creates an almost infinite set of opportunities to fail to deliver quickly and consistently on threats. While some policing programs can work even if only the police department performs as planned, prosecutors, judges, and probation officers always need cooperation from the police and from the jails, and usually from one another. A testing-and-sanctions program could work perfectly: until the jail is too full to hold an extra prisoner when a probationer has earned a two-day stay, or the police decide they have more urgent tasks than serving bench warrants for people who have missed probation appointments. A focused low-arrest drug crackdown could work perfectly: until the prosecutor insists on prosecuting the cases that the police want to hold in abeyance.

Not only do complicated criminal-justice programs require inter-organizational cooperation, they require cooperation from officials who do

---

*See page 36.

not share a common boss: the police work for the mayor, the jailers for the sheriff, the probation officers for the county administrator (or sometimes for an administrative judge), and the parole agents for the parole or corrections department. The judges, of course, answer only to themselves.

Even within a given organization, a program—even a successful program such as Ceasefire in Boston or some of the early efforts at community-oriented policing—can run afoul of budget constraints, clashing ambitions and egos, and the tendency to relax once things start to get better. Transforming a mere "program" into something durable—something built into the basic operating procedures of the host agency in a way that makes it robust to budget problems, fashions, and whims—requires either consistent support from the very top of the organization chart or some process such as CompStat that creates consistent pressure for measurably good performance.

Moreover, everyone in the system is busy; at least in the short run, higher priority for one set of cases must mean lower priority for some other set, unless, like Judge Alm's team in Honolulu, everyone is prepared to work harder at the beginning. And everyone in the system considers himself or herself a professional, with the capacity for trained judgment that requires discretion in how to handle each case. All of them, especially those wearing judges' robes, tend to resent any attempt to curb that discretion. But to some extent "consistency" and "discretion" are opposite principles: what seems to a probation officer or a judge to be tempering justice with mercy in the interests of an offender who has been making a good-faith effort to go straight may well look from the perspective of the probationer like the exercise of arbitrary authority. If the judge has the discretion *not* to punish, then if the judge decides to punish just the same, then the judge has *chosen* to do something unpleasant to the probationer, which makes the probationer think, "Why was she mad at me?" rather than, "Those are the rules, and there are costs for breaking them."

The same positive-feedback loops that make success self-reinforcing also propagate failure. Once those who have been warned learn that they can violate the rules without consistent consequences, they will violate more often, making it that much harder and more expensive to deliver those consistent consequences. That is an especially grave risk for a program that starts out too large, or without the necessary "buy-in" from one or more of the key sets of players, as happened to the Break the Cycle program in Maryland.

We can label all of these problems "failures of public management." Or we can say, "Changing addict behavior is easy; changing judge behavior is hard" or "We have met the enemy and he is us." But the labels will not make the problems go away, and sometimes the result will be failure.

DIFFERENCES OF MISSION

It is a commonplace that crime is interlinked with other personal and social problems: joblessness, homelessness, family breakdown, mental illness, somatic disease, poor educational performance, weak neighborhoods. Much of the argument of this book is that crime control and other efforts at individual and community improvement ought to be more closely coupled: that the jails ought to take more responsibility for protecting the public health from infectious disease, the schools more responsibility for preventing crimes by and against their students, the housing projects and welfare departments and child protection agencies and supervisors of foster care more responsibility for reducing crime among their residents and clients, and the police more responsibility for improving neighborhood collective efficacy.

But it is also a commonplace that an organization needs to have a clear mission, and to be managed by testing everything the organization does against the performance of that mission. One of the explanations often given for the poor performance of public schools in bad neighborhoods in terms of turning out literate and numerate graduates is that they have taken, or been given, responsibility for many aspects of students' lives that others (e.g., parents) might reasonably have been expected to bear instead. The schools provide nutrition, day care, drug abuse prevention, gang activity prevention, domestic violence prevention, health education, physical education, drivers' education, sex education, civic education: all very valuable, no doubt, but not the same as making sure that the graduates can read, write, and calculate. Part of the theory underlying No Child Left Behind is that insisting that each school perform adequately on those basic tasks will divert some effort from some of those ancillary activities back to the three Rs. By the same token, CompStat is likely to make precinct captains less cheerful about contributing officer-hours to drug abuse prevention in the form of DARE.

In theory, it would be nice to have every decision-maker consider all of the likely consequences of alternative courses of action before making a choice: that is, after all, what we teach in schools of public policy. But managerially and for purposes of accountability—to the public and to elected officials and their appointees—it is essential to have a limited set of performance measures and to keep each organization focused on its assigned tasks. Yes, if the jails delivered more infectious-disease control and the health-care system more anti-violence efforts, we might wind up both healthier and safer. But we might also wind up with worse-managed jails and hospitals as a result of divided managerial attention.

Moreover, there are not very good mechanisms for adding resources to an agency to allow it to do something that is not its central mission.* The official in charge of the jail may reasonably doubt that doing a better job on the infectious-disease front will lead whoever makes her budget to be more generous, and the manager of the hospital may reasonably have the same doubt about being able to recoup the costs of doing a better job at preventing retaliatory violence by gunshot-trauma patients.

These are not "problems" for which we might find "solutions"; they are simply facts about the world that will necessarily make our actual efforts less useful than we could achieve with ideal, rather than actual, people and organizations.

So while it seems obvious to someone focused on crime control that the high schools ought to shift their hours to reduce afternoon burglaries and perhaps adolescent pregnancies—especially since doing so would predictably improve educational outcomes as well—someone running a big-city school system might not be quite so enthusiastic. The proposals

---

*Mark H. Moore of Harvard University's Kennedy School has identified this as a central difference between public and private management: since sales generate revenue, private-sector managers are usually happy to have more users of their products and services, even using them in ways the managers never imagined. To most public managers, people using services constitute "workload" that has to be accommodated within a fixed budget, and there is always concern that a program is being "abused" if it is used in an unexpected way: for example, if working parents use the public library as informal after-school care for their children (Moore 1995, ch. 1).

to change school hours would be sure to run into objections from some parents, some teachers, some other staff members, some school-bus operators, some owners of enterprises that value the mid-afternoon student trade, and probably several other categories of potentially aggrieved parties. In addition, the school manager would worry about all the after-school activities—from athletics to the school newspaper and the orchestra—that would probably also be sacrificed to the students' disinclination to get up early.

At that point, the school manager would likely decide that there were better uses for her limited supply of time, energy, and political capital: unless the police chief were especially insistent, and able to offer in return some police activity that could directly benefit the educational enterprise, such as aggressive efforts to protect students coming to and from school. Even then, she might well find, once she had torqued her whole organization around to allow for later hours, that the next police chief had found something else to do with the officer-hours she was promised in return. That's life in the big city.

Thus the project of incorporating crime control into the agendas of non-law-enforcement public agencies and nonprofits confronts three problems:

- First, the leaders of those agencies might not want to take on the crime-control mission, and there might not be adequate political will to induce them to do it against their will. That is roughly the world we live in now.
- Second, under the proper political and budgetary inducements, the leaders of those agencies (and promoters of new programs) might latch on to "crime control" as a catch-all justification, without doing the sort of serious thinking or managing around how their activities could actually control crime that they (sometimes) do around how to perform their core missions. That would give us lots of activities with "crime control" as part of their nominal justification, but with no one actually accountable for whether those activities generate crime-control benefits.
- Third, we could persuade, bribe, or bully some non-criminal-justice agencies to really contribute to crime control, and find that we had done so at the expense of having those agencies serve their primary goals well.

Crime control is important enough in itself, and a sufficiently important contributor to the performance of other efforts to educate, treat, and
serve the populations in high-crime areas, to justify asking the managers of schools, health-care providers, and social-service agencies to think
hard about what they could do to help contain it. But there can be no
guarantee that doing so will yield good results.

Overcontrol, Oppression, and Tyranny

This would be a very different book were it written in Singapore, still
more if it were written in China, or in the Alabama of 1962. The analysis
assumes that, other things equal, more compliance with the law is better than less compliance with the law, and that achieving social control
at lower budget cost and lower cost in the suffering of those punished is
therefore a largely undiluted good. But that will not always be the case.

Lowering the cost of punishment can raise the "price" of crime to the
criminal. Where "crime" consists only of theft, fraud, and violence, that
seems unobjectionable. But some laws are better broken than enforced.

Even in a democratic setting, those who make the laws do not have
interests or opinions identical to those whom the laws control. The less
democratic the setting, the greater the gap. Older and richer people tend
to have tastes for greater order and quiet than younger and poorer ones,
and "order maintenance," if not kept under strong local control, can too
easily intrude on valued personal liberty, especially in the presence of
ethnic tensions.

Differences in both religion and religiosity can add to the gap between
the lawmakers and those who must live under them. Representatives may
vote for laws they do not actually favor in order to appear to voters to
have the "right" values; during alcohol Prohibition, the legislator who
"voted dry and drank wet" was a byword. Would the country really have
been better off if the "Noble Experiment" had not collapsed?

Some would make the same argument about all of our current drug
prohibitions. Others, including the present author, disagree. The logical
point is that improved enforcement of a law that should not have been
passed in the first place can be a loss rather than a gain.

Underenforcement is often part of the process that leads to *de facto*, and then to *de jure*, legalization. In American history, blasphemy, dancing, fornication, gambling, drinking, and sexual contact between members of different races, or of two males or two females, have all passed through those stages. Making enforcement cheaper and more effective could slow the process of liberalization, an effect many of us would bitterly regret.

Call that the problem of "overcontrol."

Related, but not identical, is the problem of "oppression." The laws against Catholicism in Elizabethan, Stuart, and Hanoverian England and against racial integration in the post-Reconstruction South were designed by one group of people to keep another group in subjection. Before those laws were repealed, they were violated: in the case of Jim Crow, violated systematically as a deliberate means toward their overthrow. It would be morally insane to regret those violations or to wish that the enforcement machinery had been more efficient.

And indeed the substantial success of the English Protestant attempt to either convert Catholics or deprive them of wealth and power depended in part on the application of some of the principles argued for above. While Parliament after Parliament was willing to pass laws of increasing ferocity against Catholics, the very squires and burgesses who composed those Parliaments proved unwilling to carry out those laws in their roles as justices of the peace. Voting for a bill to hang Catholics in the abstract was one thing; actually hanging the Catholic in your own town, whose family had lived there for generations and who might be related to you by marriage, was something else. (There was, alas, more willingness to proceed to extremes against priests, especially Jesuits, who were seen as a political and not just a religious threat.)

But while executions for Catholicism could not actually be carried out, a modest fine for not attending Anglican services each week could actually be collected. That less severe but much more certain punishment, combined with unspectacular but crippling social disabilities such as exclusion from political life and the learned professions, accomplished over generations what a more spectacular persecution might not have done: the reduction of English Catholics to a small and largely powerless minority. Lovers of religious liberty might well wish that Cecil and his successors had been less aware of the principle that severity is the enemy of certainty, and lovers of racial equality must rejoice that the opponents of the Second Reconstruction never figured out how to accomplish their aims with fines instead of jail cells and waterhoses, or how to concentrate threats to make them more effective.

Tyranny, the extreme of oppression, can also make use of the principles of certainty, of concentration, and of directly communicated threats. It was not Russian tanks alone that allowed the Communist parties of Eastern Europe to keep their societies in subjection. As important as it is for China to get control of its crime problem, the reflection that most of the liberties we take for granted are crimes in today's China puts a heavy question mark against any project to help the current Chinese government become more skilled at enforcing the law at low cost.

Tyranny is hardly a substantial threat in the contemporary United States. But the principles expounded here could be used to further burden the lives of the ten million or so people who live in the United States without legal permission; it is not unreasonable to think that a nativist majority could make bad use of what in other contexts might seem like good advice.

In sum, one thrust of this book is how to make law enforcement less clumsy. But clumsy law enforcement can both discourage the tendency to criminalize things that should not be crimes and buffer the effect of bad laws already on the books. It is reasonable to hope that falling crime rates will strengthen the political forces that prefer more liberty to less liberty. But that is a hope, not a promise.

An Agenda for Crime Control

What, then, is to be done? What follows is a bare checklist; the balance of the book provides the supporting argumentation for the general approach and some of the specific policies. This list of recommendations is exemplary rather than exhaustive. In some cases we already know enough to know what to do; in other cases, the next step is to develop and rigorously field-test programs that ought to work based on what we think we know. Not every recommendation applies to every jurisdiction; the proof of the pudding is in the eating, and local conditions—social, budgetary, and institutional—vary so widely that one size will not fit all. Where the barriers to execution are budgetary, institutional, and managerial, the challenge is to change the budgets, the institutions, and the management styles.

GENERAL AND BUDGETARY

- Treat arrests and punishments as costs, not benefits.
- Emphasize swiftness and certainty of punishment rather than severity.
- Design punishments with the maximum ratio of deterrent efficacy to (1) the suffering inflicted and (2) the damage to the noncriminal opportunities of those punished.
- Concentrate enforcement rather than dispersing it.
- Directly communicate deterrent threats.
- Shift the burdens of crime and punishment away from otherwise disadvantaged groups, especially poor African Americans who face much more of both.
- Increase the budgets of criminal-justice agencies when doing so will reduce either crime or incarceration. The dollars currently spent on criminal-justice activities are a small problem compared either to crime or to the appalling number of Americans behind bars.

- Shift the mix of correctional budgets away from institutions (prisons and jails) and toward community corrections (probation and parole). Spend more on controlling the behavior of those awaiting trial.
- Multi-offending gangs represent a substantial and growing part of the overall problem of crime. Juveniles, and prisoners, join gangs in part for reasons of self-defense. Improving the actual and perceived capacity of the criminal-justice system to protect juveniles and prisoners from assault and extortion not only benefits them, but also reduces the incentive for gang membership. From this perspective, effective tolerance of juvenile-on-juvenile and prisoner-on-prisoner assault looks like a very expensive policy.

POLICING

- Add police to areas that are under-policed, as measured by a high ratio of crimes to officers.
- Focus police attention on reducing crime and disorder, not on making arrests.
- Identify and target high-rate serious offenders, with the goal of incapacitating them by incarceration.
- Identify those who only barely miss being targeted as high-rate serious offenders—the junior varsity—and warn them that continued criminal activity will result in their being added to the varsity list.
- In making both varsity and junior-varsity lists, pay attention to driving histories and histories of domestic violence. For those already on the varsity list, and for gang members targeted for investigation and prosecution as part of a crackdown on that gang, investigate domestic violence as a potential vulnerability for targeted offenders.
- Select specific easy-to-observe crimes for "zero-tolerance" treatment, either jurisdiction-wide or in specific areas. Publicize those choices, with "narrowcast" warnings aimed at identified offenders as well as "broadcast" announcements.
- Break up flagrant retail drug markets that generate disorder, crime, and fear with pre-announced low-arrest crackdowns.

- Outside crackdown areas, choose dealers and dealing organizations as enforcement targets according to their contribution to violence and disorder and their use of minors as accomplices, rather than their volume.
- Where there are multi-offending groups such as youth gangs, identify the active participants, make a list of "zero-tolerance" offenses, starting with gunfire and then working outward, and warn the active participants, as groups, that an infraction of any "zero-tolerance" rule by any member of a group will lead to aggressive enforcement with respect to every member of that group for the entire range of offenses. Organize at the community level to make carrying out that threat politically feasible. Organize both internally and in cooperation with other agencies to make carrying out that threat operationally feasible. Zero tolerance for some behaviors does not imply an implicit license for other crimes. The "pulling levers" strategy is a threat, not a deal: "If you sell drugs or steal cars, you're at the same risk of arrest as anyone else is. But if someone from your group shoots somebody, you're at much higher risk of arrest for any illegal conduct, and a target for enforcement to the letter of probation and parole requirements, with police working actively to put you, personally, in prison for as long as possible."
- In areas with large gang problems, gang enforcement requires an information-gathering process that can distinguish active gang participants from mere color-wearers. (If in fact Los Angeles County is home to 80,000 "gang members," the 20,000 police and deputy sheriffs need to select a subset of those 80,000 people for active enforcement.)
- Adjust internal management and incentive systems to give the service of bench warrants, especially those resulting from H.O.P.E.-style probation efforts, the highest rather than the lowest priority.
- Identify recent prison releasees, put them under close scrutiny in the high-risk early months, and warn them of that scrutiny.

Prosecution, Courts, and Sentencing Rules

- Economize on the use of scarce prison and jail cells. Make them do as much crime-control work—incapacitation and deterrence—as possible by selecting prisoners carefully and not imposing excessive sentences. While prisons and jails are at capacity, an additional day behind bars for one offender means one day less behind bars for another.

- Focus long prison terms on serious high-rate offenders as demonstrated by the *rate* of arrests and convictions rather than the cumulative lifetime offense count. Try to minimize the use of scarce cell-years on older offenders who, if not incarcerated, would be semi-retired. Allow sentencing judges access to juvenile criminal records.

- Punish probation violations systematically and quickly but moderately. Punish absconders much more substantially.

- As the level of probation compliance improves, substitute probation (and probation-enforced alternative sanctions such as "community service") for prison.

- Provide some nontrivial punishment even for first-time misdemeanor offenders. (This idea will be more feasible if probation can be made into a nontrivial punishment.)

- Use pretrial release strategically. Time spent behind bars awaiting trial has more deterrent efficacy than time spent behind bars after conviction, because it comes closer in time to the crime.

- Enforce bail conditions, including desistance from the use of expensive illicit drugs.

- Offer steep punishment "discounts" for quick pleas.

- Move high-rate offenders released on bail up the queue for trial dates.

- Consider both the offender's broader criminal history and the broader driving history—especially a history of accidents with personal injury—in sentencing drunken or reckless drivers. A drunken driver who also has an assaultive personality, which might be marked by a criminal history including violent crime such as domestic violence, is much more likely to kill someone while driving drunk than someone who drinks and drives but does not otherwise enjoy hurting people; driving badly is dangerous, but not as dangerous as driving both badly and aggressively.

- Prosecute felonies committed by parolees as new crimes, rather than allowing them to be treated as mere parole violations.

- Coordinate with police to carry out specific deterrent threats aimed at individuals or at classes of behavior. A drug-dealing case arising as part of a focused attempt to break up a particular market is a better candidate for a substantial prison term than a routine drug-dealing case. This effort will be facilitated in large jurisdictions by moving toward "community prosecution" programs where policies are allowed to vary by neighborhood and are made with active consultation with both police and community leaders.

- Make some period of post-release supervision part of every prison sentence and most jail sentences.

INSTITUTIONAL CORRECTIONS

- Develop a performance-measurement system and hold wardens accountable for performance, as measured by the post-release welfare and criminal activity of the prisoners.* Measure the physical and psychological health of prisoners, including correlates of stress, and characteristics such as literacy that are demonstrably related to improving reintegration and reducing recidivism, as prisoners enter and exit each institution. Measure recidivism and measures of post-release reintegration (employment status, housing status, reporting for post-release supervision) on an institution-by-institution basis. Make recidivism a key performance measure. Mine recent releasees for detailed information on prison conditions, using interviewers who are not corrections department employees.
- Reexamine prison size and prison design. In the context of ethnic prison gangs, perhaps the optimal size of a prison is much smaller than it used to be. Be prepared to ignore currently accepted standards, where those standards are unsupported by evidence that they improve prisoner physical or psychological health, improve reintegration, or reduce recidivism.
- In designing and managing prisons, strive to reduce noise and other sources of stress. Television sets can be equipped to use wireless headphones.

*This will no doubt seem grossly unfair to the wardens, who after all control few of the key determinants of recidivism. But then school principals control few of the key determinants of educational attainment. If recidivism reduction is important—and it is hard to imagine anything more important—then it needs to be part of the wardens' scoring system, or it will continue to be neglected.

- Some of the features of prisons that make them most horrible—especially inmate-on-inmate violence—may not make them more aversive. A prison that largely reproduces the social order of an underclass street corner may be a less effective deterrent than a prison kept as quiet and orderly as possible. The therapeutic community (TC) model of drug treatment reflects a complete alternative to what now stands as ordinary prison life. Nothing about the TC process is specific to drug addiction. While TCs on the outside are very expensive compared to other forms of drug treatment because they are residential, putting someone in a TC instead of a prison, or a TC inside a prison, is only slightly more expensive and no less aversive than prison itself. A TC alternative should be offered to every prisoner who wants it, regardless of his drug history or lack thereof, with return to a regular cellblock as the ultimate sanction.

- It is possible that deterrent efficacy may relate much more closely to the aversiveness of the prison environment, especially at the end of the sentence, than to its duration. That opens the possibility of shortening sentences while making them more unpleasant, for example, with social isolation, deprivation of television and radio, lack of opportunity to exercise, and a healthy but uninteresting (e.g., low-fat, low-sodium, low-sugar) diet. Treatment that would be cruel and unusual punishment if extended over months or years can be innocuous if the duration is measured in days or weeks. The apparently common-sense practice of moving prisoners down levels of supervision, which generally means somewhat more pleasant conditions, as their release dates approach may be counterproductive; perhaps the last two weeks of every prison term should be spent in solitary confinement on bread and water.

- Since skills such as literacy are portable across the boundary between prison and the community, stress skill acquisition rather than attempts at behavior change such as drug treatment.

- Consider placing a computer in each cell. Computers can be excellent means of delivering educational programming; moreover, computer competence is now necessary for many jobs. Substituting computer use for television-watching and weight-lifting might make prisons at once less pleasant and more rehabilitative. (The cheap, hand-cranked computers being advanced for developing-country use can obviate the problem that prison cells do not—for good reasons—have electric power outlets.)

- Stop tolerating inmate-on-inmate violence. Especially for new institutions, it should be possible to design closed-circuit TV monitoring systems leaving no "blind spots" where violence can occur.

- Prison and jail populations are unhealthy. Inmates are at risk of infection with a variety of communicable diseases. Especially for jails, with their high traffic in and out, this represents a substantial threat to public health. All inmates should be tested for tuberculosis, hepatitis B and C, and the major sexually transmitted diseases at both entry and exit; this happens now in some jails, but by no means all. Because of their concentration of people with physical and mental health problems, prisons and jails are attractive targets for health-education efforts. Exit planning should include connecting prisoners who need treatment to local health-care providers.

- The movement toward for-profit prisons has not been noticeably successful. Consider a system of not-for-profit "charter prisons"—perhaps using as a legal model the "faith-based prisons" run by the Prison Fellowship—under which a variety of institutions would be allowed to try their hands at prison management, with prisoners allowed to choose placement in any institution secure enough to hold them and willing to take them. Such institutions would allow a far more rapid rate of innovation—and elimination of unsuccessful practices—than could be accomplished within the constraints of the correctional bureaucracy. Obviously, a very strong inspectorate would be a necessary adjunct to such a system.

COMMUNITY CORRECTIONS

- Manage for results, where the key result is cessation of offending and the development of behavior patterns—employment, housing, family status—correlated with desistance from crime. Both services and supervision should be managed around those goals. Evaluate probation officers, supervisors, and offices based on the frequency and seriousness of re-offending rates, adjusted for the characteristics of the caseload. Use correlates of re-offending such as job, family, and housing status as proxy measures to provide more immediate feedback.

- Impose fewer rules on probationers and parolees, with each rule linked to reductions in re-offending, and with some capacity to monitor compliance with each rule in real time. Drug testing, for example, should use techniques that provide on-the-spot results rather than sending samples out for off-site testing.

- Other than for identified serious high-rate offenders for whom incapacitation is the goal, avoid revocations for technical violations. Rule violations, and sanctions for them, should be treated as routine aspects of community supervision, not as a reason to end it.

- Develop the capacity to continuously monitor the locations of offenders. The most promising approach would be some mix of GPS and cell-phone technology mounted in a unit to be worn as an anklet with a tamper-evident band. This will allow both the imposition of time-and-place restrictions such as curfews and the linking of offender locations with the sites of new crimes. A large fraction, perhaps more than half, of those now in prison or jail could be safely released under such monitoring, and time-and-place restrictions could substitute for incarceration in creating temporary deprivation of liberty for the purpose of deterrence and retribution.

- When a probationer or parolee commits a new felony, do not substitute revocation for trial and sentencing; the penalty for a crime should be higher, not lower, for someone under community supervision than for someone not under community supervision.

- Where resources are scarce, prioritize. Better to manage some clients well by concentrating attention than to manage all clients badly by dispersing attention. As the initial group of high-supervision offenders comes into compliance, slowly expand the size of that group, making sure always to have adequate capacity to enforce whatever rules are imposed on the designated high-supervision group.

- Work with the courts to substitute swiftness and certainty for severity in sanctioning probation violations not amounting to new crimes. Where swift hearings are infeasible, use "holds" pending hearings to deliver quick consequences.

- Develop relationships with other public agencies and nonprofit organizations in which the outside entity provides "community service" supervision in return for access to unpaid labor.
- If high levels of compliance with probation officers' orders can be achieved, be ready to use substitute sanctions (such as day reporting, curfews, or hours of "community service") rather than jail for violations of probation rules. But be completely inflexible about imposing jail time for those who fail to comply with those non-jail sanctions.
- Reward good behavior as well as punishing bad behavior. Allow offenders to, in effect, set their own conditions, with compliance leading to lesser restriction and noncompliance leading to greater restriction. As rewards, reduced monitoring or loosened conditions (e.g., later curfews) are good; where feasible, financial incentives in the form of rebates on fines and fees are probably better.
- Employment greatly reduces recidivism. Probation offices, like welfare offices, can both help and encourage their clients to find and hold jobs; the Federal Probation office in St. Louis has done so successfully, greatly reducing recidivism in the process. As the capacity of the system to ensure compliance with probation and parole terms improves, probationers and parolees become more attractive employees. But those improvements are not transparent, and will not communicate themselves to employers. Community-corrections agencies need to pick up some of the slack with aggressive efforts to update employers' perceptions. Of course, those efforts must not outrun the reality on the ground.
- Assertive Community Therapy, in which the community-corrections system joins with the community mental-health system to increase treatment compliance, can improve the lives of probationers and parolees with serious mental-health problems. When those problems are linked to recidivism—or to the economic and social failure that leads to recidivism, as in the case of major depression—ACT can be good crime prevention as well as good medicine. A first step would be screening to find the large proportion of mentally ill probationers and parolees whose conditions have not been properly diagnosed.

- Concentrate both services and supervision on the days and weeks immediately following release, both to manage a high-risk period and to screen for those who need a longer period of intensive supervision.

PRETRIAL RELEASE (BAIL OR RELEASE ON RECOGNIZANCE)

While arrestees awaiting trial are innocent in law and cannot legitimately be subjected to punishment, they can be required to observe any condition of pretrial release reasonably related to securing their appearance and trial and preventing them from committing crimes while on release. Both drug testing and position monitoring could be effective in this regard.

JUVENILE CORRECTIONS

- Since most juvenile offenders—even serious juvenile offenders—do not develop into active adult criminals, there is a strong interest in avoiding any criminal-justice action that would increase that risk by reducing a juvenile's noncriminal opportunities. On the other hand, juveniles account for a substantial share of serious crime, including violent crime, and the goal of rehabilitation (or avoiding anti-rehabilitative effects) should not have complete priority over immediate deterrence and incapacitation.
- Make an offender's juvenile record available to the sentencing judge after an adult felony conviction.
- Juveniles are even more sensitive than adults to social isolation and stimulus deprivation; boredom can be much more aversive than fear or physical suffering, with the additional advantage of not making for heroic stories or memories. A weekend spent alone in something that looks like a motel room without a television set, with uninterestingly healthy food, might turn out to be a potent deterrent, and could be implemented without interfering with schooling. As with community corrections, that capacity could be used to leverage other forms of punishment: a sentence to eighty hours of "community service" would mean something if the consequence for failing to appear were a weekend of solitude and boredom.

Drug Policy

- Raise alcohol taxes.
- Consider the abolition of the age restriction in combination with tax increases to provide a net decrease in juvenile drinking and juvenile drunken driving while also decreasing the rate at which late adolescents learn to break the law (and to acquire and use false identification to do so).
- Forbid the use of alcohol, at least for some period, to those convicted of drunken assault, drunken driving, drunken vandalism, or repeated disorderly conduct under the influence. Enforce that restriction as the current age restriction is enforced, by requiring alcohol providers to verify eligibility to drink. That would require "carding" all bar and package-goods customers.
- Keep tobacco taxation below the level at which open retail markets in untaxed or smuggled products develop, because those markets can be highly criminogenic. Interstate compacts, or the substitution of federal for state and local taxation, can reduce the problem of tobacco tax evasion.
- Cut back on routine drug law enforcement and associated sentencing. As a reasonable middle-term target, aim at reducing the population behind bars for drug-defined offenses from the current half million to a quarter million.
- Permit the consumption of cannabis, and its production for personal use or gratis distribution, while maintaining the ban on commerce in the drug.
- The extreme intrusiveness of drug law enforcement, the use of criminal informants with the attendant risks, and high-hazard techniques such as "dynamic-entry" raids are hard to separate from the enforcement of laws against hard-to-observe consensual activity. But necessity does not make those techniques any less problematic. A focus on the visible problems created by drug dealing, rather than the invisible damage done by supplying drugs to drug abusers, will reduce the need for extreme enforcement tactics.
- In many cities, police concentrate prostitution enforcement on street-walking and brothels, allowing "outcall" services to operate largely untouched. Analogously, deliberate neglect of low-community-impact

forms of drug dealing, such as discreet home-delivery services, will help shrink demand for the more flagrant, and thus more neighborhood-threatening, styles of dealing involving open-air transactions or dedicated drug-selling locations.

- Use low-arrest crackdowns to break up flagrant retail markets.
- Focus enforcement attention and sentencing on violence, disorder, and the use of juveniles, not on the mere volume of drugs sold.
- Expand the availability of drug treatment, especially opiate-substitution therapies. End the prejudice against substitution therapies in diversion programs and drug courts.
- Explore the promise of cash incentive systems for abstinence by criminally active drug users not currently under community corrections supervision.
- Encourage "spontaneous desistance" and stop promoting the false belief that people with drug-abuse problems can recover only with professional help.
- Force probationers, parolees, and those on bail to desist from the use of expensive or criminogenic illicit drugs. Use occasional random drug screening to identify clients in need of more frequent testing. Do not require treatment except for those who prove incapable of desistance under the pressure of monitoring and sanctions. If appropriate capacity for remote monitoring can be developed, the ban might be extended to alcohol, especially for those with histories of alcohol-related offending.
- In neighborhoods where drug dealing is prevalent, focus in-school and community-based prevention efforts on preventing dealing.

Guns

- Reducing the number of firearms in private hands by 90 percent would no doubt reduce the homicide rate. But reducing the number by 10 percent would have only a very small effect on crime (as opposed to accident or suicide prevention). The experience with states passing "shall-issue" laws (making it far easier to acquire permits to carry concealed weapons) provides no evidence of substantial criminal violence by holders of those permits. Thus two of the major goals of gun control advocates—reducing the prevalence of firearm ownership, and preventing the passage of "shall-issue" laws—are largely irrelevant to the project of reducing victimization risk.

- On the other hand, reducing access to firearms by those whose criminal history or history of psychiatric commitment make them ineligible for legal gun possession can reduce the level of criminal violence with firearms.

- While licensed firearms dealers are required to check the eligibility of gun purchasers, private parties selling their own weapons are under no such requirement.* Eliminating that exemption by requiring that private sellers verify eligibility through licensed gun dealers would be a step in reducing access to guns by those likely to use them criminally. So would limiting the number of firearms that anyone other than a licensed dealer can purchase over the course of a month.

- Another source of weapons for criminal use is the small number of scofflaw gun dealers who knowingly or recklessly sell to ineligible users, or to professional gun traffickers or "straw purchasers" for re-sale to such users. Tracing guns used in crimes back to their most recent legal sale can help identify problem gun dealers. If it became technically feasible, requiring guns to be fired before sale and entering the ballistic signatures on the bullet and (especially) the cartridge entered into a database along with the serial number of the weapon would extend the capacity to trace guns used in the commission of a crime to situations in which the bullet or the cartridge is left at the crime scene but the gun itself is not recovered. The gun's last legal purchaser could then be asked to account for what happened to it.

- The combination of closing the private-sale loophole, limiting the number of guns purchased in a month, and more intensive crime-gun tracing and enforcement against scofflaw dealers could, in combination, provide all the crime-control benefits that would be provided by a much more politically controversial national gun registry. A package of legislation combining those tightening measures with a

---

* Because many private firearms sales take place at gun shows, this is sometimes known in political discussions as the "gun show loophole," though in fact no activity illegal elsewhere is legal at gun shows.

national "shall-issue" law and permission for someone licensed in one state to possess a weapon or to carry a concealed weapon to do so in any state might be able to command a legislative majority and to combine more freedom and convenience for gun owners with less violent crime.

SOCIAL SERVICES AND OTHER NONPUNITIVE ANTI-CRIME MEASURES

- Since social-service approaches to crime control spend only money rather than "spending" authority and liberty, and since they generally have side benefits and cost offsets rather than side costs, they deserve preference over punitive approaches even at somewhat higher costs per crime prevented.
- Crime-control benefits ought to be weighed along with other benefits in designing, funding, managing, and evaluating social programs. For programs serving high-risk populations, make prevention of crime by program participants and their children an explicit goal, reflected in internal performance-measurement and incentive systems.
- Look for ways to concentrate on people who would otherwise be at high risk of high-rate serious offending. Much higher costs per person served are justified where target efficiency is high.
- By the same token, low-cost interventions can be justified even if their target efficiency is also low.
- Try to substitute mandates to change behavior (e.g., desistance from drug use) for mandates to receive services (e.g., drug treatment), to avoid swamping the service-delivery system.
- Start middle school and high school later in the day and end them later in the day, both to improve educational and health outcomes and to prevent after-school crime.
- Replicate the "classroom management game" experiment. If the result holds up, roll out the program nationally.
- Give bullying prevention a high priority in schools. Back it up with an administrative culture that firmly rejects "boys will be boys" as an excuse for pupil-on-pupil violence.

- Do carefully designed and well-controlled studies on the impact of various youth recreation and job programs on crime.
- Emphasize order maintenance and crime prevention in managing subsidized housing. Create effective sanctions short of eviction to discourage disorderly behavior and crimes by tenants' children.
- Provide Assertive Community Therapy for offenders in the community whose mental-health problems lead to frequent offending and who will not comply with mental-health regimens on their own.
- Make aggressive attempts to eliminate, or at least drastically reduce, the remaining sources of lead exposure, chiefly the remaining lead paint in residential structures and lead in the air as a result of smelting. Treat the reckless sale of lead-containing children's toys as a criminal matter.
- Be prepared to spend money to improve parenting skills in high-risk populations. Nurse home visitation seems to be an effective approach. A universal first visit could be provided at relatively modest cost (less than \$1 billion per year nationally) and the results of that visit could be used as a screen to focus further services where they are most needed. Long-term intensive visitation (e.g., weekly for two years) is obviously much more expensive on a per-client basis, but with even modest target efficiency it may well pay for itself in crime-prevention terms alone, with many other benefits and cost offsets as a bonus.
- Enlist social-service programs (e.g., TANF and WIC) to deliver services and incentives aimed at improving child-raising skills to at-risk parents.

Some crime control efforts are easy. Others are harder. But in general this is common sense, not rocket science. A sensible crime-control agenda would satisfy neither the conservative impulse to punish as many people as possible as severely as possible nor the liberal impulse to substitute facilitation for coercion and social reform for law enforcement. Liberals will have to swallow the idea that improved coercion is as necessary as improved conditions. Conservatives will have to swallow the ideas that punishment is a cost and not a benefit and that the measure of the efficacy of a threat is how often it does not need to be carried out, plus the fact that providing services to actual and potential offenders can in some circumstances control crime more effectively and more cost-effectively than law enforcement.

Criminal-justice institutions need to give crime control priority over institutional habit and managerial comfort. Public and private institutions that do not have crime control in their mission statements need to acknowledge that, where their actions and omissions can make the crime problem better or worse, they are, willy-nilly, in the crime-control business.

Just by making effective use of things we already know how to do, we could reasonably expect to have half as much crime and half as many people behind bars ten years from now. There are a thousand excuses for failing to make that effort, but not one good reason.

NOTES

Introduction: How to Have Less Crime and Less Punishment

1. Jens Ludwig, "The Costs of Crime," testimony, United States Committee on the Judiciary, September 19, 2006; John J. Donohue III and Jens Ludwig, "More COPS," policy brief no. 158 (Washington, D.C.: Brookings Institution, March 2007), http://judiciary.senate.gov/testimony.cfm?id=2068&wit_id=5749.

2. Atul Gawande, "Hellhole," *New Yorker*, March 25, 2009, http://www.newyorker.com/reporting/2009/03/30/090330fa_fact_gawande?yrail.

3. James Q. Wilson, "Penalties and Opportunities," in Duff and Garland, eds., *A Reader on Punishment*, p. 195.

4. Raaj K. Sah, "Social Osmosis and Patterns of Crime," *Journal of Political Economy*, 99, 6 (1991): 1272–95; Mark Kleiman, "Enforcement Swamping: A Positive-Feedback Mechanism in Rates of Illicit Activity," *Mathematical and Computer Modeling* 17, 2 (1993): 65–75; Joel Schrag and Suzanne Scotchmer, "The Self-Reinforcing Nature of Crime," *International Review of Law and Economics* 17, 3 (1997): 325–35.

5. Kleiman 1993.

6. Thomas Schelling (1968, 1976) made such "tipping" phenomena famous among social scientists, and Malcolm Gladwell made them famous more generally. The first use of the term in this context is in Grodzins (1958). Engineers call such systems "bi-stable."

7. David Kennedy, *Deterrence and Crime Prevention: Reconsidering the Prospect of Sanction* (Toronto: Routledge, 2009), 54–58.

8. James Q. Wilson and Richard J. Herrnstein, *Crime and Human Nature* (New York: Simon and Schuster, 1985).

9. S. G. Kellam, G. W. Rebok, N. Ialongo, and L. S. Mayer, "The Course and Malleability of Aggressive Behavior from Early First Grade into Middle School: Results of a Developmental Epidemiologically-based Preventive Trial," *Journal of Child Psychology and Psychiatry* 35 (1994): 259–81.

10. Daniel S. Nagin and Kenneth C. Land, "Age, Criminal Careers and Population Heterogeneity: Specification and Estimation of a Nonparametric, Mixed Poisson Model," *Criminology* 31 (2006): 327–62; Daniel S. Nagin, David P. Farrington, and Terrie E. Moffitt, "Life-Course Trajectories of Different Types of Offenders," *Criminology* 33 (1995): 111–39.

11. Elena Garces, Thomas Duncan, and Janet Currie, "Longer-Term Effects of Head Start," *American Economic Review* 92, 4 (September 2002): 999–1012.

12. Lawrence W. Sherman et al., *Preventing Crime: What Works, What Doesn't, What's Promising*, report to the U.S. Congress (Washington, D.C.: U.S. Dept. of Justice, 1997); Rick Nevin, "Understanding International Crime Trends: The Legacy of Preschool Lead Exposure," *Environmental Research* 104, 3 (July 2007): 315–36.

CHAPTER 1: THE TRAP

1. Leonard Berkowitz and Jacqueline Macaulay, "The Contagion of Criminal Violence," *Sociometry* 34, 2 (1971): 238–60.

2. Richard A. Easterlin, *Birth and Fortune: The Impact of Numbers on Personal Welfare* (Chicago: University of Chicago Press, 1987).

3. Lee N. Robins, *The Vietnam Drug User Returns*, Special Action Office Monograph, Series A, No. 2 (Washington, D.C.: U.S. Government Printing Office, 1974).

4. Alfred Blumstein, "Youth Violence, Guns, and the Illicit-drug Industry," *The Journal of Criminal Law and Criminology* 86 (1995): 26–29.

5. Kerner Commission, *Report of the National Advisory Commission on Civil Disorders* (Washington, D.C.: U.S. Government Printing Office, 1968).

6. Robert Martinson, "What Works—Questions and Answers about Prison Reform," *Public Interest* 35, 22 (Spring 1974): 22–54.

7. Philip J. Cook, "Punishment and Crime: A Critique of Current Findings Concerning the Preventive Effects of Punishment," *Law and Contemporary Problems* 41, 1 (1977): 164–204.

8. James Q. Wilson, *Thinking About Crime* (New York: Basic Books, 1975).

9. Gary Becker and William Landes, *Essays in the Economics of Crime and Punishment* (New York: Columbia University Press, 1974).

10. Mark Kleiman, Kerry D. Smith, Richard A. Rogers, and David P. Cavanagh, "Imprisonment-to-Offense Ratios," BOTEC Analysis Corporation, August 1988; Mark Kleiman and David P. Cavanagh, "Cost Benefit Analysis of Prison Cell Construction and Alternative Sanctions," BOTEC Analysis Corporation, prepared for the National Institute of Justice, June 19, 1990.

11. Kleiman, 1993; Raaj K. Sah, "Social Osmosis and Patterns of Crime," *Journal of Political Economy* 99, 6 (1991): 1272–95.

12. Pew Center on the States, "One in 100: Behind Bars in America 2008," 2008.

13. P. J. Cook and J. H. Laub, "After the Epidemic: Recent Trends in Youth Violence in the United States," *Crime and Justice* (2002): 1–37; Alfred Blumstein and

Joel Wallman, eds., *The Crime Drop in America* (rev. ed., Cambridge: Cambridge University Press, 2006); Franklin E. Zimring, *The Great American Crime Decline* (New York: Oxford University Press, 2007).

14. Kennedy 2009, 63–56; E.Glaeser, B. Sacerdote, and J. Scheinkman, "Crime and Social Interactions," (NBER Working Paper No. 5026, 1995), citing E. L. Glaeser, *Two Essays on Information and Labor Markets* (Ph.D. diss., University of Chicago, 1992.)

15. Jeremy Travis, *But They All Come Back: Facing the Challenges of Prisoner Reentry* (Washington, D.C.: Urban Institute Press, 2005).

16. J. M. Chaiken and M. R. Chaiken, *Varieties of Criminal Behavior* (Santa Monica, Calif.: RAND, 1982); John DiIulio, Jr., and Ann Morrison Piehl, "Does Prison Pay? The Stormy National Debate Over the Cost-Effectiveness of Imprisonment," *Brookings Review* (1991): 28–35; James Q. Wilson, "Penalties and Opportunities," in R. A. Duff and David Garland, eds., *A Reader on Punishment* (New York: Oxford University Press, 1994), 195.

17. Raymond V. Liedka, Anne Morrison Piehl, and Bert Useem, "The Crime-Control Effect of Incarceration: Does Scale Matter? *Criminology and Public Policy* 5, 2 (2006): 245–76.

CHAPTER 2: THINKING ABOUT CRIME CONTROL

1. Philip J. Cook, "The Demand and Supply of Criminal Opportunities," in M. Tonry and N. Morris (eds). *Crime and Justice* 7 (1986):1–27.

2. Mark A. Cohen, Roland T. Rust, and Sara Steen, "Measuring Public Perceptions of Appropriate Prison Sentences," Executive Summary, National Institute of Justice, April 2003, http://www.ncjrs.gov/pdffiles1/nij/grants/199364.pdf.

3. Anthony N. Doob and Glenn E. Macdonald, "Television Viewing and Fear of Victimization: Is the Relationship Causal?" *Journal of Personality and Social Psychology* 37 (1979): 170–79.

4. Kenworthy Bilz, "The Puzzle of Delegated Revenge," *Boston University Law Review* 87 (2007): 1059–112.

5. "Crime in the United States, 2005," Uniform Crime Reporting Program, U.S. Department of Justice, Federal Bureau of Investigation, 2005. Hsiang-Ching Kung, Donna L. Hoyert, Jiaguan Xu, and Sherry L. Murphy, *National Vital Statistics Report*, April 24, 2008, vol. 56, no. 10, Center for Disease Control and Prevention, U.S. Department of Health and Human Services.

6. "Poisoning in the United States: Fact Sheet," Center for Disease Control and Prevention, U.S. Department of Health and Human Services, http://www.cdc.gov/ncipc/factsheets/poisoning.htm.

7. Robert H. Frank, *Luxury Fever: Why Money Fails to Satisfy in an Era of Excess* (New York: Free Press, 1999); Steven Shavell, "Individual Precautions to Prevent Theft: Private Versus Socially Optimal Behavior," NBER Working Paper 3560, 1990.

8. Steven Raphael and Michael A. Stoll, *Modest Progress: The Narrowing Spatial Mismatch Between Blacks and Jobs in the 1990s*, Living Cities Census Series (Washington, D.C.: Brookings Institution, 2002).

9. Jeffrey Grogger, "Arrests, Persistent Youth Joblessness, and Black/White Employment Differentials," *Review of Economics and Statistics* 74 (1992): 100–106.

10. Wesley Skogan, *Disorder and Decline: Crime and the Spiral of Decay in American Neighborhoods* (Berkeley: University of California Press, 1990).

11. Philip J. Cook, *Assessing Urban Crime and Its Control: An Overview*, NBER Working Paper No. W13781 (February 2008).

12. Shannan M. Catalano, "Criminal Victimization, 2003," *National Crime Victimization Survey*, Bureau of Justice Statistics, U.S. Department of Justice, September 2004, NCJ 205455.

13. "Homicide Trends in the US—Trends by Race," Bureau of Justice Statistics, U.S. Department of Justice, 2005.

14. *Sourcebook of Criminal Justice Statistics*, 2002.

15. Glenn C. Loury, "Why Are So Many Americans in Prison?" *Boston Review*, July/August 2007.

16. Randall Kennedy, *Race, Crime, and the Law* (New York: Pantheon, 1997), 69–75.

17. John Adams, *Risk* (London: UCL Press, 1995).

18. Cohen et al., "Willingness-to-Pay for Crime Control Programs," *Criminology* 43 (1) (2006): 89–110.

19. Peter Greenwood et al., *Three Strikes You're Out: Estimated Benefits and Costs of California's New Mandatory Sentencing Law* (Santa Monica, Calif.: RAND, 1994).

20. William J. Stuntz, "Law and Disorder: The Case for a Police Surge," *The Weekly Standard* 14 (22), February 22, 2009.

CHAPTER 3: HOPE

1. Mark A. R. Kleiman et al., "Opportunities and Barriers in Probation Reform: A Case Study of Drug Testing and Sanctions" (Berkeley: California Policy Research Center, 2003).

2. John Kaplan, *The Hardest Drug: Heroin and Public Policy* (Chicago: University of Chicago Press, 1985); Robert L. Dupont and Eric D. Wish, "Operation Tripwire Revisited," *Annals of the American Academy of Political and Social Science* 521, 1 (1992):

91–111; Mark A. R. Kleiman, "Coerced Abstinence: A Neo-Paternalist Drug Policy Initiative" in Lawrence Mead, editor, *The New Paternalism* (Washington, D.C.: Brookings Institution Press, 1997); Kleiman, "Controlling Drug Use and Crime with Testing, Sanctions, and Treatment," in *Drug Addiction and Drug Policy: The Struggle to Control Dependence*, edited by Philip B. Heymann and William N. Brownsberger (Cambridge, Mass.: Harvard University Press, 2001).

3. J. J. Gallegher, "Project Sentry Final Program Report" (Lansing, Mich.: Project Sentry, 1996).

4. John A. Carver, "Using Drug Testing to Reduce Detention," *Federal Probation* 57 (1993): 42.

5. Adele Harrell, Shannon Cavanagh, and John Roman, "Final Report: Findings from the Evaluation of the D.C. Superior Court Drug Intervention Program" (Washington, D.C.: Urban Institute, May 1999).

6. Mark Kleiman, David P. Cavanagh, Adele Harrell, and Merle Frank, "Evaluation of the Multnomah County Drug Testing and Evaluation Program," BOTEC Analysis Corporation, February 1995.

7. Angela Hawken and Mark Kleiman, "H.O.P.E. for Reform," *The American Prospect*, April 10, 2007, web only, http://www.prospect.org/cs/articles?article Id=12628.

8. William Bratton and Peter Knobler, *Turnaround: How America's Top Cop Reversed the Crime Epidemic* (New York: Random House, 1998).

9. Steven Lee Myers, "'Squeegees' Rank High on Next Police Commissioner's Priority List," *New York Times*, December 4, 1993; David A. Kaplan, "These Guys Do Windows," *Newsweek*, January 17, 1994, 48.

10. Aric Press, *Piecing Together the System: The Response to Crack* (New York: Bar Association, 1987).

11. Brendan O'Flaherty and Rajiv Sethi, "The Racial Geography of Vice," Columbia University Department of Economics Discussion Paper No. 0809-11, 2008, http://www.columbia.edu/cu/economics/discpapr/DP0809-11.pdf.

12. Mark Kleiman, "Crackdowns: The Effects of Intensive Enforcement on Retail Heroin Dealing," in *Street Level Drug Enforcement: Examining the Issues*, edited by Marcia R. Chaiken (Washington, D.C.: National Institute of Justice, 1988).

13. M. Sviridoff, S. Sadd, R. Curtis, and R. Grinc, *The Neighborhood Effects of Street-Level Drug Enforcement: Tactical Narcotics Teams in New York* (New York: Vera Institute of Justice, 1992).

14. David M. Kennedy, "Reconsidering Deterrence," a report to the Office of Justice Programs, U.S. Department of Justice, December 2003.

15. David M. Kennedy, *Deterrence and Crime Prevention* (Toronto: Routledge, 2009), ch. 7.

CHAPTER 4: TIPPING, DYNAMIC CONCENTRATION, AND THE LOGIC
OF DETERRENCE

1. Thomas C. Schelling, *The Strategy of Conflict* (Cambridge, Mass.: Harvard University Press, 1960).

2. James Joyce, "Bayes' Theorem," *The Stanford Encyclopedia of Philosophy* (Fall 2008 ed.), edited by Edward N. Zalta, http://plato.stanford.edu/archives/fall2008/entries/bayes-theorem/.

3. R. MacCoun, B. Kilmer, and P. Reuter, "Research on Drug Crime Linkages: The Next Generation, Exhibit 1" (commissioned paper), in *Toward a Drugs and Crime Research Agenda for the Twenty-first Century* (National Institute of Justice Special Report, September 2003); J. Caulkins, and R. MacCoun, "Limited Rationality and the Limits of Supply Reduction," *Journal of Drug Issues* 33, 2 (2003): 433–64.

CHAPTER 5: CRIME DESPITE PUNISHMENT

1. Jack Katz, *Seductions of Crime: Moral and Sensual Attractions in Doing Evil* (New York: Basic Books, 1988).

2. Kennedy 2009, ch. 11 ("Listening to Lysistrata").

3. Peter Reuter, Robert J. MacCoun, P. J. Murphy, Allan F. Abrahamse, and Barbara Simon, *Money from Crime: A Study of the Economics of Drug Dealing in Washington, D.C.* (Santa Monica, Calif.: RAND, 1990).

4. Steven D. Levitt and Sudhir Alladi Venkatesh, "An Economic Analysis of a Drug-Selling Gang's Finances," *Quarterly Journal of Economics* 115, 3 (2000): 755–89.

5. John M. Walsh, "Are We There Yet? Measuring Progress in the U.S. War on Drugs in Latin American," *Drug War Monitor*, from the Washington Office on Latin America (December 2004).

6. Daniel Kahneman and Amos Tversky, "Availability: A Heuristic for Judging Frequency and Probability," *Cognitive Psychology* 5 (1973): 207–32.

7. Amos Tversky and Daniel Kahneman, "Judgment under Uncertainty: Heuristics and Biases," *Science* 185, 4157 (September 1974): 1124–31; R. K. MacCoun, "Drugs and the Law: A Psychological Analysis of Drug Prohibition," *Psychological Bulletin* 113 (1993): 497–512; Caulkins and MacCoun 2003.

8. Ola Svenson, "Are We All Less Risky and More Skillful Than Our Fellow Drivers?" *Acta Psychologica* 47, 2 (1981): 143–48; Isabelle Brocas and Juan D. Carillo, "Are We All Better Drivers than Average? Self-Perception and Biased Behaviour," Centre for Economic Policy, October 2002.

9. Maurice Allais and Ole Hagen, eds., *Expected Utility Hypotheses and the Allais Paradox* (Dordrecht, Holland: Reidel, 1979); D. Ellsberg, "Risk, Ambiguity

and the Savage Axioms," *Quarterly Journal of Economics* 75 (Spring 1961): 643–69; J. D. Hey, "Experimental Investigations of Errors in Decision Making under Risk," *European Economic Review* 39 (1995): 633–40; C. Starmer, "Developments in Non-Expected Utility Theory: The Hunt for a Descriptive Theory of Choice under Risk," *Journal of Economic Literature* 38 (2000): 332–82.

10. H. G. Grasmick, C. R. Tittle, R. J. Bursik, and B. J. Arneklev, "Testing the Core Empirical Implications of Gottfredson and Hirschi's General Theory of Crime," *Journal of Research in Crime and Delinquency* 30 (1): 5–29; Douglas Longshore, "Self-Control and Criminal Opportunity: A Prospective Test of the General Theory of Crime," *Social Problems* 45, 1 (1998): 102–13; Hans J. Eysenck, "Personality and Criminality: A Dispositional Analysis," *Advances in Criminological Theory* 1 (1989): 89–110; Richard Herrnstein, "Some Criminogenic Traits of Offenders," in *Crime and Public Policy*, edited by James Q. Wilson (San Francisco: Institute for Contemporary Studies, 1983); J. L. White et al., "Measuring Impulsivity and Examining Its Relationships to Delinquency," *Journal of Abnormal Psychology* 103 (1994): 192–205; James Q. Wilson and Richard J. Herrnstein, *Crime and Human Nature* (New York: Simon and Schuster, 1985).

11. Daniel Kahneman and Amos Tversky, "Availability: A Heuristic for Judging Frequency and Probability," *Cognitive Psychology* 5 (1973): 207–32; and "Prospect Theory and Analysis of Decision under Risk," *Econometrica* 47, 2 (1979): 263–91.

12. B. L. Fredrickson and Daniel Kahneman, "Duration Neglect in Retrospective Evaluations of Affective Episodes," *Journal of Personality and Social Psychology* 65 (1993): 45–55.

13. D. Kahneman, "Objective Happiness," In *Well-Being: Foundations of Hedonic Psychology*, edited by D. Kahneman, E. Diener, and N. Schwarz (New York: Russell Sage Foundation Press, 1999), 3–25; Philip Brickman, Daniel Coates, and Ronnie Janoff-Bulman, "Lottery Winners and Accident Victims: Is Happiness Relative?" *Journal of Personality and Social Psychology* 36, 8 (1978): 917–27.

14. Fredrickson and Kahneman 1993.

15. D. Kahneman and A. Tversky, eds. *Choices, Values and Frames* (New York: Cambridge University Press and the Russell Sage Foundation, 2000).

16. Donald A. Redelmeier and Daniel Kahnemann, "Patients' Memories of Painful Medical Treatments: Real-Time and Retrospective Evaluations of Two Minimally Invasive Procedures," *Pain* 66, 1 (1996): 3–8.

17. Wilson and Herrnstein 1985.

18. Kris N. Kirby and Nancy M. Petry, "Heroin and Cocaine Abusers Have Higher Discount Rates for Delayed Rewards than Alcoholics or Non-drug-using Controls," *Addiction* 99, 4 (2004): 461–71.

19. George Ainslie, "Derivation of 'Rational' Economic Behavior from Hyperbolic Discount Curves," *American Economic Review* 81, 2 (1991): 334–40.

20. Thomas C. Schelling, *Choice and Consequence: Perspectives of an Errant Economist* (Cambridge, Mass.: Harvard University Press, 1984).

21. Warren K. Bickel, Frank J. Chaloupka, Michael Grossman, and Henry Saffer, eds., *The Economic Analysis of Substance Use and Abuse: An Integration of Econometric and Behavioral Economic Research*, National Bureau of Economic Research Conference (NBER-C) Report, 1999.

22. George Loewenstein, "Out of Control: Visceral Influences on Behavior," *Organizational Behavior and Human Decision Processes* 65 (3) (1996): 272–92.

23. Thomas C. Schelling, "Self-Command in Practice, in Policy, and in a Theory of Rational Choice," *American Economic Review* 74 (1984): 1–11.

24. Daniel Nagin and Greg Pogarsky, "Integrating Celerity, Impulsivity, and Extralegal Sanction Threats into a Model of General Deterrence: Theory and Evidence," *Criminology* 39 (2001): 865–92.

25. Philip J. Cook, "The Demand and Supply of Criminal Opportunities," *Crime and Justice* 7 (1980): 1–27.

26. Kennedy 2009, 61; Todd Clear, Dina Rose, Elin Waring, and Kristen Scully, "Coercive Mobility and Crime: A Preliminary Examination of Concentrated Incarceration and Social Disorganization," *Justice Quarterly* 20, 1 (March 2003): 33–64.

27. Ernesto Dal Bó and Marko Tervio, "Self-Esteem, Moral Capital, and Wrongdoing," NBER working paper no. 14508, 2008.

CHAPTER 6: DESIGNING ENFORCEMENT STRATEGIES

1. Schelling 1984.

2. Chaiken and Chaiken 1982. See also Anne Morrison Piehl and John DiIulio, "Returning to the Crime Scene," *Brookings Review* (Winter 1995): 21–24.

3. Peter Greenwood and Allan Abrahamse, *Selective Incapacitation* (Santa Monica, Calif.: RAND, 1982).

4. State of California, Department of Corrections and Rehabilitation, *California Prisoners and Parolees 2007: Summary Statistics on Adult Felon Prisoners and Parolees, Civil Narcotic Addicts and Outpatient and Other Populations*, table 12, p. 22.

5. Peter W. Greenwood, C. Peter Rydell, Allan F. Abrahamse, Jonathan Caulkins, James Chiesa, Karyn Model, and Stephen P. Klein, *Three Strikes and You're Out: Estimated Benefits and Costs of California's New Mandatory-Sentencing Law* (Santa Monica, Calif.: RAND, 1994); *A Primer: Three Strikes—The Impact After More Than a Decade*, California Legislative Analyst's Office, October 2005, http://www.lao.ca.gov/2005/3_Strikes/3_strikes_102005.htm.

6. J. M. Chaiken and M. R. Chaiken, *Who Gets Caught Doing Crime?* (Rockville, Md.: Bureau of Justice Statistics, 1985).

7. William Spelman, *Criminal Incapacitation* (New York: Plenum Press, 1994).

8. Philip J. Cook, "Reducing Injury and Death Rates in Robbery," *Policy Analysis*, 6 (Winter 1980): 21–45.

9. Ibid.

10. Pew Center on the States, "One in 31: The Long Reach of American Corrections" (Washington, D.C.: Pew Charitable Trusts, 2009).

11. Ibid.

12. Kleiman et al. 2003.

13. Stuntz 2009.

14. James Q. Wilson and George L. Kelling, "Broken Windows: The Police and Neighborhood Safety," *Atlantic Monthly* 249, 3 (March 1982): 29–38.

15. George Kelling and Catherine Coles, *Fixing Broken Windows: Restoring Order and Reducing Crime in Our Communities* (New York: Free Press, 1996).

16. Thomas Schelling, "On the Ecology of Micromotives," *Public Interest* 25 (Fall 1971): 61–98.

17. Kees Keizer, Siegwart Lindenberg, and Linda Steg, "The Spreading of Disorder," *Science* 322, 5908 (December 12, 2008): 1681–685.

18. Bernard E. Harcourt and Jens Ludwig, "Broken Windows: New Evidence from New York City and a Five-City Social Experiment," *University of Chicago Law Review* 73 (2006): 271–320.

19. Robert J. Sampson, Stephen Raudenbush, and Felton Earls, "Neighborhoods and Violent Crime: A Multilevel Study of Collective Efficacy," *Science* 277, 5328 (August 15, 1997): 918–24.

20. Kennedy 2009, ch. 9.

21. Mark H. Moore, "Sizing Up Compstat: An Important Administrative Innovation in Policing," *Criminology and Public Policy* 2: 469–94.

22. David M. Kennedy, Anthony A. Braga, Anne M. Piehl, and Elin J. Waring, "Reducing Gun Violence: The Boston's Gun Project's Operation Ceasefire," National Institute of Justice, September 2001.

23. Loïc Wacquant, "Deadly Symbiosis: When Ghetto and Prison Meet and Mesh," *Punishment and Society* 3, 1 (2001): 95–133.

24. Glenn Loury, *The Anatomy of Racial Inequality* (Cambridge, Mass.: Harvard University Press, 2002).

25. William J. Stuntz, "Unequal Justice," *Harvard Law Review* 121 (2008): 1969–2040.

26. John J. Donohue, "Economic Models of Crime and Punishment," *Social Research* 74, 2 (2007): 379–412.

27. Steven D. Levitt and Thomas J. Miles, "The Empirical Study of Criminal Punishment," in *The Handbook of Law and Economics*, edited by A. Mitchell Polinsky and Steven Shavell (2007), 453–95.

28. William Spelman, "What Recent Studies Do (and Don't) Tell Us about Imprisonment and Crime," *Crime and Justice* 27 (2000): 419–94.

29. José A. Canela-Cacho, Alfred Blumstein, and Jacqueline Cohen, "Relationship Between the Offending Frequency (λ) of Imprisoned and Free Offenders," *Criminology* 35, 1 (2006): 133–76.

30. Nagin, "Imprisonment and Reoffending," *Crime and Justice* 31 (forthcoming).

31. Kennedy 2009, 63–65; E. Glaeser, B. Sacerdote, and J. Scheinkman, "Crime and Social Interactions," NBER Working Paper No. 5026, 1995, citing E. L. Glaeser, *Two Essays on Information and Labor Markets*, Ph.D. diss., University of Chicago, 1992.

32. Raymond V. Liedka, Anne Morrison Piehl, and Bert Useem, "The Crime-Control Effect of Incarceration: Does Scale Matter? *Criminology and Public Policy* 5, 2 (2006): 245–76.

33. Bert Useem and Anne Morrison Piehl, *Prison State: The Challenge of Mass Incarceration* (New York: Cambridge University Press, 2008), ch. 3.

34. Bureau of Justice Statistics, *Felony Defendants in Large Urban Counties, 2002*, table 7, http://www.ojp.usdoj.gov/bjs/pub/pdf/fdluc02.pdf.

35. Joan Petersilia, "Community Corrections," in *Crime*, edited by James Q. Wilson and Joan Petersilia (Oakland, Calif.: ICS Press, 2002).

36. Joan Petersilia, Susan Turner, James Kahan, and Joyce Peterson, *Granting Felons Probation: Public Risks and Alternatives* (Santa Monica, Calif.: RAND, 1985).

37. Presentation of Roland Burris, Chief Federal Probation Officer for the Eastern District of Missouri, to the U.S. Sentencing Commission's Seminar on Alternatives to Incarceration, July 14, 2008, http://www.ussc.gov/SYMPO2008/Material/02_FINAL_Overview%20of%20Alternative%20SentencingOptions.pdf.

CHAPTER 7: CRIME CONTROL WITHOUT PUNISHMENT

1. Office of National Drug Control Policy, "National Drug Control Strategy: FY 2003 Budget Summary" (Washington, D.C.: Office of the President, February 2002), table 2, p. 6.

2. Peter Greenwood et al., *Diverting Children from a Life of Crime: Measuring Costs and Benefits* (Santa Monica, Calif.: RAND, 1998).

3. William N. Trumbull, "Who Has Standing in Cost-Benefit Analysis?" *Journal of Policy Analysis and Management* 9, 2 (Spring 1990): 210–12; John Burghardt et al., "Does Job Corps Work? Summary of the National Job Corps Study" (Princeton, N.J.: Mathematica Policy Research, June 2001); Peter Z. Schochet et al., "Does Job Corps Work? Impact Findings from the National Job Corps Study," *American*

Economic Review 98, 5 (December 2008): 1864–86. See also Kevin Barry, "The Job Corps and Crime," unpublished manuscript, UCLA School of Public Affairs, 2008.

4. Anirban Basu, A. David Paltiel, and Harold A. Pollack, "Health Economics, Social Costs of Robbery and the Cost-Effectiveness of Substance Abuse Treatment," *Health Economics* 17 (2008): 927–946.

5. But see Anirban Basu, A. David Paltiel, and Harold A. Pollack, "Social Costs Of Robbery And The Cost-Effectiveness Of Substance Abuse Treatment," *Health Economics* 17 (2008): 927–46.

6. Martha Hansen, Imke Janssen, Adam Schiff, Phyllis C. Zee, and Margarita L. Dubocovich, "The Impact of School Daily Schedule on Adolescent Sleep Pediatrics," *Pediatrics* 115 (2005): 1555–561.

7. Joseph A. Durlak, *Successful Prevention Programs for Children and Adolescents*, (New York: Springer, 1997), 37–38.

8. Jonathan Caulkins et al., *An Ounce of Prevention, A Pound of Uncertainty* (Santa Monica, Calif.: RAND, 1999).

9. S. G. Kellam, G. W. Rebok, N. Ialongo, and L. S. Mayer, "The Course and Malleability of Aggressive Behavior from Early First Grade into Middle School: Results of a Developmental Epidemiologically-Based Preventive Trial," *Journal of Child Psychology and Psychiatry* 35 (1994): 259–81.

10. Richard E. Tremblay and Wendy M. Craig, "Developmental Crime Prevention," *Crime and Justice* 19 (1995): 151–236.

11. David P. Weikart, James T. Bond, and J. T. McNeil, *Ypsilanti Perry Preschool Project: Preschool Years and Longitudinal Results Through Fourth Grade* (Ypsilanti, Mich.: High/Scope Press, 1978).

12. Elena Garces, Duncan Thomas, and Janet Currie, "Longer-Term Effects of Head Start," *American Economic Review* 92, 4 (September 2002): 999–1012. But see John M. Love et al., *Head Start Research: Making a Difference in the Lives of Infants and Toddlers and Their Families: The Impacts of Early Head Start*, Mathematica Policy Research Inc., prepared for the U.S. Department of Health and Human Services, 2002.

13. Monica A. Sweet and Mark I. Appelbaum, "Is Home Visiting an Effective Strategy? A Meta-Analytic Review of Home Visiting Programs for Families with Young Children," *Child Development* 75, 5 (September/October 2005): 1435–456.

14. Garry Mendez, Jr., "Annals of the American Academy of Political and Social Science," *African American Male in American Life and Thought* 569 (May 2000): 101.

15. J. M. Goldenring and E. Cohen, "Getting into Adolescent Heads," *Contemporary Pediatrics* 5 (7) (1988): 75–90; J. M. Goldenring and D. Rosen, "Getting into Adolescent Heads: An Essential Update," *Contemporary Pediatrics* 21 (1) (2004): 64–90.

16. Steven D. Levitt and Sudhir Venkatesh, "An Analysis of the Long-Run Consequences of Gang Involvement," prepared for the Harvard Summer Inequality Institute, National Science Foundation and American Bar Foundation, 2001.

17. David Mechanic and Donna D. McAlpine, "Mission Unfulfilled: Potholes on the Road to Mental Health Parity," *Health Affairs* (September 1999): 7–21.

18. James Gilligan, "The Last Mental Hospital," *Psychiatric Quarterly* 72 (1) (2001): 45–61.

19. H. Richard Lamb and Leona L. Bachrach, "Some Perspectives on Deinstitutionalization," *Psychiatric Services* 52 (August 2001): 1039–45.

20. Susan D. Phillips et al., *Moving Assertive Community Treatment Into Standard Practice*, http://ps.psychiatryonline.org/cgi/content/full/52/6/771#otherarticles.

21. Dina Greenberg, "Fighting The Bullet," University of Pennsylvania Medical Center, *Penn Medicine* 16, 1 (2003): 6–12.

22. Ricardo J. Wray, "Public Health Communication Theory and Strategies for Interpersonal Violence Prevention," *Journal of Aggression, Maltreatment and Trauma* 13 (3/4) (2006), 41–61.

23. B. P. Lanphear, K. Dietrich, P. Auinger, and C. Cox, "Cognitive Deficits Associated with Blood Lead Concentrations <10 microg/dL in U.S. Children and Adolescents," *Public Health Rep.* 115 (2000): 521–29.

24. Herbert L. Needleman et al., "Bone Lead Levels and Delinquent Behavior," *Journal of the American Medical Association* 275, 5 (1996): 363–69.

25. Richard Nevin, "How Lead Exposure Relates to Temporal Changes in IQ, Violent Crime and Unwed Pregnancy," *Environmental Research* 83, 1 (2000): 1–22.

26. Ibid. The article also mentions the benefit in dollars, though it does not mention how much it costs to switch from lead to unleaded.

27. Joel Schwartz, Hugh Pitcher, Ronnie Levin, Bart Ostro, and Albert L. Nichols, *Costs and Benefits of Reducing Lead in Gasoline: Final Regulatory Impact Analysis*, U.S. Environmental Protection Agency, 1985.

28. J. Julian Chisolm, Jr., "The Road to Primary Prevention of Lead Toxicity in Children," *Pediatrics* 102 (1998): 227–29.

29. Ellen K. Silbergeld, "Preventing Lead Poisoning in Children," *Annual Review of Public Health* 18 (1997): 187–210; Herbert L. Needleman, "The Future Challenge of Lead Toxicity," *Environmental Health Perspectives* 89 (1990): 85–89.

30. Nevin 2000.

31. Gary W. Evans, Staffan Hygge, and Monika Buinger, "Chronic Noise and Psychological Stress," *Psychological Science* 6, 6 (1995): 333–38.

32. Eric V. Copage, "Neighborhood Report: Lower East Side; Last of the Midnight Hoops," *New York Times*, August 29, 1999.

CHAPTER 8: GUNS AND GUN CONTROL

1. Franklin E. Zimring, "Is Gun Control Likely to Reduce Violent Killings?" *University of Chicago Law Review* 35 (1968): 21–37; Franklin E. Zimring, "Firearms, Violence, and Public Policy," *Scientific American* 265, 5 (1991): 48–54.

2. Ben Totter, "Outmanned and Outgunned: Miami Officials Unite to End Street 'Arms Race,' " *Miami Sun Post*, February 21, 2008. http://www.miamisunpost.com/archives/2008/02-21/022108newsmiamiweapons.htm.

3. Scott H. Decker and Richard Rosenfeld, "The St. Louis Consent-to-Search Program," National Institute of Justice Research Reports, NCJ 191332, November 2004.

4. Juan Pena-Acosta et al., "Gun Bounty Program: Program Design and Evaluation for the City of Pittsburgh," Heinz School, Carnegie Mellon University, May 1998.

5. David M. Kennedy, Anthony A. Braga, Anne M. Piehl, and Elin J. Waring. *Reducing Gun Violence: The Boston Gun Project's Operation Ceasefire* (Washington, D.C.: National Institute of Justice, 2001). http://www.ncjr.gov/pdffiles1/nij/188741.pdf.

6. Jens Ludwig, "Concealed-Gun-Carrying Laws and Violent Crime: Evidence from State Panel Data," *International Review of Law and Economics* 18 (1998): 239–54.

7. Philip J. Cook and Jens Ludwig, "Aiming for Evidence-Based Gun Policy," *Journal of Policy Analysis and Management* 25, 3 (2007): 691–735.

8. John Lott, *More Guns, Less Crime*, 2nd ed. (Chicago: University of Chicago Press, 2000).

9. Cook and Ludwig, 2007.

10. Gary Kleck and Marc Gertz, "Armed Resistance to Crime: The Prevalence and Nature of Self-Defense with a Gun," *Journal of Criminal Law and Criminology* 86, 1 (1995); David Hemenway, "Survey Research and Self-Defense Gun Use: An Explanation of Extreme Overestimates," *Journal of Criminal Law and Criminology* 87, 4 (Summer 1997): 1430–45; Philip J. Cook and Jens Ludwig, "Guns in America: National Survey on Private Ownership and Use of Firearms," NIJ Research in Brief, National Institute of Justice, May 1997.

11. Philip J. Cook, Jens Ludwig, Sudhir Venkatesh, and Anthony A. Braga, "Underground Gun Markets," *Economic Journal* 117 (November 2007): F1–F29.

12. Philip J. Cook, Jens Ludwig, and Anthony A. Braga, "Criminal Records of Homicide Offenders," *Journal of the American Medical Association* 294, 5 (2005): 598–601.

13. Philip J. Cook and Jens Ludwig, "The Social Costs of Gun Ownership," *Journal of Public Economics* 90, 1–2 (2006): 379–91.

14. Jens Ludwig and Philip J. Cook, "Homicide and Suicide Rates Associated with Implementation of the Brady Handgun Violence Prevention Act," *Journal of the American Medical Association* 284, 5 (2000): 585–91.

15. Mark G. Duggan, "More Guns, More Crime," *Journal of Political Economy* 109 (2001): 1086–114; Cook and Ludwig 2006.

16. John Kaplan, "Controlling Firearms," *Cleveland State Law Review* 28 (1979): 1–28.

17. Fox Butterfield, "The Woman Who Changed the Illegal-Gun Landscape," *New York Times*, December 23, 2000: A12.

18. Sam S. Kamin, "Law and Technology: The Case for a Smart Gun Detector," *Law and Contemporary Problems* 59, 1 (1996): 220–62.

19. Lawrence W. Sherman, James W. Shaw, and Dennis P. Rogan, *The Kansas City Gun Experiment* (Washington, D.C.: National Institute of Justice, 1995).

20. George Orwell, "Wells, Hitler, and the World State," in *Orwell: The Collected Essays, Journalism and Letters*, vol. 3, edited by Sonia Orwell and Ian Angus, *My Country Right or Left* (London: Secker and Warburg, 1968), 139–47. Originally published in *Horizon*, August 1941.

21. Charlton Heston, "The Second Amendment: America's First Freedom," speech delivered at the National Press Club, September 17, 1997, http://www .varmintal.com/heston.htm.

22. "Temperance Address," Springfield, Ill., February 22, 1842, in *The Collected Works of Abraham Lincoln*, vol. 1, edited by Roy P. Basler (New Brunswick, N.J.: Rutgers University Press, 1953).

23. *District of Columbia et al. v. Heller*, 557 U.S, 2008.

24. Eugene Volokh, "The Mechanisms of the Slippery Slope," *Harvard Law Review* 116, 1026 (2003): 1077–114.

CHAPTER 9: DRUG POLICY FOR CRIME CONTROL

1. National Institute of Justice, *1999 Annual Report on Drug Use among Adult and Juvenile Arrestees* (Washington, D.C.: U.S. Department of Justice, 2000).

2. U.S. Department of Justice, *Substance Abuse and Treatment, State and Federal Prisoners*, Bureau of Justice Statistics, NCJ-172871 (Washington, D.C.: U.S. Department of Justice, January 1999).

3. Daniel Cork, "Examining Space-Time Interaction in City-Level Homicide Data: Crack Markets and the Diffusion of Guns among Youth," *Journal of Quantitative Criminology* 15 (1999): 379–406.

4. Office of National Drug Control Policy, *National Drug Control Strategy* (Washington, D.C.: The White House, 1994).

5. Ethan A. Nadelman, "The Case for Legalization," *The Public Interest* 92 (Summer 1988): 3–31.

6. John Stuart Mill, *On Liberty*, ch. 3.

7. *2005 National Survey on Drug Use and Health: National Results*, Substance Abuse and Mental Health Services Administration, U.S. Department of Health and Human Services, http://www.drugabusestatistics.samhsa.gov/NSDUH/2k5NSDUH/2k5results.htm#Ch7.

8. Philip J. Cook, *Paying the Tab: The Costs and Benefits of Alcohol Control* (Princeton, N.J.: Princeton University Press, 2007); Cook 2008.

9. Philip J. Cook and George Tauchen, "The Effect of Liquor Taxes on Heavy Drinking," *Bell Journal of Economics* 13, 2 (1982): 379–90.

10. Philip J. Cook, "A Free Lunch," *Journal of Drug Policy Analysis* 1(1): Article 2.

11. Mark Kleiman, *Against Excess: Drug Policy for Results* (New York: Basic Books, 1992), p. 250.

12. Philip J. Cook, "The Demand and Supply of Criminal Opportunities," in *Crime and Justice* 7 (1986): 1–29.

13. Mark Kleiman, "Reducing the Prevalence of Cocaine and Heroin Dealing among Adolescents," *Valparaiso University Law Review* 31 (2): 551–64; see Reuter et al. 1990, on the prevalence of part-time dealing.

14. Mark Kleiman and David A. Boyum, "Breaking The Drug-Crime Link," *Public Interest* 152 (Summer 2003): 19–38.

15. Boyum and Reuter, *An Analytic Assessment of U.S. Drug Policy* (Washington, D.C.: AEI Press, 2005).

16. John Haaga and Peter Reuter, "Prevention: The (Lauded) Orphan of Drug Policy," in *Handbook on Drug Abuse Prevention*, edited by Robert Coombs and Douglas Ziedonis (Englewood Cliffs, N.J.: Allyn and Bacon, 1995).

17. Caulkins et al. 1999.

18. Kleiman 1997.

19. M. Douglas Anglin and George Speckart, "Narcotics Use, Property Crime and Dealing: Structural Dynamics Across the Addiction Career," *Journal of Quantitative Criminology* 2 (1986): 355–75; David N. Nurco, Thomas E. Hanlon, Timothy W. Kinlock, and Karen R. Duszynski, "Differential Criminal Patterns of Narcotic Addicts over an Addiction Career," *Criminology* 26 (1988): 407–23; M. Douglas Anglin, and Yih-Ing Hser, "Treatment of Drug Abuse," *Crime and Justice* 13 (1990): 393–460.

20. Robert L. Hubbard et al., *Drug Abuse Treatment: A National Study of Effectiveness* (Chapel Hill: University of North Carolina Press, 1989).

21. Gene Heyman, *Addiction: A Disorder of Choice* (Cambridge, Mass.: Harvard University Press, 2009).

22. Susan S. Everingham and C. Peter Rydell, *Controlling Cocaine: Supply Versus Demand Programs* (Santa Monica, Calif.: RAND, 1994).

23. Douglas Longshore et al., "Evaluation of the Substance Abuse and Crime Prevention Act: Cost Analysis Report (first and second years)," UCLA Integrated Substance Abuse Programs (April 5, 2006), p. 34.

24. Ibid.

25. National Institute of Justice, *Drug Courts: The Second Decade* (Washington, D.C.: U.S. Department of Justice, 2006).

26. C. W. Huddleston, III., D. Marlowe, and R. Casebolt, *Painting the Current Picture: A National Report Card on Drug Courts and Other Problem-Solving Court Programs in the United States* (Washington, D.C.: National Drug Court Institute, 2008).

27. Kleiman 1997.

BIBLIOGRAPHY

Adams, John. 1995. *Risk*. London: UCL Press.

Ainslie, George. 1991. "Derivation of 'Rational' Economic Behavior from Hyperbolic Discount Curves." *American Economic Review* 81 (2): 334–40.

Ali, R., et al. 1999. "Report of the External Panel on the Evaluation of the Swiss Scientific Studies of Medically Prescribed Narcotics to Drug Addicts." *Sucht* 45: 160–70.

Allais, Maurice, and Ole Hagen, eds. 1979. *Expected Utility Hypotheses and the Allais Paradox*. Dordrecht, Holland: Reidel.

Anglin, M. Douglas, and Y.h-Ing, Hses. 1990. "Treatment of Drug Abuse," *Crime and Justice* 13: 393–460.

Anglin, M. Douglas, and George Speckart. 1986. "Narcotics Use, Property Crime and Dealing: Structural Dynamics Across the Addiction Career." *Journal of Quantitative Criminology* 2: 355–75.

Aos, Steve, Marna Miller, and Elizabeth Drake. 2006. *Evidence-Based Public Policy Options to Reduce Future Prison Construction, Criminal Justice Costs, and Crime Rates*. Olympia: Washington State Institute for Public Policy.

Balko, Radley. 2006. *Overkill: The Rise of Paramilitary Police Raids in America*. Washington, D.C.: Cato Institute.

Barry, Kevin. 2008. "The Job Corps and Crime." Unpublished manuscript, UCLA School of Public Affairs.

Basu, Anirban, A. Daniel Paltiel, and Harold A. Pollack. 2008. "Health Economics, Social Costs of Robbery and the Cost-Effectiveness of Substance Abuse Treatment." *Health Economics* 17: 927–46.

Bazos, Audrey, and Jessica Hausman. 2003. "Correctional Education as a Crime Control Program." Applied Policy Project, UCLA School of Public Affairs.

Beccaria, Cesare. 1764/1986. *On Crimes and Punishments*. Translated from the Italian in the author's original order, with notes and introduction by David Young. Indianapolis, Ind.: Hackett.

Becker, Gary, and William Landes. 1974. *Essays in the Economics of Crime and Punishment*. New York: Columbia University Press.

Bentham, Jeremy. 1830. *The Rationale of Punishment*. London: R. Heward.

Berkowitz, Leonard, and Jacqueline Macaulay. 1971. "The Contagion of Criminal Violence." *Sociometry* 34 (2): 238–60.

Bickel, Warren K., Frank J. Chaloupka, Michael Grossman, and Henry Saffer, eds. 1999. "The Economic Analysis of Substance Use and Abuse: An

Integration of Econometric and Behavioral Economic Research." National Bureau of Economic Research Conference (NBER-C) report.

Bilz, Kenworthy. 2007. "The Puzzle of Delegated Revenge." *Boston University Law Review* 87: 1059–112.

Blumstein, Alfred. 1995. "Youth-Violence, Guns, and the Illicit-Drug Industry." *Journal of Criminal Law and Criminology* 86: 26–29.

Blumstein, Alfred, and Allen J. Beck. 2005. "Reentry as a Transient State between Liberty and Recommitment." In *Prisoner Reentry and Crime in America*, edited by Jeremy Travis and Christy Visher. New York: Cambridge University Press.

Blumstein, Alfred, Jacqueline Cohen, Jeffrey A. Roth, and Christy A. Visher, eds. 1986. *Criminal Careers and "Career Criminals,"* vol. 1. Washington, D.C.: National Academies Press.

Blumstein, Alfred, and Daniel Nagin. 1978. "On the Optimum Use of Incarceration for Crime Control." *Operations Research* 26 (3): 381–405.

Blumstein, Alfred, and Joel Wallman. 2000. *The Crime Drop in America*. New York: Cambridge University Press.

———. 2006. "The Crime Drop and Beyond." *Annual Review of Law and Social Science* 2: 125–46.

Boyum, D. A. 1992. "Reflections on Economic Theory and Drug Enforcement." Ph.D. diss., Harvard University.

Boyum, David, and Peter Reuter. 2005. *An Analytic Assessment of U.S. Drug Policy*. Washington, D.C.: AEI Press.

Braga, Anthony A. 2005. "Hot Spots Policing and Crime Prevention: A Systematic Review of Randomized Controlled Trials." *Journal of Experimental Criminology* 1: 317–42.

Bratton, William, and Peter Knobler. 1998. *The Turnaround: How America's Top Cop Reversed the Crime Epidemic*. New York: Random House.

Brickman, Philip, Daniel Coates, and Ronnie Janoff-Bulman. 1978. "Lottery Winners and Accident Victims: Is Happiness Relative?" *Journal of Personality and Social Psychology* 36 (8): 917–27.

Brocas, Isabelle, and Juan D. Carillo. 2002. "Are We All Better Drivers Than Average? Self-Perception and Biased Behaviour." Centre for Economic Policy. October.

Bureau of Justice Statistics. 2000. "Correctional Populations in the United States, 1997." Office of Justice Programs, U.S. Department of Justice. NCJ 177614.

———. 2005. "Homicide Trends in the U.S.—Trends By Race." U.S. Department of Justice.

———. 2001. *Prison and Jail Inmates at Mid-Year.*

———. 1991. *Profile of Jail Inmates.*

———. 2005. *Sourcebook of Criminal Justice Statistics Online,* http://www.albany.edu/sourcebook/pdf/t122005.pdf.

———. 1996. *Survey of State Prison Inmates.*

Burghardt, John, et al. 2001. "Does Job Corps Work?" Summary of the National Job Corps Study. Princeton, N.J.: Mathematica Policy Research, Inc.

Burke, Peggy. 1997. "Policy-Driven Responses to Probation and Parole Violations." Silver Spring, Md.: Center for Effective Public Policy.

Butterfield, Fox. 2005. "Guns and Jeers Used by Gangs to Buy Silence." *New York Times,* January 16.

———. 2000. "The Woman Who Changed the Illegal-Gun Landscape." *New York Times,* December 23, A12.

Canela-Cacho, José A., Alfred Blumstein, and Jacqueline Cohen. 2006. "Relationship Between the Offending Frequency (λ) of Imprisoned And Free Offenders." *Criminology* 35 (1): 133–76.

Carver, John A. 1993. "Using Drug Testing to Reduce Detention." *Federal Probation* 57: 42.

Catalano, Shannan M. 2004. *Criminal Victimization, 2003.* National Crime Victimization Survey, Bureau of Justice Statistics, U.S. Department of Justice, NCJ 205455.

Caulkins, Jonathan P. 1990. "The Distribution and Consumption of Illicit Drugs: Some Mathematical Models and Their Policy Implications." Ph.D. diss., MIT.

Caulkins, Jonathan P., Susan S. Everingham, C. Peter Rydell, James Chiesa, and Shawn Bushway. 1999. *An Ounce of Prevention, a Pound of Uncertainty: The Cost Effectiveness of School Based Drug Prevention Programs.* Santa Monica, Calif.: RAND.

Caulkins, J., and R. MacCoun. 2003. "Limited Rationality and the Limits of Supply Reduction." *Journal of Drug Issues* 33: 433–64.

Cavanagh, D. P. ,and A. Harrell. 1995. "Evaluation of the Multnomah County Drug Testing and Evaluation Program." Final report to the National Institute of Justice. Cambridge: BOTEC Analysis Corporation.

Center for Disease Control and Prevention. "Poisoning in the United States: Fact Sheet." U.S. Department of Health and Human Services.

Chaiken, J. M., and M. R. Chaiken. 1982. *Varieties of Criminal Behavior.* Santa Monica, Calif.: RAND.

———. 1995. "Returning to the Crime Scene." *Brookings Review* (Winter): 21–24.

Chisholm, J. Julian, Jr. "The Road in Primary Prevention of Lead Toxicity in Children." *Pediatrics.* http://pediatrics.aappublications.org/cgi/content/full/107/3/581.

Clear, Todd, Dina Rose, Elin Waring, and Kristen Scully. 2003. "Coercive Mobility and Crime: A Preliminary Examination of Concentrated Incarceration and Social Disorganization," *Justice Quarterly* 20 (1): 33–64.

Cohen, Mark A., Roland T. Rust, and Sara Steen. 2003. "Measuring Public Perceptions of Appropriate Prison Sentences." Executive Summary, National Institute of Justice. April. http://www.ncjrs.gov/pdfillliles1/nij/grants/199364.pdf.

Cohen, Mark A., Roland T. Rust, Sara Steen, and Simon T. Tidd. 2006. "Willingness-to-Pay for Crime Control Programs. *Criminology* 43 (1): 89–110. March.

Coleman, James. 1988. "Social Capital in the Creation of Human Capital." *American Journal of Sociology* supplement 94: S95–S120.

Cook, Philip J. 2008. "A Free Lunch." *Journal of Drug Policy Analysis* 1 (1): Article 2.

———. 2008. "Assessing Urban Crime and Its Control: An Overview." NBER working paper no. W13781. February.

———. 2007. *Paying the Tab: The Costs and Benefits of Alcohol Control.* Princeton, N.J.: Princeton University Press.

———. 1977. "Punishment and Crime: A Critique of Current Findings Concerning the Preventive Effects of Punishment." *Law and Contemporary Problems* 41 (1): 164–204.

———. 1980. "Reducing Injury and Death Rates in Robbery." *Policy Analysis* (Winter): 21–45.

———. 1986. "The Demand and Supply of Criminal Opportunities." *Crime and Justice* 7: 1–27.

Cook, Philip J., and John H. Laub. 2002. "After the Epidemic: Recent Trends in Youth Violence in the United States." In *Crime and Justice: A Review of Research*, edited by Michael Tonry. Chicago: University of Chicago Press, 117–53.

Cook, Philip J., and Jens Ludwig. 2007. "Aiming for Evidenced-based Gun Policy." *Journal of Policy Analysis and Management* 25 (3): 691–735.

———. 2006. "The Social Costs of Gun Ownership." *Journal of Public Economics* 90 (1–2): 379–91.

Cook, Philip J., Jens Ludwig, and Anthony A. Braga. 2005. "Criminal Records of Homicide Offenders." *Journal of the American Medical Association* 294 (5): 598–601.

Cook, Philip J., Jens Ludwig, Sudhir Venkatesh, and Anthony A. Braga. 2007. "Underground Gun Markets." *Economic Journal* 117: F1–F29.

Cook, Philip J., and George Tauchen. 1982. "The Effect of Liquor Taxes on Heavy Drinking." *Bell Journal of Economics* 13 (2): 379–90.

Copagne, Eric V. 1999. "Neighborhood Report: Lower East Side; Last of the Midnight Hoops." *New York Times*, August 29.

Core Health Indicators: United States of America. 2007. *WHO Statistical Information System*, World Health Organization.

Cork, Daniel. 1999. "Examining Space-Time Interaction in City-Level Homicide Data: Crack Markets and the Diffusion of Guns among Youth." *Journal of Quantitative Criminology* 15: 379–40.

Crime in the United States. 2005. "Uniform Crime Reporting Program." U.S. Department of Justice, Federal Bureau of Investigation.

Dal Bó, Ernesto, and Marko Tervio. 2008. "Self-Esteem, Moral Capital and Wrongdoing." NBER working paper no. 14508.

Decker, Scott H., and Richard Rosenfeld. 2004. "The St. Louis Consent-to-Search Program." National Institute of Justice Reports, NCJ 191332. November.

Diamond, Peter. 1982. "Aggregate Demand Management in Search Equilibrium." *Journal of Political Economy* 90 (5): 881–94.

DiIulio, John. 1998. "Reinventing Probation and Parole." *Brookings Review* 16 (4): 40–42.

DiIulio, John, Jr., and Ann Morrison Piehl. 1991. "Does Prison Pay? The Stormy National Debate over the Cost-Effectiveness of Imprisonment." *Brookings Review* 9 (4): 28–35.

DiNardo, James. 1985. *Power in Numbers. The Political Strategy of Protest and Rebellion*. Princeton, N.J.: Princeton University Press.

District of Columbia et al. v. Heller, No. 07–290. Argued March 18, 2008; decided June 26, 2008.

Donohue, John J. 2007. "Economic Models of Crime and Punishment." *Social Research* 74 (2): 379–412.

Donohue, John J., and Jens Ludwig. 2007. "More COPS." Policy brief no. 158. Washington, D.C.: Brookings Institution.

Donohue, John J., and Peter Siegelman. 1998. "Allocating Resources among Prisons and Social Programs in the Battle Against Crime." *Journal of Legal Studies* 27: 1–43.

Doob, Anthony N., and Glenn E. Macdonald. 1979. "Television Viewing and Fear of Victimization: Is the Relationship Causal?" *Journal of Personality and Social Psychology* 37: 170–79.

Dupont, Robert L., and Eric D. Wish. 1992. "Operation Tripwire Revisited." *Annals of the American Academy of Political and Social Science* 521 (1): 91–111.

Duggan, Mark G. 2001. "More Guns, More Crime." *Journal of Political Economy* 109: 1086–114.

Durlak, Joseph A. 1997. *Successful Prevention Programs for Children and Adolescents.* New York: Springer.

Easterlin, Richard A. 1987. *Birth and Fortune: The Impact of Numbers on Personal Welfare.* Chicago: University of Chicago Press.

Ehrlich, Isaac. 1974. "Participation in Illegitimate Activities: An Economic Analysis." In *Essays in the Economics of Crime and Punishment,* edited by Gary S. Becker and William M. Landes. New York: National Bureau of Economic Research.

Ellsberg, D. 1961. "Risk, Ambiguity and the Savage Axioms." *Quarterly Journal of Economics* 75 (Spring): 643–69.

Evans, Gary W., Staffan Hygge, and Monika BuUinger. 1995. "Chronic Noise and Psychological Stress." *Psychological Science* 6 (6): 333–38.

Everingham, Susan S., and C. Peter Rydell. 1994. *"Controlling Cocaine: Supply Versus Demand Programs."* (Santa Monica, Calif.: RAND).

Eysenck, Hans J. 1989. "Personality and Criminality: A Dispositional Analysis." *Advances in Criminological Theory* 1:89–110.

Farrel, M., and W. Hall. 1998. "The Swiss Heroin Trials: Testing Alternative Approaches." *British Medical Journal* 316: 639.

Federal Bureau of Investigation. 2001. "Uniform Crime Reports."

Fredrickson, B. L., and Daniel Kahneman. 1993. "Duration Neglect in Retrospective Evaluations of Affective Episodes." *Journal of Personality and Social Psychology* 65: 45–55.

Freeman, Scott, Jeffrey Grogger, and Jon Sonstelie. 1996. "The Spatial Concentration of Crime." *Journal of Urban Economics* 40 (September): 216–31.

Gallegher, J. J. 1996. "Project Sentry Final Program Reporting." Lansing, Mich.: Project Sentry.

Gawande, Atul. 2009. "Hellhole." *New Yorker,* March 25. http://www .newyorker.com/reporting/2009/03/30/090330fa_fact_gawande?yrail.

Gilligan, James. 2001. "The Last Hospital." *Psychiatric Quarterly* 72 (1): 45–61.

Gladwell, Malcolm. 2002. *The Tipping Point: How Little Things Can Make a Big Difference.* Boston: Little, Brown.

Glaeser, E., B. Sacerdote, and J. Scheinkman. 1995. "Crime and Social Interactions." NBER working paper no. 5026, citing E. L. Glaeser, "Two Essays on Information and Labor Markets," Ph.D. diss., University of Chicago, 1992.

Glaze, Lauren, and Seri Palla. 2004. "Probation and Parole in the United States, 2003." Bureau of Justice Statistics Bulletin NCJ 205336.

Godine, David R. 1941. *Horizon* 4 (20): 133–39.

Goldenring, J. M., and E. Cohen. 1988. "Getting into Adolescent Heads." *Contemporary Pediatrics* 5 (7): 75–90.

Goldenring, J. M., and D. Rosen. 2004. "Getting into Adolescent Heads: An Essential Update." *Contemporary Pediatrics* 21 (1): 64–90.

Grasmick, H. G., C. R. Tittle, R. J. Bursik, and B. J. Arneklev. 1993. "Testing the Core Empirical Implications of Gottfredson and Hirschi's General Theory of Crime." *Journal of Research in Crime and Delinquency* 30 (1): 5–29.

Greenberg, Dina. 2003. "Fighting the Bullet." University of Pennsylvania Medical Center, *Penn Medicine* 16 (1): 6–12.

Greenwood, Peter, C. Peter Rydell, Allan F. Abrahamse, Jonathan Caulkins, James Chiesa, Karyn Model, and Stephen P. Klein. 1994. *Three Strikes You're Out: Estimated Benefits and Costs of California's New Mandatory Sentencing Law*. Santa Monica, Calif.: RAND.

Greenwood, Peter, and Allan Abrahamse. 1982. *Selective Incapacitation*. Santa Monica, Calif.: RAND.

Greenwood, Peter, et al. 1998. *Diverting Children from a Life of Crime: Measuring Costs and Benefits*. Santa Monica, Calif.: RAND.

Grodzins, Morton. 1958. *The Metropolitan Area as a Racial Problem*. Pittsburgh: University of Pittsburgh Press.

Grogger, Jeffrey. 1992. "Arrests, Persistent Youth Joblessness, and Black/White Employment Differentials." *Review of Economics and Statistics* 74: 100–106.

Haaga, John, and Peter Reuter. 1995. "Prevention: The (Lauded) Orphan of Drug Policy." In *Handbook on Drug Abuse Prevention*, edited by Robert Coombs and Douglas Ziedonis. Englewood Cliffs, N.J.: Allyn and Bacon.

Hanlon, E., Timothy W. Kinlock, and Karen R. Duszynski. 1988. "Differential Criminal Patterns of Narcotic Addicts over an Addiction Career." *Criminology* 26: 407–23.

Hansen, Martha, Imke Janssen, Adam Schiff, Phyllis C. Zee, and Margarita L. Dubocovich. 2005. "The Impact of School Daily Schedule on Adolescent Sleep Pediatrics." *Pediatrics* 115 (6): 1555–561.

Harcourt, Bernard E. 2006. "From the Asylum to the Prisons: Rethinking the Incarceration Revolution." *Texas Law Review* 84: 1751–86.

Harcourt, Bernard E., and Jens Ludwig. 2006. "Broken Windows: New Evidence from New York City and a Five-City Social Experiment." *University of Chicago Law Review* 73: 271–320.

Harrell, Adele, William Adams, and Caterian Gouvis Roman. 1994. "Evaluation of the Impact of Systemwide Drug Testing in Multnomah County, Oregon." Research report. April.

Harrell, Adele, Shannon Cavanagh, and John Roman. 1999. "Final Report: Findings from the Evaluation of the D.C. Superior Court Drug Intervention Program." Washington, D.C.: Urban Institute.

Hawken, Angela, and Mark Kleiman. 2007. "H.O.P.E. for Reform." *The American Prospect*, April 10. http://www.prospect.org/cs/articles?article?articleId =12628.

Hemenway, David. 1997. "Survey Research and Self-Defense Gun Use: An Explanation of Extreme Overestimates." *Journal of Criminal Law and Criminology* 87 (4): 1430–45.

Herrnstein, Richard. 1983. "Some Criminogenic Traits of Offenders." In *Crime and Public Policy*, edited by James Q. Wilson. San Francisco: Institute for Contemporary Studies.

Heston, Charlton. 1997. "The Second Amendment: America's First Freedom," speech delivered at the National Press Club, September 17. http://www .varmintal.com/heston.htm.

Hey, J. D. 1995. "Experimental Investigations of Errors in Decision Making Under Risk." *European Economic Review* 39: 633–40.

Heyman, Gene M. 2009. *Addiction: A Disorder of Choice*. Cambridge, Mass.: Harvard University Press.

Holzer, Harry J., Steven Raphael, and Michael A. Stoll. 2003. "Employment Dimensions of Reentry: Understanding the Nexus between Prisoner Reentry and Work." Paper presented at Urban Institute Reentry Roundtable, May, New York.

Howard, Ronald A. 1980. "On Making Life and Death Decisions." In *Societal Risk Assessment: How Safe Is Safe Enough?* edited by Richard C. Schwing and Walter A. Albers, Jr. New York: Plenum Press.

Hubbard, Robert L., et al. 1989. *Drug Abuse Treatment: A National Study of Effectiveness*. Chapel Hill: University of North Carolina Press.

Huddleston, C. W. III., D. Marlowe, and R. Casebolt. 2008. *Painting the Current Picture: A National Report Card on Drug Courts and Other Problem-Solving Court Programs in the United States*. Washington, D.C.: National Drug Court Institute.

Inciardi, James A. 1996. "Corrections-Based Continuum of Effective Drug Abuse." Research brief. Washington, D.C.: U.S. Department of Justice, National Institute of Justice.

Joyce, James. 2008. "Bayes' Theorem." In *The Stanford Encyclopedia of Philosophy*, edited by Edward N. Zalta. Fall. http://plato.stanford.edu/archives/ fall2008/entries/bayes-theorem.

Kahneman, Daniel, and Amos Tversky. 1992. "Advances in Prospect Theory: Cumulative Representation of Uncertainty." *Journal of Risk and Uncertainty* 5: 297–323.

———. 1973. "Availability: A Heuristic for Judging Frequency and Probability." *Cognitive Psychology* 5: 207–32.

———, eds. 2000. *Choices, Values and Frames*. New York: Cambridge University Press and Russell Sage Foundation Press.

———. 1999. "Objective Happiness." In *Well-Being: Foundations of Hedonic Psychology*, edited by D. Kahneman, E. Diener, and N. Schwarz. New York: Russell Sage Foundation Press.

———. 1979. "Prospect Theory and Analysis of Decision under Risk." *Econometrica* 47 (2): 263–91.

Kamin, S. 1996. "Law and Technology: The Case for a Smart Gun Detective." *Law and Contemporary Problems* 59 (1): 220–62.

Kaplan, David A. 1994. "These Guys Do Windows." *Newsweek* 48 (January 17).

Kaplan, John. 1979. "Controlling Firearms." *Cleveland State Law Review* 28: 1–28.

———. 1985. *The Hardest Drug: Heroin and Public Policy*. Chicago: University of Chicago Press.

Katz, Jack. 1988. *Seductions of Crime: Moral and Sensual Attractions in Doing Evil*. New York: Basic Books.

Keizer, Kees, Siegwart Lindenberg, and Linda Steg. 2008. "The Spreading of Disorder," *Science* 322, 5908: 1681–86.

Kellam, S. G., G. W. Rebok, N. Ialongo, and L. S. Mayer. 1994. "The Course and Malleability of Aggressive Behavior from Early First Grade into Middle School: Results of a Development Epidemiologically-Based Preventive Trial." *Journal of Child Psychology and Psychiatry* 35: 259–81.

Kelling, George, and Catherine Coles. 1996. *Fixing Broken Windows: Restoring Order and Reducing Crime in Our Communities*. New York: Free Press.

Kelling, George, and James Wilson. 1982. "Broken Windows: The Police and Neighborhood Safety." *Atlantic Monthly* 249 (3): 29–38.

Kennedy, David M. 1997. "Pulling Levers: Chronic Offenders, High-Crime Settings, and a Theory of Prevention." *Valparaiso University Law Review* 31, 2 (Spring): 449–84.

Kennedy, David M. 1998. "Pulling Levers: Getting Deterrence Right." *National Institute of Justice Journal* 236 (July).

Kennedy, David M., Anthony A. Braga, Anne M. Piehl, and Elin J. Waring. 2001. *Reducing Gun Violence: The Boston Gun Project's Operation Ceasefire*. Washington, D.C.: National Institute of Justice. http://www.ncjrs.gov/pdffiles1/nij/188741.pdf.

Kennedy, David M. 2003. "Reconsidering Deterrence." A Report to the Office of Justice Programs. U.S. Department of Justice. December.

Kennedy, David M. 2009. *Deterrence and Crime Prevention: Reconsidering the Prospect of Sanction*. Toronto: Routledge.

Kennedy, Randall. 1997. *Race, Crime, and the Law*. New York: Pantheon.

Kerner Commission. 1968. *Report of the National Advisory Commission on Civil Disorders*. Washington, D.C.: U.S. Government Printing Office.

Kleck, Gary, and Marc Gertz. 1995. "Armed Resistance to Crime: The Prevalence and Nature of Self-Defense with a Gun." *Journal of Criminal Law and Criminology* 86 (1): 150–87. http://guncite.com/gcdgklec.html.

Kleiman, Mark. 1992a. *Against Excess: Drug Policy for Results*. New York: Basic Books.

———. 1997b. "Coerced Abstinence: A Neopaternalist Drug Policy Initiative." In *The New Paternalism*, edited by Lawrence M. Mead. Washington, D.C.: Brookings Institution.

———. 2001. "Controlling drug use and crime with testing, sanctions, and treatment." In *Drug Addiction and Drug Policy: The Struggle to Control Dependence*, edited by Philip B. Heymann and William N. Brownsberger. Cambridge, Mass.: Harvard University Press.

———. 1988a. "Crackdowns: The Effects of Intensive Enforcement on Retail Heroin Dealing." In *Street Level Drug Enforcement: Examining the Issues*, edited by Marcia R. Chaiken. Washington, D.C.: National Institute of Justice.

———. 1993. "Enforcement Swamping: A Positive-Feedback Mechanism in Rates of Illicit Activity." *Mathematical and Computer Modeling* 17 (2): 65–75.

———. 2003. "Faith-Based Fudging: How a Bush-Promoted Christian Prison Program Fakes Success by Massaging Data." Slate.com. August.

———. 1988b. *Imprisonment-to-Offense Ratios*. BOTEC Analysis Corporation.

———. 1989. *Marijuana: Costs of Abuse, Costs of Control*. Greenwich, Conn.: Greenwood Press.

———. 1992b. "Neither Prohibition Nor Legalization: Grudging Toleration in Drug Control Policy." *Daedalus* 121 (3): 353–83.

———. 1987. "The Punishment Deficit and the Prosecutor's Job." Kennedy School working paper no. 87-02-01.

———. 1997a. "Reducing the Prevalence of Cocaine and Heroin Dealing among Adolescents." *Valparaiso University Law Review* 31 (2): 551–64.

Kleiman, Mark, and David A. Boyum. 2003. "Breaking the Drug-Crime Link." *Public Interest* 152 (Summer): 19–38.

Kleiman, Mark, and David P. Cavanagh. 1990. *Cost Benefit Analysis of Prison Cell Construction and Alternative Sanctions*. BOTEC Analysis Corporation, prepared for the National Institute of Justice.

Kleiman, Mark, David P. Cavanagh, Adele Harrell, and Merle Frank. 1995. *Evaluation of the Multnomah County Drug Testing and Evaluation Program*. BOTEC Analysis Corporation. February.

Kleiman, Mark A. R., Thomas H. Tran, Paul Fishbein, Maria-Teresa Magula, Warren Allen, and Gareth Lacy. 2003. "Opportunities and Barriers in Probation Reform: A Case Study of Drug Testing and Sanctions." Berkeley: California Policy Research Center. http://www.ucop.edu/cprc/documents/sanctionsrpt.pdf.

Kirby, Kris N., and Nancy M. Petry. 2004. "Heroin and Cocaine Abusers Have Higher Discount Rates for Delayed Rewards than Alcoholics or Non-drug-using Controls." *Addiction* 99 (4): 461–71.

Kung, Hsiang-Ching, Donna L. Hoyert, Jiaguan Xu, and Sherry L. Murphy. 2008. *National Vital Statistics Report*. Center for Disease Control and Prevention, 56 (10) (April).

Laffont, Jean-Jacque, and Jean Tirole. 1991. "Decision-Making: A Theory of Regulatory Capture." *Quarterly Journal of Economics* 106, 4 (November): 1089–127.

Lamb, Richard H., and Leona L. Bachrach. 2001. "Some Perspectives on Deinstitutionalization." *Psychiatric Services* 52 (August): 1039–45.

Lanphear, B. P., K. Dietrich, P. Auinger, and C. Cox. 2000. "Cognitive Deficits Associated with Blood Lead Concentration in U.S. Children and Adolescents." *Public Health Rep.* 115: 521–29.

Levitt, Steven D., and Thomas J. Miles. 2007. "The Empirical Study of Criminal Punishment." In *The Handbook of Law and Economics*, vol. 1, edited by A. Mitchell Polinsky and Steven Shavell. Amsterdam: North-Holland.

Levitt, Steven D., and Sudhir Alladi Venkatesh. 2000. "An Economic Analysis of a Drug-Selling Gang's Finances." *Quarterly Journal of Economics* 115 (3): 755–89.

Liedka, Raymond V., Anne Morrison Piehl, and Bert Useem. 2006. "The Crime-Control Effect of Incarceration: Does Scale Matter?" *Criminology and Public Policy* 5 (2): 245–76.

Lincoln, Abraham. 1842/1953. "Temperance Address." In *The Collected Works of Abraham Lincoln*, vol. 1, edited by Roy P. Basler. New Brunswick, N.J.: Rutgers University Press.

Lochner, Lance, and Enrico Moretti. 2004. "The Effect of Education on Crime: Evidence from Prisoner Inmates, Arrests, and Self-Reports." *American Economic Review* 94, 1 (March): 155–89.

Loewenstein, George. 1996. "Out of Control: Visceral Influences on Behavior." *Organizational Behavior and Human Decision Processes* 65 (3): 272–92.

Longshore, Douglas. 1998. "Self-Control and Criminal Opportunity: A Prospective Test of the General Theory of Crime." *Social Problems* 45 (1): 102–13.

Longshore, Douglas, et al. 2006. *Evaluation of the Substance Abuse and Crime Prevention Act: Cost Analysis Report*. UCLA Integrated Substance Abuse Programs. P. 34. April 5.

Lott, John. 2000. *More Guns, Less Crime*. 2nd ed. Chicago: University of Chicago Press.

Loury, Glenn. 2002. *The Anatomy of Racial Inequality*. Cambridge, Mass.: Harvard University Press.

Loury, Glenn C. 1977. "A Dynamic Theory of Racial Income Differences." In *Women, Minorities, and Employment Discrimination*, edited by P. A. Wallace and A. M. La Mond. Lexington, Mass: Heath, 153–86.

———. 2007. "Why Are so Many Americans in Prison?" *Boston Review*, July/August.

Loury, Glenn, Pamela Karlan, Loic Wacquant, and Tommie Shelby. 2008. *Race, Incarceration, and American Values*. A Boston review book. Cambridge, Mass.: MIT Press.

Love, John M., et al. 2002. *Head Start Research: Making a Difference in the Lives of Infants and Toddlers and Their Families: The Impacts of Early Head Start*. Mathematica Policy Research Inc., prepared for the U.S. Department of Health and Human Services.

Ludwig, Jens. 1998. "Concealed-Gun-Carrying Laws and Violent Crime: Evidence from State Panel Data." *International Review of Law and Economics* 18: 239–54.

———. 2006. "The Costs of Crime." Testimony. United States Committee on the Judiciary, September 19.

Ludwig, Jens, and Philip J. Cook. 2001. "The Benefits of Reducing Gun Violence: Evidence from Contingent-Valuation Survey Data." *Journal of Risk and Uncertainty* 22, 3 (2001): 207–26.

———. 2000. "Homicide and Suicide Rates Associated with Implementation of the Brady Handgun Violence Prevention Act." *Journal of the American Medical Association* 284 (5): 585–91.

MacCoun, R. J. 1993. "Drugs and the Law: A Psychological Analysis of Drug Prohibition." *Psychological Bulletin* 113: 497–512.

MacCoun, R., B. Kilmer, and P. Reuter. 2003. "Research on drug crime linkages: The next generation, Exhibit 1. Toward a drugs and crime research agenda for the Twenty-first Century." National Institute of Justice Special Report.

MacCoun, Robert J., and Peter Reuter. 2001. *Drug War Heresies: Learning from Other Vices, Times, and Places*. Cambridge: Cambridge University Press.

Manski, Charles R., John V. Pepper, and Carol V. Petrie, eds. 2001. *Informing America's Policy on Illegal Drugs: What We Don't Know Keeps Hurting Us*. Washington, D.C.: National Academy Press.

Martinson, Robert. 1974. "What Works—Questions and Answers about Prison Reform." *Public Interest* 35, 22 (Spring): 22–54.

Mechanic, David, and Donna D. McAlpine. 1999. "Mission Unfulfilled: Potholes on the Road to Mental Health Parity." *Health Affairs* (September): 53–69.

Mendez, Garry, Jr. 2000. "Annals of the America Academy of Political and Social Science." *African Male in American Life and Thought* 569: 101.

Mill, John Stuart. 1859. *On Liberty.*

Moore, M. H. 1995. *Creating Public Value: Strategic Management in Government.* Cambridge, Mass.: Harvard University Press.

Moore, Mark H. 2006. "Sizing Up Compstat: An Important Administrative Innovation in Policing." *Criminology and Public Policy* 2: 469–94.

Moore, Mark H., Susan Estrich, Daniel McGillis, and William Spelman. 1985. *Dangerous Offenders: The Elusive Target of Justice.* Cambridge, Mass.: Harvard University Press.

Myers, Steven Lee. 1993. " 'Squeegees' Rank High on Next Police Commissioner's Priority List." *New York Times*, December 4.

Nadelman, Ethan A. 1988. "The Case for Legalization." *Public Interest* 92 (Summer): 3–31.

Nagin, Daniel S., Francis T. Cullen, and Cheryl Lero Jonson. 2009. "Imprisonment and Reoffending." *Crime and Justice* 38 (forthcoming).

Nagin Daniel S., and Kenneth C. Land. 2006. "Age, Criminal Careers, and Population Heterogeneity: Specification and Estimation of a Nonparametric, Mixed Poisson Model." *Criminology* 31: 327–62.

Nagin, Daniel, and Greg Pogarsky. 2001. "Integrating Celerity, Impulsivity, and Extralegal Sanction Threats into a Model of General Deterrence: Theory and Evidence." *Criminology* 39: 865–92.

Naik, Ashish V., Alok Baveja, Rajan Batta, and Jonathan P. Caulkins. 1996. "Scheduling Crackdowns on Illicit Drug Markets." *European Journal of Operational Research* 88: 231–50.

National Institute of Justice. 2000. *1999 Annual Report on Drug Use among Adult and Juvenile Arrestees.* Washington, D.C.: U.S. Department of Justice.

National Institute of Justice. 2006. *Drug Courts: The Second Decade.* Washington, D.C.: U.S. Department of Justice. http://www.ncjrs.gov/pdffiles1/nij/211081.pdf.

Needleman, Herbert L. 1990. "The Future Challenge of Lead Toxicity." *Environmental Health Perspectives* 89: 85–89.

Needleman, Herbert L., et al. 1996. "Bone Lead Levels and Delinquent Behavior." *Journal of the American Medical Association* 275 (5): 363–69.

Nevin, Richard. 2000. "How Lead Exposure Relates to Temporal Changes in IQ, Violent Crime and Unwed Pregnancy." *Environmental Research* 83 (1): 1–22.

Office of National Drug Control Policy. 1994. *National Drug Control Strategy*. Washington, D.C.: The White House.

O'Flaherty, Brendan, and Rajiv Sethi. 2008. "The Racial Geography of Vice." Columbia University Department of Economics Discussion Paper No. 0809-11. http://www.columbia.edu/cu/economics/discpapr/DP0809-11.pdf.

Orwell, George. 1968. "Wells, Hitler and the World State." In *Orwell: The Collected Essays, Journalism and Letters*, vol. 3, *My Country Right or Left*, edited by Sonia Orwell and Ian Angus, pp. 139–45. London: Secker and Warburg.

Pena-Acosta, Juan, et al. 1998. "Gun Bounty Program: Program Design and Evaluation for the City of Pittsburgh." Heinz School, Carnegie Mellon University.

Perneger, T. V., F. Giner, M. Del Rio, and A. Mino. 1998. "Randomized Trial of Heroin Maintenance Program for Addicts Who Fail in Conventional Drug Treatments." *British Medical Journal* 317: 13–18.

Petersilia, Joan. 2002. "Community Corrections." In *Crime*, edited by James Q. Wilson and Joan Petersilia. Oakland, Calif.: ICS Press.

———. 1997. "Probation in the United States." *Crime and Justice* 22: 149–200.

———. 2009. *When Prisoners Come Home*. New York: Oxford University Press, 215–16.

Petersilia, Joan, Susan Turner, James Kahan, and Joyce Peterson. 1985. *Granting Felons Probation: Public Risks and Alternatives*. Santa Monica, Calif: RAND.

Pew Center on the States. 2008. *One in 100: Behind Bars in America 2008*. Washington, D.C.: Pew Charitable Trusts. http://www.pewcenteronthestates .org/uploadedFiles/8015PCTS_Prison08_FINAL_2-1-1_FORWEB.pdf.

———. 2009. *One in 31: The Long Reach of American Corrections*. Washington, D.C.: Pew Charitable Trusts.

Piehl, Anne Morrison. 1994. "Learning While Doing Time." Kennedy School working paper no. R94-25, Harvard University.

Press, Aric. 1987. *Piecing Together the System: The Response to Crack*. New York: New York City Bar Association.

Public Elementary-Secondary Education Finance Data. 2005. *United States Census Bureau*.

Raiffa, Howard. 1982. *The Art and Science of Negotiation*. Cambridge, Mass.: Harvard University Press.

Raphael, Steven. 2003. "The Socioeconomic Status of Black Males: The Increasing Importance of Incarceration." Working paper, Goldman School of Public Policy, University of California, Berkeley.

Raphael, Steven, and Michael A. Stoll. 2002. *Modest Progress: The Narrowing Spatial Mismatch Between Blacks and Jobs in the 1990s*, Living Cities Census Series. Washington, D.C.: Brookings Institution.

————. 2007. "Why Are so Many Americans in Prison?" In *Do Prisons Make Us Safer? The Benefits and Costs of the Prison Boom*, edited by Steven Raphael and Michael Stoll. New York: Russell Sage Foundation Press.

Redelmeier, Donald A., and Daniel Kahnemann. 1996. "Patients' Memories of Painful Medical Treatments: Real-time and Retrospective Evaluations of Two Minimally Invasive Procedures." *Pain* 66 (1): 3–8.

Rehm, J., P. Gschwend, T. Steffen, F. Gutzwiller, A. Dobler-Mikola, and A. Uchtenhagen. 2001. "Feasibility, Safety, and Efficacy of Injectable Heroin Prescription for Refractory Opioid Addicts: A Follow-Up Study." *Lancet* 358: 1417–420.

Reuter, Peter, Robert J. MacCoun, P. J. Murphy, Allan F. Abrahamse, and Barbara Simon. 1990. *Money from Crime: A Study of the Economics of Drug Dealing in Washington D.C.* Washington, D.C.: RAND.

Reuter, Peter, and Mark Kleiman. 1986. "Risks and Prices: An Economic Analysis of Drug Enforcement." In *Crime and Justice: An Annual Review of Research*, vol. 7, edited by Michael Tonry and Norval Morris.

Robins, Lee N. 1974. *The Vietnam Drug User Returns*. Special Action Office Monograph, Series A, No. 2. Washington, D.C.: U.S. Government Printing Office.

Rosenfeld, Richard, Robert Fornango, and Eric Baumer. 2005. "Did Ceasefire, Compstat, and Exile Reduce Homicide?" *Criminology and Public Policy* 4: 419–50.

Rosenfeld, Richard, Robert Fornango, and Andres Rengifo. 2007. "The Impact of Order-Maintenance Policing on New York City Robbery and Homicide Rates: 1988–2001." *Criminology* 45, 2: 355–84.

Rotter, Julien. 1966. "Generalized Expectancies for Internal versus External Control of Reinforcements." *Psychological Monographs* 80: 1–28.

Rydell, Peter C., and Susan S. Everingham. 1994. *Controlling Cocaine: Supply Versus Demand*. Santa Monica, Calif.: RAND.

Sah, Raaj K. 1991. "Social Osmosis and Patterns of Crime." *Journal of Political Economy* 99 (6): 1272–295.

Samaha, Joel. 2005. *Criminal Justice*. Belmont, Calif.: Thomson Wadsworth.

Sampson, Robert J., Stephen Raudenbush, and Felton Earls. 1997. "Neighborhoods and Violent Crime: A Multilevel Study of Collective Efficacy." *Science* 277: 918–24.

Schelling, Thomas C. 1984a. *Choice and Consequence: Perspectives of an Errant Economist*. Cambridge, Mass.: Harvard University Press.

————. 1971. "On the Ecology of Micromotives." *Public Interest* 25: 61–98.

————. 2003. Foreword to *Collective Choice: Essays in Honor of Mancur Olson*, edited by Jac Heckelman and Dessin Coates. Berlin: Springer.

————. 1978. *Micromotives and Microbehavior*. New York: W. W. Norton.

————. 1984b. "Self-Command in Practice, in Policy, and in a Theory of Rational Choice." *American Economic Review* 74: 1–11.

————. 1960. *The Strategy of Conflict*. Cambridge, Mass.: Harvard University Press.

Schochet, Peter Z., et al. 2008. "Does Job Corps Work? Impact Findings from the National Job Corps Study." *American Economic Review* 98, 5 (December): 1864–86.

Schuck, Peter H., and Richard J. Zeckhauser. 2006. *Targeting in Social Programs Avoiding Bad Bets, Removing Bad Apples*. Washington, D.C.: Brookings Institution Press.

Schwartz, Amy Ellen, Scott Susin, and Ioan Voicu. 2003. "Has Falling Crime Driven New York City's Real Estate Boom?" *Journal of Housing Research* 14 (1): 101–35.

Schwartz, Joel, Hugh Pitcher, Ronnie Levin, Bart Ostro, and Albert L. Nichols. 1985. *Costs and Benefits of Reducing Lead in Gasoline: Final Regulatory Impact Analysis*. U.S. Environmental Protection Agency.

The Sentencing Project. 2004. "New Incarceration Figures: Rising Population Despite Falling Crime Rates." Report at www.sentencingproject.org/pdfs/1044.pdf.

Shavell, Steven. 1990. "Individual Precautions to Prevent Theft: Private Versus Socially Optimal Behavior." NBER working paper no. 3560.

Sherman, Lawrence W., James W. Shaw, and Dennis P. Rogan. 1995. *The Kansas City Gun Experiment*. Washington, D.C.: National Institute of Justice.

Silbergeld, Ellen K. 1997. "Preventing Lead Poisoning in Children." *Annual Review of Public Health* 18: 187–210.

Skogan, Wesley. 1990. *Disorder and Decline: Crime and the Spiral of Decay in American Neighborhoods*. Berkeley: University of California Press.

Skogan, Wesley, and Kathleen Frydl. 2004. *Fairness and Effectiveness in Policing: The Evidence*. Washington, D.C.: National Academy Press.

Spelman, William. 1994. *Criminal Incapacitation*. New York: Plenum Press.

————. 2002. "The Limited Importance of Prison Expansion." In *The Crime Drop in America*, edited by Alfred Blumstein and Joel Wallman. Cambridge: Cambridge University Press.

————. 2000. "What Recent Studies Do (and Don't) Tell Us about Imprisonment and Crime." *Crime and Justice* 27: 419–94.

Starmer, C. 2000. "Developments in Non-Expected Utility Theory: The Hunt for a Descriptive Theory of Choice Under Risk." *Journal of Economic Literature* 38: 332–82.

State of California, Department of Corrections and Rehabilitation. 2008. *California Prisoners and Parolees 2007: Summary Statistics on Adult Felon Prisoners and Parolees, Civil Narcotic Addicts and Outpatient and Other Populations.* http://www.cdcr.ca.gov/Reports_Research/Offender_Information_Services_Branch/Annual/CalPris/CALPRISd2008.pdf.

———. 1999. *California Prisoners and Parolees 1997 and 1998: Summary Statistics on Adult Felon Prisoners and Parolees, Civil Narcotic Addicts and Outpatient and Other Populations.* http://www.cdcr.ca.gov/Reports_Research/Offender_Information_Services_Branch/Annual/CalPris/CALPRISd1999.pdf

Stuntz, William J. 2009. "Law and Disorder: The Case for a Police Surge." *Weekly Standard* 14, 22 (February 22). http://www.weeklystandard.com/Content/Public/Articles/000/000/016/157ehmas.asp.

———. 2008. "Unequal Justice." *Harvard Law Review* 121: 1969–2040.

Substance Abuse and Mental Health Services Administration. 2005. "2005 National Survey on Drug Use and Health: National Results." U.S. Department of Health and Human Services.

Svenson, Ola. 1981. "Are We All Less Risky and More Skillful Than Our Fellow Drivers?" *Acta Psychologia* 47 (2): 143–48.

Sviridoff, M., S. Sadd, R. Curtis, and R. Grinc. 1992. *The Neighborhood Effects of Street-Level Drug Enforcement: Tactical Narcotics Teams in New York.* New York: Vera Institute of Justice.

Sweet, Monica A., and Mark I. Appelbaum. 2005. "Is Home Visiting an Effective Strategy? A Meta-Analytic Review of Home Visiting Programs for Families with Young Children." *Child Development* 75, 5 (September/October): 1435–56.

Thaler, Richard H., and Cass R. Sunstein. 2008. *Nudge: Improving Decisions about Health, Wealth, and Happiness.* New Haven, Conn.: Yale University Press.

Totter, Ben. 2008. "Outmanned and Outgunned: Miami Officials Unite to End Street Arms Race." *Miami Sun Post*, February 21. http://www.miamisunpost.com/archives/2008/02-21/022108/newsmiamiweapons.htm.

Travis, Jeremy. 2005. *But They All Come Back: Facing the Challenges of Prisoner Reentry.* Washington, D.C.: Urban Institute Press.

Tremblay, Richard E., and Wendy M. Craig. 1995. "Developmental Crime Prevention." *Crime and Justice 19:* 151–236.

Trumbull, William N. 1990. "Who Has Standing in Cost-Benefit Analysis?" *Journal of Policy Analysis and Management* 9 (2): 210–12.

Tversky, Amos, and Daniel Kahneman. 1974. "Judgment under Uncertainty: Heuristics and Biases." *Science* 185, 4157 (September): 1124–31.

United States Census, 2000.

U.S. Department of Justice. 1999. "Truth in Sentencing in State Prisons." U.S. Department of Justice, Office of Justice Programs, NCJ 170032, January 1999.

———. 1999. *Substance Abuse and Treatment, State and Federal Prisoners.* Bureau of Justice Statistics, NCJ-172871. Washington, D.C.: U.S. Department of Justice.

U.S. Probation and Pretrial Services System. 2004. "Year in Review Report, Fiscal Year 2003." August 2004.

U.S. Sentencing Commission. 2002. "Report to the Congress: Cocaine and Federal Sentencing Policy May 2002." http://www.ussc.gov/r_congress/02crack/ch6.pdf.

Useem, Bert, and Anne Morrison Piehl. 2008. *Prison State: The Challenge of Mass Incarceration.* New York: Cambridge University Press.

Van den Brink, W., V. M. Hendriks, and J. Van Ree. 1999. "Medical Co-prescription of Heroin to Chronic, Treatment-Resistant Methadone Patients in the Netherlands." *Journal of Drug Issues* 29: 587–608.

Viscusi, W. Kip. 1993. "The Value of Risks to Life and Health." *Journal of Economic Literature* 31 (4): 1912–46.

Volokh, Eugene. "The Mechanisms of the Slippery Slope." *Harvard Law Review* 116 (1026) (2003): 1077–14.

Wacquant, Loic. 2001. "Deadly Symbosis: When Ghetto and Prison Meet and Mesh." *Punishment and Society* 3 (1): 95–133.

Wakeling, Stewart. 2003. "Ending Gang Homicide: Deterrence Can Work." *Perspectives on Violence Prevention*, 1. California Attorney General's Office, California Health and Human Services Agency. http://safestate.org/index.cfm?navId=12.

Walsh, John M. 2004. "Are We There Yet? Measuring Progress in the U.S. War on Drugs in Latin American." *Drug War Monitor*, from the Washington Office on Latin America (December).

Weikart, David P., James T. Bond, and J. T. McNeil. 1978. *Ypsilanti Perry Preschool Project: Preschool Years and Longitudinal Results Through Fourth Grade.* Ypsilanti, Mich.: High/Scope Press.

White, J. L., et al. 1994. "Measuring Impulsivity and Examining Its Relationships to Delinquency." *Journal of Abnormal Psychology* 103: 192–205.

Wilson. James Q. 1994. "Penalties and Opportunities." In *A Reader on Punishment*, edited by R. A. Duff and David Garland. New York: Oxford University Press.

Wilson, James Q. 1975. *Thinking About Crime.* New York: Basic Books.

Wilson, James Q., and Richard J. Herrnstein. 1985. *Crime and Human Nature.* New York: Simon and Schuster.

Wood, Peter, and David C. May. 2003. "Racial Differences in Perceptions of Severity of Sanctions: A Comparison of Prison with Alternatives." *Justice Quarterly* 20 (3): 605–31.

Wray, Ricardo J. 2006. "Public Health Communication Theory and Strategies for Interpersonal Violence Prevention." *Journal of Aggression, Maltreatment and Trauma* 13 (3/4): 41–61.

Zimring, Franklin E. 1968, "Is Gun Control Likely to Reduce Violent Killings?" *University of Chicago Law Review* 35: 21–27.

——— 1991. "Firearms, Violence and Public Policy." *Scientific American* 265 (5): 48–54.

Zimring, Franklin E. 2007. *The Great American Crime Decline*. New York: Oxford University Press.

Zimring, Franklin E., and Gordon Hawkins. 1997. *Crime Is Not the Problem: Lethal Violence in America*. New York: Oxford University Press.

———. 1991. *The Scale of Imprisonment*. Chicago: University of Chicago Press.

INDEX

The letter *f* following a page number refers to a figure on that page.

African Americans: crime impacts and, 23–24, 175; statistical discrimination and, 84, 111; under-policing and, 100

agendas for crime control: community corrections and, 181–84; drugs and, 185–86; general and budgetary and, 175–76; guns and, 186–88; institutional corrections and, 179–81; juvenile corrections and, 184; policing and, 176–77; pretrial release and, 184; prosecution, courts and sentencing rules and, 177–79; social services and nonpunitive measures and, 188–89. *See also specific issues*

Aggressive Community Therapy. *See* Assertive Community Therapy (ACT)

Alm, Judge, 34–38, 168

Armed Career Criminal (ACC) statute, 107

Assertive Community Therapy (ACT), 130–31, 183, 189

Balko, Radley, 155

Bayes' Rule/Theorem, 51–52

Beccaria, Cesare, 74

Becker, Gary, 12

behavioral triage, 99

benefits and costs, 2, 5, 6–7, 21–22, 25–32, 45–46, 49–50, 87, 90n, 112–16, 121–23, 133–34, 151–53, 188, 189

Brady Law, 142–43

Bratton, William, 42–43

Break the Cycle (Maryland), 36, 168–69

broken windows, 67, 100–104; collective efficacy and, 103–4; drug markets and, 157; enforcement and, 101–2; enforcement swamping and, 102; positive feedback and, 103

bullying, 123–24, 188

burglary, 68; punishment and, 73–74; risk-seeking and, 74; victimization losses and, 17–19; wages of, 68–70

cannabis, 151–52

Carnevale, John, 149

CeaseFire (Chicago), 131–32

Ceasefire project (Boston), 107–8, 138–39

Chaiken, Jan and Marcia, 90–91, 114

Coles, Catherine, 100–101

collective social capital, 20

community corrections, 5–6, 27, 29, 31, 97–98, 112–13; agenda for crime control and, 176, 181–84; management of, 181–82. *See also* probation(ers); social services

CompStat process, 106–7, 168, 170

Cook, Philip J., 81, 118

cost-benefit analysis. *See* benefits and costs

cost-effectiveness, 6, 7, 32, 115, 116, 119–21, 127, 134, 159, 161–62, 190

crack cocaine, 8

crime: Baby Boom generation and, 8; civil rights movement and, 9; damage from, 2; drugs and, 8; economic theory of, 11–12; education and, 6; existential pleasures of, 69; financial costs of, 26–28; nonmonetary costs of, 30–32; punishment and, 10f, 12; root causes and, 11, 32–33; the Sixties and, 8; social costs of, 9; social disadvantage and, 2, 117; suffering and, 30–31; uneven impacts of, 23–24

crime-avoidance behavior, 20–22

crime control, 10f; avoiding victimization and, 19–22; budgets and, 27; bullying and, 123–24; communication of deterrent threats and, 5, 46–47; community supervision and, 5–6; concentration of

CPSIA information can be obtained
at www.ICGtesting.com
Printed in the USA
LVOW11s0820201017

553134LV00002B/4/P